Trust the Mystery

Library and Archives Canada Cataloguing in Publication

Shoroplova, Nina, 1947-, author
Trust the mystery : questions, quotes, & quantum wisdom / Nina Shoroplova.

Issued in print and electronic formats.
ISBN 978-1-77141-130-1 (paperback).--ISBN 978-1-77141-139-4 (pdf)

1. Spiritual life. I. Title.

BL624.S475 2015 204'.4 C2015-904231-3
C2015-904232-1

Trust the Mystery

Questions, Quotes, and Quantum Wisdom

To Nina
Trust the mystery
to align fully with
your true self.
Nina Shoroplova

Nina Shoroplova

First Published in Canada 2015 by Influence Publishing

Book Cover Design: Marla Thompson
Editor: Catherine Kerr
Assistant Editor: Sue Kehoe
Typeset: Greg Salisbury
Portrait Photographer: Adam and Kev Photography
Front Cover Photographer: Hubert Dumont

To Kenneth and Vera McGregor
without whose loving parenting I would not be here
to tell my story and express my beliefs.

To my children and their spouses and their children, my grandchildren:
Alun and Dana, Zael, Aidan, and Esmé
Jessica and Ari, Eliana, Morgan, and Dasha
Grant and Carole, Liam, Léa, and Lana
Ian
without whom I would have far less reason to express my beliefs.

To my husband Christian Shoroplov
without whom I would be unable to believe.

I love you all. Thank you for being in my life.

Testimonials

"In *Trust the Mystery,* Nina Shoroplova shares a lifetime of deep thought-provoking concepts. This book can fulfill your quest to get the answers to many heartfelt questions. It also will help to expand your consciousness to ask the deeper questions with confidence that you can get those answers yourself. This book is a gift that each reader will open at just the perfect time, for there are no coincidences."

The Reverend Christina Lunden

Creator mediator and author of *Your Divine Life: Angelic Guidance for the Ascension, The Angel Connection: Divinity in the New Energy,* and *Angelic Affirmations, Daily Inspirations*

"Wisdom shared in bite-sized pieces ... I intuitively know this book will help its readers."

Brock Tully

Co-founder of the Kindness Foundation of Canada, three epic bicycle trips around North America for Kindness (50,000 km/30,000 miles), and author of *The Great Gift for Someone Special* and five *Reflections* books; brocktully.com

"*Trust the Mystery* is a great tool for individuals seeking to improve and develop their character in both the third dimension and in spiritual reality. The compilation of various esoteric modalities, Spiritual teachings, and common practices available in one book makes it a great reference tool for developing conscious souls on their spiritual path. You will find yourself reflecting on the questions being asked to see if you have asked yourself the same ones, a personal 'check and balance.'"

Tim Doyle

Spiritual teacher, www.ThePathToOneness.com

"*Trust the Mystery* is a wonderful, delightful, and inspiring read. Shoroplova delicately weaves unique principles together into an understandable fabric of oneness that we all can use in our personal, professional, and mystical lives. I was so moved by the teachings she presented that it sparked a cascade of creative endeavoring in my own mind and Spirit. Her work in this book got me back to my writing chair, in the same way that it will inspire any one of us to reach out to the potential the Universe has to offer us."

George Baxter-Holder, D.N.P.

Author of *Drugs, Food, Sex and God: An Addicted Drug Dealer Goes from Convict to Doctor through the Power of Intention*

"Nina's metaphysical ponderings and spiritual insights inspire not just self-discovery, but discovering the truth of all things in our experience to live more fulfilling lives."

JZ Bown

Medical Intuitive, ThetaHealer®, Dr. TCM Dip.

"Nina's book is unlike anything else you will ever read. It is full of wisdom, true discovery, mystery, a testament and guide to being fully one's Self. I especially enjoyed her perception of 'words' and their unique meanings. It has truly opened my eyes and ears!"

Michèle Bisson-Somerville

A personal intuitive trainer, Juice Plus+ dealer, and author of *Voodoo Shit for Men: Flex Your Intuitive Muscle*

"A beautiful collection of wisdom, insight, and powerful perspectives designed to unwind the mind and align with our inner truth."

Sue Dumais

Intuitive healer, international speaker, Heart Led Living Coach, and best-selling author of *Heart Led Living*

"Nina Shoroplova shows her passion for helping people learn more about themselves. Using her own experiences as examples and the wisdom she's gained, she is able to ask just the right questions to allow a person to learn more about who they truly are. So grab a journal and record your own answers to the questions she asks at the end of each scene, and you will learn some interesting things about yourself."

Margarett Mae Monzo Ruthford

Certified spiritual and personal counsellor, hypnotherapist, Reiki master, and non-denominational holistic minister

"*Trust the Mystery* creates an accessible roadmap for a life fully lived, distilling essence from a potent mix of personal experiences and interdisciplinary teachings. Nina journeys beyond time-honoured gates to universal wisdom and invites us to apply the gathered insights to our own life. The likely result of this invitation? Inspiration, clarity, and a greater trust in the great unfolding."

Keith Condliffe, B.A., N.D.

Naturopathic Physician

"Nina's book is very thought provoking and full of great fuel for contemplation. It demonstrates the rewards of living life as if every event has meaning, and provides great prompts for sucking the juice out of life by sinking more deeply into the motivations for your actions and decisions. The personal stories provide inspiration for what it means to live from a place of consciousness and choice in alignment with one's values."

Andrea Jacques

Meaningful Work and Workplace Transformation Expert, Kyosei Consulting

"*Trust the Mystery* inspires us to live a life with love and passion—to trust in our own Divinity, to follow our bliss, and to know that our Soul's purpose in life 'is to be who we are as fully as possible.' Through the author's own trust in life and love of life, and with the power of words, she weaves together inspirational stories of her journey of self-healing and discovery, personal experiences, wisdom, her love-of-learning, and she encourages us to question ourselves, and to go deep within our Souls to find wholeness. Beautifully blended with her own thoughts and understandings, as well as quotations from the insight of other authors, we are reminded of our connection to Spirit, that we are intuitive beings, intimately connected to everyone and everything, to trust life and ourselves, that everything is energy and that we co-create our reality through the power of our thoughts and words. *Trust the Mystery* shows us how beautiful life is and how powerful we are!"

Kelly Kiss, RHN

Holistic Healer, Registered Holistic Nutritionist, ThetaHealing® practitioner and teacher, Reiki Master/Teacher

"Nina delights and inspires with her unique insights into life and living. Her call to 'trust the mystery' of life opens doors of possibility for the reader. This balance of grounding and inspiration assists the reader in finding purpose and passion, and provides a guidebook that enables the reader to dig deeper and look higher. Her words combine both heart and head and are fresh and enlightening. This truly is an exceptional book that will uncover the magic and mystery that is part of our everyday lives."

Alyson Jones, MA, RCC

Clinical Director of Alyson Jones & Associates, and author of *M.O.R.E. A New Philosophy for Exceptional Living*

"*Trust the Mystery* has warmly lured me into deeper acknowledgement and commitment to what I already know are the elements of my spiritual calling."

LARAAJI

American recording artist, sound healer, and laughter therapist

"Nina Shoroplova has written an amazing portrayal of unlocking the connections that almost anyone can understand relating to some of the best unsolved mysteries of the 21st century. These mysteries go back through the ages, have been questioned, but still in most areas hold an element of continued mystery. Her information draws from many contemporaries such as Dr. Deepak Chopra and Dr. Bruce Lipton who have become leaders in the field of seeking commonality between science and spirit. I feel what I love most is Nina's personal experiences shared in this most thought-induced experience of *Trust the Mystery*."

Marilyn Parkin, Ph.D.

Founder of the International College of Medical Intuition, Inc.

"When I first encountered Nina Shoroplova, she was a godsend as the editor of my book, *Sunshine before the Dawn*. Now that she has written her book—*Trust the Mystery: Questions, Quotes, and Quantum Wisdom*—I find her an even greater godsend, for she will reach those souls who are considering whether they are ready to pursue the spiritual path. After reading her book, they will be. Nina's readers will have far more tools at their disposal and a wonderful path ahead of them."

Judy Satori Way shower, activator, catalyst for human transformation, and author of *Sunshine before the Dawn*

Acknowledgements

I am grateful to all the authors, writers, speakers, healers, nutritionists, musicians, and friends who have inspired me, drawn me along, and kept my belief alive in the growth of my own spiritual wisdom. I will name a few (alphabetically): Frederick Bailes, M.D., Edgar Cayce, Deepak Chopra, M.D., Tim Doyle, the Reverend Markus Dünzkofer, Tania Gabrielle, Jonathan Goldman, Andrrea Hess, Anodea Judith, Kelly Kiss, the Reverend Christina Lunden, Barbara Y. Martin, Drunvalo Melchizedek, Caroline Myss, Michael Newton, Ph.D., Julie Salisbury, the Reverend Jessica Schaap, Vianna Stibal, James Twyman, Doreen Virtue, Ambika Wauters, and Paramahansa Yogananda. Without examples like theirs to follow, I would not be where I am in my life's journey today, able to relate those parts that illustrate ideas likely to be of value to you my reader.

A wide variety of teachings have shaped my perception of the spirit's journey, from the Bible to *I Ching*, from texts old and new, from various trainings, courses, workshops, and readings, and through the lessons I have gained from the spiritual books I have edited. I have sought out quotes that strengthen what I believe; I hope you find them helpful and provocative. I am very grateful to all the authors, speakers, website owners, and journalists who have granted me permission to quote their words.

Also, as an editor with Influence Publishing, I receive constant opportunities to learn from others—the authors whose books I edit—about some of the intricate ways in which we answer the questions in our lives. I am very grateful to all the Influence Publishing authors who have granted me permission to quote their words within these pages.

I am especially grateful to the entire team that has brought my book from a collection of ideas to a substantial object in the world. To Julie Salisbury, my publisher, thank you dear friend for your constant enthusiasm and trust. To the Influence Publishing team—Gulnar Patel, Alina Wilson, Lisa Halpern, Jennifer Kaleta, Sue Kehoe, Lyda Mclallen, Greg Salisbury, and Marla Thomas—thank you. To Hubert Dumont, for his wonderful photograph of the nuns praising the divine energy of the Atlantic Ocean, merci. And to my exacting editor, Catherine Kerr, for her wise counsel and questions that have raised my book to the next level, many heartfelt thanks.

My sincere thanks to the Honourable Judith Guichon, Lieutenant Governor of British Columbia, for her generous words in the Foreword.

Finally, I wish to acknowledge you, my reader. If reading my book helps you with your spiritual growth, then mine becomes another name in a long list of people who inspire each of us to be our best, to grow during our lives, to progress our spirit. That's all I want for this work: for it to be a stepping stone along the way. Thanks for reading and growing and contemplating the questions. Let me know how you answer them, at trustthemystery.ca.

Contents

Foreword

Government House
Victoria
June 6, 2015

It was a pleasure to read Nina Shoroplova's new book, *Trust the Mystery: Questions, Quotes and Quantum Wisdom*. As with her previous book, *Cattle Ranch: The Story of the Douglas Lake Cattle Company*, this new publication represents a prodigious amount of research, organization of material and years of dedicated work. *Trust the Mystery* is an accumulation of years of enquiry and experience. The depth of research is evident in Nina's comprehension of spirituality and she generously shares the revelations she's gathered over a lifetime of learning. This work illuminated for me the many spiritual and inner workings of our very beings and shed light on experiences of the past that hovered semiconsciously in my mind and body.

I look forward to the publication of *Trust the Mystery* as it will be the perfect gift for many friends and family. For all who believe in wholeness and the connected nature of this world, this work helps to explain the process.

Thank you, Nina, for the gift of this work.

Sincerely,

The Honourable Judith Guichon, OBC
Lieutenant Governor of British Columbia

When I Get Out of My Own Way

I am a Divine drop of the vast ocean of consciousness
When I get out of my own way
I am a lighthouse
I am a sunbeam
I am a vessel
I am a conduit
I am a messenger
I am a channel

Breath inspires me
Spirit seeks me
Fire creates me
Water pours me
Earth grounds me
Air lifts me
Tone vibrates and moves and heals me
Music sounds me
Song sings me
Poetry speaks me
Words write me
Dance skips me
Laughter laughs me
My hands touch me
My eyes see me
My Higher Self knows me

The present moment gifts me with its presence
Divine Love loves me
When I get out of my own way
I know I am a Divine drop of the vast ocean of consciousness

Nina Shoroplova, July 28, 2013, Channelled from Archangel Metatron

Introduction

Part I of *Trust the Mystery* explores how we negotiate our way through our lives using our basic tools of emotions, senses, energy connections, thoughts, and words. I offer some anecdotes and reminiscences of observing myself through using these tools and explain how they have powered my actions and deeds. Why? Because these tools serve for more than survival and social bonding. They give us access to the countless mysteries of life. Engagement with these mysteries is, in my view, the secret to improving one's actions and deeds and living at a higher octave. As Daniel C. Matt writes in *The Essential Kabbalah,* "By cleaving in love and full awareness to the source of life, the soul shines from supernal light, and all feelings, thoughts, and actions are refined."[1]

Part II looks at phenomena we often ignore or don't notice, such as early mysteries, effective alternative healing modalities, paranormal events, coincidences, synchronicities, and channelled wisdom. Part II also suggests how we might engage with these mysteries through our time, talent, and treasure. Part III provides examples of how we can expand our ability to observe ourselves and some of the ways we can embody the mystery. It concludes with suggested ways for integrating our body, mind, and soul more effectively.

You and I

Recently, I have begun to see that a writer gains authenticity when he expresses a judgment or perception with "I, me, my," and "myself"—the first-person point of view—rather than addressing the reader as "you." For myself, I would prefer to read "I find that this is so" over being told, "you will find that this is so," which sometimes is irksome. So rather than instructing and advising, I am just going to write about what works for me; it may work for you; it may not. (Please let me know! I would love

[1]Daniel C. Matt, *The Essential Kabbalah* (HarperOne, 1996), p. 32.

to hear from you.)

My decision in favour of first-person narrative involves the knowledge that, despite being individuals, we are also one, for we all come from the same Divine Source. So I shall refer to myself when relating a lesson of probable value to you as well as me. I leave the rest up to you. As you the reader reads "I," you will know that whatever I state for myself is a potential for you. You can therefore accept it or reject it. I hope that you will experience *Trust the Mystery* as your own journey, seeing yourself as the person who has lived these stories.

The Framework for Your Reading

I present my suggestion to trust the mystery mathematically and logically. That is, an understanding of Part I along with an acceptance of Part II leads to an ability to live a fuller life as portrayed in Part III.

I + II = III.

These three parts have three chapters each, divided into three sections, each of which has several scenes (to borrow a theatrical term) introduced by quotations. The quotations are there to provoke contemplation. Questions at the end of each scene in Parts I, II, and III stimulate self-reflection, encouraging you to witness your personal process. I ask these, because, although we all carry quantum wisdom deep inside ourselves, within our very cells, we sometimes fail to access that wisdom. The questions I ask are designed to provoke you into greater awareness of your part in the mystery of life.

Part IV has just one chapter with sections and scenes, and no questions. After reading the first nine chapters, you'll be asking yourself appropriate questions. Chapter ten suggests how to stay in the now, to continue asking questions, and to research and trust the mystery.

There are between three and six scenes per section for a total of 128 in all. How interesting that the Kabbalah says there are 125 steps from each of us to our Creator!

The order of this entire book will guide you along a path toward your true self, that unchangeable part of yourself that is your soul. It will also take you further toward that higher aspect of yourself, your Higher Self. As you start to recognize this eternal self, you cannot help but live more fully, with greater awareness.

The Terms I Use

Let me define the terms I use. In using the term "mind," I am referring to an individual's ability to perceive their world through their thoughts. This perception might take place through their subconscious, unconscious, or conscious minds or through their link to the collective conscious and unconscious minds. In scientific circles, the brain is presumed to be the only site where thoughts are processed, and yet specialized collections of neurons gather elsewhere in the body—for instance, the heart and gut have neurons that gather and feed information back to the brain. Michael Gershon, professor and chair of pathology and cell biology at Columbia University, says the gut is "another independent center of integrative neural activity."

And the gut and the heart are not the only additional locations of mind; our entire body is mindful, and our mind collides with the minds of others in many ways and places.

Consciousness is greater than mind, being that energetic aspect of ourselves that predates, is present during, and postdates this Earthly lifetime. Thus, it is more expansive than our mind that is connected with just this lifetime. Our consciousness is that part of each of us that continues to exist after the death of our physical body. It is less than our spirit. Our consciousness connects with Divine Mind.

Sometimes, I may use the term "spirit" interchangeably with "soul," not as in "she has such spirit," meaning life force and energy, but rather as in "she heard the call of her spirit." An individual's spirit includes her Higher Self in the afterlife plus her embodied spirit, known also as "soul."

Each of us is a spiritual being embodied and living a physical life on

Earth. Our soul is that aspect of our spirit that connects our consciousness through our mind and our breath to our physical body; however, it exists as a background to our physical, emotional, and mental self. Our spirit has come to Earth as a soul with a purpose and lessons to learn. These may or may not become apparent through our lives. However, once we recognize our purpose, it becomes hard to ignore. And, if we don't learn the lessons the first time around, they continue to present themselves in different guises until we understand them.

"Spirit" with a capital "S" refers to the entire aggregate of all beings on the Other Side of this Earthly life. It particularly refers to the more highly evolved beings, such as Ascended Masters, Archangels, Guides, Teachers, and Angels, to all of whom we can appeal for Divine guidance and wisdom.

I would like to define "wisdom" and "quantum wisdom"; let me work up to them, starting with "information." A bus timetable, a map, and a play poster provide us with information. Combining information about, say, Cuba from a map, a guidebook, a university course, and a history book creates knowledge of Cuba. This knowledge or cognizance is different from experience, which involves actual personal participation in living through time spent in Cuba. A "knowing" is something different again, being synonymous with claircognizance (see the section in chapter five, "The Clairs and Intuition"); it is more of a paranormal awareness. Claircognizance provides us with a deep knowing. In much the same way, intuition, which may be no more than the skillful recognition of behavioural, environmental, and cognitive patterns, can also be brought to an acute level whereby we gain wisdom. Wisdom is the next level in this progression. A person who is able to display wisdom about the potential future of Cuba (this might be called "predicting" and it might also be called "prophesying") is probably combining a lot of information, knowledge, and experience of Cuba along with claircognizance and intuition. Wisdom involves combining intellect with what many refer to as gut instinct and others value as intuition.

The wisdom that especially interests me is Divine Wisdom: the inner wisdom each of us is able to access via our inner wise self. The Divine is the source of all wisdom, all knowledge, and all experience. We are alive on this Earth to add to that knowledge and wisdom base. We add to it and we can access it whenever we wish. Let me expand on the term "Divine Wisdom" by also defining "quantum wisdom."

While I explain fully what I mean by quantum wisdom in chapter four, under "Mysteries We Ignore," I will say here that we connect with Divine Mind, our source of all wisdom, all knowledge, and all experience, through our quantum wisdom. By accessing our quantum wisdom, we are aligning ourself with our divinity. An analogy might be "the still small voice within" that we can seek out at any moment of the day or night.

More terms. Most of the time, I like to use the term "dis-ease" with a hyphen (pronounced 'diss-eaze) rather than the words "disease" (pronounced di-'zeaze) or "illness," both of which seem to suggest that an outside force or event has overtaken an unsuspecting victim. Dis-ease instead implies that the participant's lack of ease has some bearing on why she is suffering, and may even throw light on a possible cure for the malady.

The difference between "religious" and "spiritual" also bears discussion. I consider myself more spiritual than religious, the difference for me being that spirituality conveys a unique, personal experience of the Divine, whereas each religion, no matter which, requires the intervention of other people, liturgies, symbols, ceremonies, rules, and customs. Even so, I believe strongly in the power and importance of adhering to a religion. Although I have A *Course in Miracles, The Urantia Book, The Gnostic Gospels, I Ching*, and several editions of the *Bhagavad Gita* and *The Dead Sea Scrolls* on my bookshelves, the Bible is the religious text I know best. On my laptop, I have even more—*Confucian Analects, The Emerald Tablet of Hermes, The Divine Pymander of Hermes Mercurius Trismegistus,* and more. I have been reinterpreting and translating the Bible and the Anglican Church's liturgy for myself for so long that it now makes sense to me in a whole new way. Reading other sacred texts and current metaphysical teachings expands my understanding of humanity's desire to experience and trust the mystery.

I trust that my stance, with one foot on biblical soil and the other on esoteric wisdom, will help you examine your beliefs, your own stance.

My Hope for You

You and I are alive on this Earth to embody a particular and unique aspect of Divine wisdom. Each of us can strengthen our soul by accessing Creation's wisdom with an observant, self-reflective mind. After reading *Trust the Mystery,* my hope for you, dear reader, is that you will know more about yourself and how you are living your life; you will be closer to knowing and living your purpose and being on your path. I am honoured to be walking beside you for this brief part of your journey.

Part I ~ Our Basic Tools

Chapter 1—Emotions and Senses

Bathing in Emotions

~ Bathing in Our Mothers' Emotions ~

"Befriend Your Emotions."

Judith Orloff, M.D.[2]

Most of us got our start as cuddly, innocent beings; demanding because helpless and weak; sometimes puzzling; invariably lovable. Babies.

Few of us can remember our birth. We have instead some early memories that usually carry emotions. I have an early memory of fear. I know that, moments before the memory begins, I was holding my mother's hand on a busy sidewalk in Cardiff, the town in Wales where I was born. We were shopping for groceries using war rations. I don't know how old I was: old enough to run.

My mother is now ahead of me. Between us are two tall, dark-clad men walking close together. I am frightened of the strange men. But I am even more frightened at the thought of not being connected to my mother. I don't even think; I just feel the fear. I duck down (even though I am already very little) and run between the two men to catch up with my mother. I hold her hand again.

That's the whole memory.

I was born right after the Second World War: after my father returned from completing his final war duty as acting Town Major of the City of Graz in Austria. Once he had returned the city to its fathers, he came

[2] *Dr. Judith Orloff's Guide to Intuitive Healing: Five Steps to Physical, Emotional, and Sexual Wellness* (Three Rivers Press, 2000), p. 135.

home. Nine months later, I became one of the millions of children born during the postwar baby boom.

The first emotions we ever feel are our mother's, when she carries us in her womb. The emotions my mother felt—relief and joy at the return of my father, who had been away for five years during the war; worry for her mother, who was already extremely ill and living downstairs in our three-storey duplex; exasperation at trying to quieten my energetic and noisy older sister so as not to disturb her own mother—became my emotions as I grew within her; I was benefitting from the nutrients she ingested as well as the hormones she released.

Theo Fleury and Kim Barthel explain in their book *Conversations with a Rattlesnake* how all the chemicals in a pregnant mother that are capable of crossing the mother's blood-brain barrier are also capable of crossing the fetus's blood-brain barrier. Those chemicals include the organic substances created by the mother's brain and the rest of her body, and others ingested as food, alcohol, medicine, and drugs.

The foods my mother ate when she carried me were the ones that fed me. I was blessed; they were all nourishing foods. I was born healthy and I have stayed that way, despite experiencing my share of dis-eases.

Author Sue Dumais knew that the world would be a frightening place, even when she was still in her mother's womb; even more frightening when all was quiet than when there was sound. She describes this knowing in her book *Heart Led Living*. "When my mother was pregnant with me, she and my father were still together. At that point in their relationship my parents argued a lot. As a baby I was in some way comforted by the yelling and the noise. At least when I heard them fighting, I knew my mother was okay. I have a memory of feeling the need to protect my mother. I could sense her fear and stress. My father was never physically abusive, but for whatever reason I became afraid of silence while in my mother's uterus."[3]

---

[3]Sue Dumais, *Heart Led Living: When Hard Work Becomes Heart Work* (North Vancouver: Influence Publishing, 2014), p. 147.

Barthel explains to Fleury in their conversational bestseller that a newborn baby is hyperalert to the emotions of her caregivers, able to "read" her caregivers' faces in less than a second. She also explains that mirror neurons in the right side of the baby's brain mimic the mood of the mother. An unhappy mother thus promotes unhappiness in a baby. Aloof mothering distances a baby. Unwelcoming caregivers give off emotions that their babies absorb. And that's just in the first few days.

I feel as though I always knew that.

Apparently, "our brains are like Velcro to all negative thoughts and Teflon toward our positive ones. So it's the negatives thoughts that stick."[4] And "stick" they do, in the right side of the brain.[5] Not until around the age of eighteen months does the left side of a baby's brain develop; psychologists consider the left side to be "the positive side of the brain." So in order to grow positively through the first eighteen months of our lives, we have to rely on the emotions of our primary caregivers.

I am deeply grateful that my mother was the loving woman she was. What a fabulous start she and my father gave me.

What are your predominant emotions? Do you know the emotional state of your mother when she carried you? Does that explain anything? Thinking about your emotions as a child, what emotions do you think you might have hung onto? Can you morph those emotions into others these days?

~ *Bathing My Baby in My Emotions* ~

"Although children of all ages have special and specific needs to grow and develop normally, the first eighteen months of life are crucial.... [T]he nine months of pregnancy are equally important."

Paul Roumeliotis, M.D.[6]

---

[4]Theo Fleury and Kim Barthel, *Conversations with a Rattlesnake* (North Vancouver: Influence Publishing, 2014), p. 139.
[5]Ibid., p. 140
[6]Paul Roumeliotis, M.D., *Baby Comes Home: A Parent's Guide to a Healthy and Well First 18 Months* (North Vancouver: Influence Publishing, 2014), p. 4

I feel very grateful and privileged to have had the opportunity to carry, give birth to, and raise four children, now so fully grown that I am shorter and lighter than each of them and I am still learning from them and from their children.

By the time I knew I was carrying my first child—my son Alun—I was married and living at Douglas Lake Ranch in British Columbia's (BC's) Interior. It was early 1971. I had emigrated from Wales to Canada two years earlier.

As I carried Alun, I went through a lot of apprehension: around the delivery, around how healthy my baby would be, misgivings about my possible inadequacy as a mother. On one occasion, I attended a very noisy car race. Alun told me in the only way he knew how that he did not want us to be there, by kicking with all his might at the lining of my womb and abdominal muscles. I left quickly.

Once Alun was born, I counted his fingers and toes and marvelled at their perfection. I gradually worked my way through the challenges facing every first-time parent—holding my baby, changing his diaper, bathing him, and taking him out into the world. I remember the first time I took Alun out. It was a cold November day and cattle buyers were bidding for steers at an auction at the holding pens at English Bridge, on the ranch, a short drive from my home. Usually a decisive person, I dithered as I struggled to decide what I needed to take with me. It wasn't as if I had to take any milk or baby bottles, because I was breastfeeding. Anyhow, I'm happy to say, things became much easier.

As a baby, Alun was content yet curious. I remember wheeling him around in an old-fashioned English pram in the early days. His eyes were wide open, observing; he was quiet and calm. What a joy.

When I carried my daughter, I experienced a lot of false labour. The contractions were strong enough to have me heading off to the hospital—sixty miles away—more than once. Finally, in the middle of the first snowstorm of the year, just days after we had put winter tires on the car and toward the end of a family gathering to celebrate Christmas, the real labour pains came along.

Jessica was a miniature beauty, responsive but also contented. Just two years apart, she and Alun became wonderful if noisy companions, curious and playful together.

Seven years later, during my third pregnancy, I was exceptionally busy; I had to be very determined to complete everything. All through the first and second trimester of carrying Grant, I was completing the publication of my first book, *Cattle Ranch: The Story of Douglas Lake Cattle Company.*[7] I was checking galleys, proofreading, and going on a publication tour across BC and Alberta. At the same time, because my then-husband and I were preparing to emigrate from Canada to New South Wales, Australia to a sheep and cattle property we had bought, I was busy emptying our home, packing, planning our journey, wondering what we'd need. And I was probably stressed.

Grant, the child I carried through this stressful time, is the most driven of my four children. He was busy from the start, pushing away from feeding because he had to get on with tackling life. I feel his drive is due hugely to the brain chemicals and hormones that were flowing through my body during the whole nine months of his gestation.

In comparison, my fourth pregnancy was the most laid back of all. I enjoyed being pregnant, I loved being a mum, and I looked forward to holding and caring for another baby. Even though I was caring for three children under ten already and it looked as though we were entering another Australian drought, life was orderly. We were living off the land, raising cattle and sheep, and selling cattle, sheep, and wool. I was growing vegetables, so that when I did the weekly or two-weekly shopping trip to the nearest supermarket—sixty miles away at Armidale or seventy-five miles away at Tamworth—I only bought staples because we grew much of our food on the property. That was a very healthy time.

Ian was a quiet, happy baby, easily brought to smiles by the loving care he received from everyone around him. He and Grant were great pals; they still are. One of my favourite photos of the two of them is of

[7]My name then was Nina Woolliams. *Cattle Ranch* was published out of North Vancouver by Douglas & McIntyre in 1979.

Grant looking straight at the camera, proudly attired as a carpenter, with various tools hanging from his belt. He is aged about four. Ian, aged about two, is looking up at his big brother and he has one small hammer tucked into his pants, too.

My understanding of the ways my emotions during my pregnancies affected my babies has taught me that, sure enough, my babies were bathing in my emotions.

If you are a woman, have you ever been pregnant? What were your emotions at the time? What are your child's emotions? If you are a man, or if you are a woman who has not been pregnant, have you ever had an opportunity to observe a woman during pregnancy and her children later? Do you see the influence?

~ *Releasing Emotions* ~

"Sometimes any empathic listener will do. In medical school I'd often pour my heart out to my dog. Ears pointed, eyes fixed on me, she listened unconditionally to every word."

Judith Orloff, M.D.[8]

One of the working titles for this book was "Words in the Iceberg"; I was using the premise that our emotional lives are like an iceberg, floating nine tenths under the surface of the ocean. What people see, hear, and know of us is the tip of our iceberg.

Kelli Benis, a woman who decided to come to terms with childhood abuse, has created a life that is now about helping others. "For years, I had stuffed my emotions down so deeply that they could not be found, and now they were bubbling up and I truly felt like I could and would make a difference. I had been called, and I will honour that calling any, and every, way that I can."[9]

[8] Orloff, *Guide to Intuitive Healing*, p. 131.
[9] Kelli Bellis, *Shredding the Shame* (North Vancouver: Influence Publishing, 2014), p. 5.

I believe if we can process our emotions, the emotions that inform our words, we can keep the "ice" circulating. If not, we must push our feelings down, freezing them. Our emotions will pack down until they have nowhere else to go. The more densely packed old emotional stuff becomes, the more likely it is that negative emotions will erupt at the slightest provocation into anger or terror or dis-ease. And, of course, the emotion that emerges might be several degrees from its source, way colder or way hotter, having evolved along the way.

Sometimes, stuffed emotions erupt, like a volcano. During my early teens, my mother used a pressure cooker to shorten cooking time. Pressure cookers have a handled lid and a handled base; the two handles lock together and a weight covering a tiny hole in the lid slows the escape of the steam, cooking the food much faster.

The first few times she used the cooker, Mum neglected to take it off the stove in time. The steam built up to such a degree that it blew off the weight, which went flying somewhere in the kitchen, and then the contents of the cooker spewed out through the tiny hole in the lid. You can only imagine how long it would take to scrape steamed potato off the walls and ceiling. Mum adjusted quickly!

We are veritable masses of energy ourselves, ranging from fiery hot to icy cold. And we, too, are capable of being pressure cookers if we do not tend ourselves with care.

As suggested by the words of intuitive Judith Orloff, any good pair of attentive ears can provide a pressure-relief valve. They can belong to a pet, a friend, a hairdresser, or a counsellor; a plant, a fellow traveller, a sibling, or a priest. The advice that sometimes comes back is not an essential part of the exchange. To release emotions, we just need to get in touch with what we're feeling and put that into words.

World-renowned conservationist and environmentalist Lawrence Anthony describes in *The Elephant Whisperer* how he would "chat" with one of his young elephants: "As he approached I studied his demeanour and decided he was fine. We had a wonderful ten minutes or so interacting, chatting about life—well, me doing that while Mnumzane contentedly browsed…."[10]

I just love that image, the freedom of Anthony being able to say whatever came to his mind in the wide spaces of Africa with his elephant munching nearby.

Shirley Valentine is a one-woman play that was very popular in Vancouver for many years. The character Shirley, acted over six hundred times by BC's beloved Nicola Cavendish, shares her full range of frustrated emotions with the wall in her kitchen. She addresses the wall: "Wall, blah, blah, blah." Very funny. Very human. Very efficient.

When something causes me to stomp off in my mind into some name-and-blame space, my first step is noticing what is happening; the second is asking myself why it is happening; and the third is listening to the answers that come. With the answers, I can identify the feelings that are fueling my emotions and go deeper with the "why." This releases any level of frustration that might build up.

My sister, who lost her husband very soon after they had both retired, struggled during the anger phase of her grief. She experienced a great release when she was driving along the Coquihalla—an Interior BC highway—hollering at her deceased husband at the top of her lungs: "Why did you have to leave so soon? We were having such a good time. I'm lonely. I'm angry with you. Why did you have to go?"

As soon as we give voice to our regrets, our pains, and our concerns, as soon as we name our emotions—e.g., anger fuelled by huge sadness at the loss of a loved one—we allow some of the steam to escape. It can be the start of a healthy ongoing process, depending on how deeply we have packed our emotions into our iceberg or our volcano.

Which of your emotions do you hide from yourself? Do you have a venting process? How do you feel after you share your deepest feelings with your wall, your elephant, the thundering ocean?

[10]Lawrence Anthony, *The Elephant Whisperer* (Thomas Dunn Books, St. Martin's Griffin, 2009), p. 343.

~ *Chakra Connections* ~

"Described as a wheel-like spinning vortex, a chakra is a point of intersection between various planes.... Chakras are also called lotuses, symbolizing the unfolding of flower petals, which metaphorically describes the opening of a chakra. These beautiful flowers are sacred in India.... Both chakras and lotuses are terms referring to seven basic energy centers within what is called the subtle body."

Anodea Judith[11]

I will be referring again to our chakra energies in this book. There are seven major chakras—energy vortices or wheels—in the human body. Clairvoyants can see them protruding out of the front and back of the torso. Our health—physically, emotionally, and mentally—is very dependent on the balanced state of our energetic chakras. Here are some accepted facts about them.

1. The root chakra at the base of the spine is associated with our grounding, our home, our birth family, and our physical health.
2. The sacral chakra, low in the belly, is associated with our relationships, our sexual health, and our financial affairs.
3. The solar plexus chakra is in the region of the belly button. Being roughly in the centre of the physical body, it is connected with being balanced and being in integrity, with ensuring we are being true to who we are.
4. The heart chakra has a unique role as the bridge between Heaven above and Earth below; it is the waistline of the hourglass. In the centre of the chest cavity, over the heart, it governs our emotions, especially loving and healing, bestowing importance on our heart's

[11]Anodea Judith, *Wheels of Life: A User's Guide to the Chakra System* (Llewellyn Publications, 1999), p. 13.

involvement in our lives. Below it are three physical chakras; their purposes are grounding, relating, and balancing. Above it are three spiritual chakras; their purposes are expressing our truth; connecting body, mind, and soul; and connecting with our Higher Self.

5. The throat chakra is the communication centre of the body from where listening, hearing, speaking, singing, and writing are governed. It is closely connected with the third chakra, ensuring that we are expressing our truth with integrity.
6. The third eye or brow chakra is the first of the spiritual chakras and is in the centre of the forehead. Hindu women who adorn themselves with a *bindi* dot between and slightly above their eyebrows are claiming spiritual insight at their third eye.
7. The crown chakra is at the fontanel, the place where the plates of the skull are yet to join together in a baby, the "soft spot." It is commonly held that the spirit enters and leaves the human body through the crown, and it is there that spiritual devotees can connect with their Higher Self and spiritual wisdom.

For a while, I was distracted by trying to number the chakras beyond the first seven major ones. In the process, I researched the eight-chakra system, the nine-, ten-, eleven-, and on up to the twenty-two-chakra system. I kept an open mind in trying to align my beliefs, understandings, and awarenesses with one of them. My favourite became the twelve-chakra system.

Michelle Pilley, Publisher and Managing Director of Hay House U.K., interviewed Diana Cooper during the Hay House World Summit 2015. Diana is a prolific author of books for adults and children, and creator of card sets and DVDs. During the interview—"10 Steps to Ascension with the Archangels"—Diana led a meditation connecting listeners with the Archangels who govern each of the twelve chakras. She went from the throat chakra governed by Archangel Michael, down to the Earth

Star chakra governed by Archangel Sandalphon, and eventually up to the Stellar Gateway governed by Archangel Metatron.

Seven-Chakra System	Twelve-Chakra System
	Earth Star chakra
root *aka* base chakra	root *aka* base chakra
sacral chakra	sacral chakra
	navel chakra
solar plexus chakra	solar plexus chakra
heart chakra	heart chakra
throat *aka* communication chakra	throat *aka* communication chakra
third eye *aka* brow chakra	third eye *aka* brow chakra
crown chakra	crown chakra
	Causal chakra
	Soul Star chakra *aka* Higher Self
	Stellar Gateway chakra

My rational left brain so appreciates understanding the equivalence between the Soul Star chakra and my Higher Self. My right brain is already playing the xylophone connection between my Earth Star and Stellar Gateway chakras.

Able to see the human aura from early childhood, another of today's foremost clairvoyants and metaphysical teachers Barbara Y. Martin applies the training she received from hermetic scientist Dorothy LaMoss to the energies she sees. The beautiful illustrations in her books—*Change Your Aura, Change Your Life; The Healing Power of Your Aura; Karma and Reincarnation*; and *Communing with the Divine*—show the chakras and spiritual energies as she sees them. Martin places extra emphasis on four chakras, giving them their hermetic names: she calls the third chakra "the spiritual heart";[12] the fourth "the hermetic centre"; the fifth "eternal

[12]In other systems, the spiritual heart (*aka* the solar plexus chakra) is known as the core star.

ego"; and the sixth "the trinity chalice." She explains the benefits to be gained from working directly with these four. She also explains that she sees the seventh chakra, the crown chakra, six inches above the head rather than directly at the crown.

Number	chakra names	hermetic wisdom names
3rd chakra	solar plexus chakra	spiritual heart
4th chakra	heart chakra	hermetic centre
5th chakra	communication chakra	eternal ego
6th chakra	brow chakra	trinity chalice
7th chakra	crown chakra	crown chakra

I particularly like the term "trinity chalice," for it shows the chakra's "one in three" and "three in one" aspect. At the trinity chalice, spiritual energy from Higher Self integrates with personal mind and physical body to embody as soul. Martin has helped my understanding of the major chakras with her knowledge of hermetic wisdom and her clairvoyance.

There is one more chakra that she does not mention: Reverend Lunden calls it the "high heart chakra" and Andrrea Hess says it is where the godspark connects soul to spirit. In the area of the thymus gland under the sternum, the high heart chakra governs unconditional love. It is in the region of what Martin calls the "Magnetic Division," which brings in talents and abilities.

Is the term "chakra" new to you? Can you accept that you have energy centres where you store spiritual energy to enliven your life force? Which chakra system do you work with?

Voicing Emotions

~ Crying Out ~

"Eight lashes later and the skin on the man's back was a pulped bloody mess and he was pulled to his feet and led groggily out of the door. Yet still he did not utter a sound.

"'He didn't cry out once,' I said to the aide.... 'I'm impressed.'

"'He must not,' he replied. 'A criminal gets an extra two lashes every time he squeals.'"

Lawrence Anthony[13]

This event took place in a tribal court in Zululand in the early part of the 21st century.

Allowing some kind of emergent sound—whichever one comes naturally to our lips at the moment we experience pain, shock, awe, and surprise—allows us to process that pain, shock, awe, and surprise more rapidly and efficiently. When we hurt ourselves, when we suffer in any way, we can launch our own healing by letting out whatever sound comes automatically, unconsciously.

Every parent knows this; she learns it from the way she responds to her child. A child falls and scrapes his knee. He soon feels the pain of the torn skin as well as the shock of the fall. He lowers his head, puts his hand to his knee, and cries. The parent moves in and instinctively soothes her child with attention, sound, and touch: looking at the injured area; stroking, holding, and cuddling the child gently; making "aahs" and "oohs," and often crooning to the child.

At some point in our acculturation from childhood, we are expected to "suck it up" and be silent about our sudden aches and pains. Lawrence Anthony, the observer of the trial in Zululand, saw how the violent physical punishment of lashings was worsened by the threat of

[13]Anthony, *The Elephant Whisperer*, p. 173.

even more lashings—triple the number in that case—if the guilty party (he had stabbed someone) made any sound whatsoever.

Imagine pain to that degree being turned inward! No wonder the man was groggy. He must have been almost unconscious. We can only endure that severity of pain by leaving our body.

I experienced severe pain on Christmas Day in 1996; an automatic cry emerged from my mouth. To make it more acceptable—or perhaps less unacceptable in our Western world where we are totally discouraged from making a noise when we suffer in some way—I altered the sound I was involuntarily making.

Let me describe the event more fully.

My husband Christian and I were spending that Christmas Day at the home of our eldest son Alun and his wife Dana, along with Dana's father and our three other children. It was a beautiful day: the sun was shining in between snow showers, just as it had the day before. Snow sparkled on tree branches and atop fence posts: a perfect winter scene.

We opened our gifts and played "Om Namaha Shivaya" from the CD of the same name, a gift to me from Christian.[14] Very relaxing. Then three of us girls—Dana, Jessica, and I—decided to go for a walk. The beauty of the outdoors was calling us.

We set out, taking photographs of each other in front of this snow-decorated tree, and that sparkling bush, when, all of a sudden, my feet flew out from under me and I landed with a hard crack on the ground and instant pain flared in my left forearm. I had slid on an area that just the day before—unbeknownst to us—had become slick where some children had been tobogganing.

Clearly from the pain, my left wrist was broken; the bones had displaced rather awkwardly.

From a nearby house, we called back to Dana's house. Her dad Dave was a volunteer ambulance driver and he took charge of getting me and Christian to the emergency department at Burnaby General, the closest

[14]Sung by Robert Gass and On Wings of Song.

hospital. Dave asked me to say on a scale of 1 to 10 how high my pain was. "Seven," I remember saying. What a useful exercise, both for myself to realize my injury wasn't life-threatening and for the paramedics to know it was worse than a bruise!

We didn't have to wait long. An orderly quickly took me in a wheelchair to one of the emergency beds. A doctor took a short history of what had happened, told me I had a Colles' fracture, and decided to reduce it then and there. He called in a nurse—to restrain me, I discovered—and then proceeded to "reduce" the break.

A reduction of a fracture is required when broken bones are lying haphazardly, perhaps on top of each other. The theory is that if the two ends of the bone are pulled apart, the ragged ends where the break has occurred will fit back together in the same way that a cup that is broken in two or three pieces can be reassembled. The only difference with the human body is that the moment a bone breaks, the body responds with a rapid series of steps from muscles and blood vessels to minimize damage and stabilize the break.

So when the doctor started pulling one way on my hand and the nurse started pulling the other way on my elbow, the injured soft tissues in my forearm started to scream at me with pain. My natural response was to scream out to release the pain. And I started to do so. Instantly, I realized two things: there are signs in hospitals to encourage us to be quiet; also, I am a singer and I knew that if I were to scream at the level that would match the pain, the only level that would be beneficial, I would injure my vocal cords, those tiny muscles in the larynx that allow us to make the majority of sounds we make.

So I decided to sing—as high and as loudly as I could. Perhaps it was a high C; I don't know. But anyhow, I maintained it for a very long time, as long as the pain continued. At one point, the doctor said, rather impatiently, "It's all right. You can stop now! We've reduced the fracture." Well, they might have stopped pulling and the bones might by then have been realigned, but my muscles were still screaming at me and I continued to vent that pain with the purest tone and note that I could sing.

Finally, things settled and I was wheeled back to the waiting room where my husband laughingly told me that when he heard the high and loud note, he knew it was me. And even though he suffered along with me and my injury, at the same time he proudly told the other people waiting that his wife was the one singing through the pain.

There was a funny epilogue to this story. Six weeks later, Christian and I kept an appointment with the emergency doctor who had seen me. We pushed open the door of his surgery and there sat fifteen other patients, young and old, all sporting my identical wrist cast, on either their right or left forearms. Apparently, that fresh fall of snow hiding black ice had made it a record day for Colles' fractures; many holidayers had been charmed by the beauty of the outdoors.

Sixteen of us with identical breaks were all waiting to see the same doctor at the same time! And he wasn't even there! That was the final insult. An air of hostility arose in that surgery, which was only quelled one person at a time when the doctor finally arrived and began seeing each of us. As I waited for my turn, I wanted to cry out again, to release my frustration; almost as though it was his fault I had fallen in the first place! Talk about emotions flying around!

Even though I had clearly irritated the doctor by making so much sound when he reduced my break, I knew it was one of the ways that I had launched my own healing after that accident. I took charge, automatically, by letting an instinctive sound—somewhat altered—escape my lips.

So, the next time you find yourself unwittingly responding with sound to an injury to your body, realize that you are starting your healing process. What is your response to injury, to insult, to shock? Could you respond vocally and engage instantly with the emotion rather than bury it?

~ *Cursing* ~

"And you, you serpent, you who ridicule
a father's grief, my curse upon you!"
Francesco Maria Piave[15]

People curse situations, themselves, and others; sometimes they curse with profanities and expletives; sometimes with much gentler versions.

"Shitsky," said our friend Danièle, after losing a trick she had hoped to win in her bridge contract. We all laughed. She had dissipated her own mood with her playful swear word and avoided creating any tension that might have built up had she actually sworn.

The word "cursing" has several meanings to me. It means to swear about a situation, as in "Damn this flat tire" or "To hell with that vase" that just landed on my foot.

One of my authors lost his manuscript after revising it for four or five hours. Despite the fact that he's writing about unconditional love and Divine grace, his reaction was, "My God! Damn! I've lost the file!" He added a couple of "blank blanks." Then he realized he should start using his own advice; he looked at the situation in a different light and managed to see that he'd be able to do an even better job of revising the next time. He cursed the situation spontaneously, moved through it, and improved his mood on the other side.

"Cursing" also means wishing ill on oneself, another person, or a group. "Damn you!" and similar curses express malice and assign blame. Unfortunately, malice and blame cause the anger, frustration, or annoyance that can make a curse stagnate.

Opera abounds with curses: Verdi's and Piave's *Rigoletto* tells the story of the court jester Rigoletto bringing a curse upon himself and his daughter Gilda, one that results in the devastating irony of Rigoletto's heartbreak when he realizes he has paid assassins to kill his own daughter

[15]Piave is the librettist and Giuseppe Verdi the composer of the opera *Rigoletto*.

rather than the one she foolishly loves, his immoral master, the Duke.

A high priest in the service of a Philistine fertility god curses the awesome strength and impregnability of Samson, leader of the Hebrews. This curse, accompanied by another one that moves Delilah to seduce Samson, results in the betrayal and tragedy captured in Camille Saint-Saens's and Ferdinand Lemaire's *Samson and Delilah.*

Rusalka the water sprite in the opera of the same name (music by Antonin Dvořák and libretto by Jaroslav Kvapil) is cursed once she decides to leave her watery home and become human.

As a Soul Realignment Practitioner™, I saw curses afflicting many of my clients—curses inflicted upon them by others, and self-inflicted curses. The self-inflicted curse is the hardest for the person to acknowledge and understand.

My practitioner training, which I acquired from psychic and author Andrrea Hess starting in 2010, brought me to the understanding that a curse causes ongoing harm for both the person who inflicts the curse and its recipient; a curse actually ties curser and "cursee" together from one lifetime to the next. I accept this insight that a curse carries a potent form of energy. If people were aware of this truth, they would not set the energy of a curse loose on their worst enemies.

Many times, we have the power to choose what happens to us in our lives. So if someone curses you in any way that feels vengeful, choose right away to reject rather than accept that energy; make it clear that you do not hold a grudge. This way, the curse falls flat, unable to accomplish its intention, and you walk away free from all ties that such a curse could inflict on you. Meanwhile, the energy of karma causes the curse to boomerang on its originator.

Have you ever intentionally cursed a situation or a person? Would you still willingly curse another person if you knew that curses can rebound?

~ *Reading Body Language* ~

"Implicitly, we read faces, interpret body language, and listen to tones of voice for survival cues."

Theo Fleury and Kim Barthel[16]

I remember attending a half-day course on the true meanings behind interpersonal communications. The instructor first paired the participants and then brought four of us up to face the others. I stood diagonally behind my seated partner; the other pair was positioned the same: one standing and one sitting.

The instructor gave us a conflict to discuss. My seated partner would declare her position on the conflict with the other seated person through regular conversation, while the two of us standing behind spoke aloud the full meaning of their words. It was astonishing how accurate our understanding of the unspoken message was. And because of that, it was also funny. For instance, my partner said something like, "I am disappointed that you did that." And, from behind her, I said, "You had absolutely no right to do that. I am furious with you." And I was able to do that based on what I saw on my partner's face and in the rest of her body. It was her body language.

In *Conversations with a Rattlesnake*, therapist Kim Barthel explains that babies have an innate ability to read body language, understanding and responding accordingly. This skill continues throughout our lives.

Have you ever wondered what body vibe you are giving off? It's actually one of the reasons I enjoy acting, because I do wonder. The discipline of acting makes me more aware of how I am holding myself, walking, sitting, speaking, and gesticulating. Do my gestures match my words? Do my words match my gestures? Am I being authentic?

Sometimes I will copy the gait of someone walking in front of me, not to mock but to learn. Having worked as a physiotherapist and also being

---

[16]Fleury and Barthel, *Conversations with a Rattlesnake*, p. 47.

an actor, I learn a lot from copying someone's gait. Every walk means something different—late for lunch, annoyed with the teller, happy about the weather, on long-term disability, trying to hold something steady, and on it goes.

Me as Jean Perkins in 2002 in *Funny Money* by Ray Cooney. Photograph by Gary Schwartz.

Body language shares its message before we even open our mouths. Are you responding to the words your friend says or to her body language? Do her words match her body language? Do yours?

ॐ

~ *Judging and Being Judged* ~

"What are the generic qualities of a 'good person'?
Why do I select the word 'good' as a starting point?
Because that word and the qualities that go with it
are inherent in the progression of good to better to best.
Those are our three categories: Good, Better, Best."

Caroline Myss[17]

We might as well give up trying to know what others think about us. We cannot begin to think of the criteria by which others are judging us, using us as their mirrors to judge themselves. They might judge us by our height, our clothes, our "good" or "plain" looks. Or by the length of our fingernails, by whether we love hockey, by which newspaper we read or television show we watch. They might judge us by whether or not we keep a pen in our pocket, a business card in our wallet, or a comb in our car. They might judge us by whether we arrive on time or late, by how clean our shoes are, by whether we do yoga, how loud we like our music, or by whether or not we have a university degree.

And what are the emotions attached to these judgments?

In the end, it's very freeing to know that when one person judges another, they are using the criteria they use on themselves. It's their stuff, not ours.

I remember as a girl, I discounted people who wore glasses. They just didn't count. Their opinions were of no value. At some point in my later teens, I recognized how horrible that judgment was, but it was still there. Of course, you can imagine how all that changed when I started wearing glasses myself in my mid-thirties!

I remember our family once received a letter from my mother's sister in which she criticized my mother for writing her letters chronologically. It's important now for me to understand that at the time my aunt was

[17]January 2014 Salon, www.facebook.com/201192805715/posts/10154205814365716; accessed February 7, 2015.

teaching creative writing at Douglas College and perhaps she was trying to make her students use their imaginations in different ways. Did her criticism also feed into her own insecurities as a writer? I'll never know. But I'll wonder.

Can you pinpoint some of the criteria you employ to judge people? Turn those criteria on their heads and realize they are merely values you hope you can always demonstrate.

Introducing this scene, I quote best-selling author and mystic Caroline Myss discussing her answers to the question, "What Are You Willing to Do to Become a Better Person?" Her range of good to best begs me to enlarge the range of descriptors from "worst" to "best": "worst, worse, bad, good, better, best." I could add "evil" and "virtuous" at the bottom and the top; that would give us quite a range.

worst | worse | bad | good | better | best

I agree that comparisons are odious, comparisons that have us ranking ourselves compared with others. But how about comparisons of ourselves in different roles, in different times of our lives, in different settings, in the future compared with the past? Can we compare ourselves with ourselves? Can we look at ourselves objectively, freeing ourselves of the emotions attached to judging our personalities and behaviour, and see where we fall within this range of "worst, worse, bad, good, better, best"? I believe we can, without being either vain or self-effacing.

And of course, we might be bad at one thing and good at another, priding ourselves in the good thing and cursing ourselves for the bad. It is a rare person who realizes that both self-blame and self-approval hold us in rigid positions of conforming to others' and our own criteria. By recognizing that we judge our own behaviour and others', we can start to be more in charge of our lives.

Caroline Myss offers us the opportunity to see how she is considering improving herself—by setting herself commitments to improve. I do the same. First, I commit to dissolving all anger within myself when I am in the presence of someone who is angry. Second, I commit to being patient with myself when I am not able to do things to the standard I set myself. And third, I commit to striving toward being a wisdom-bearer—if not in this lifetime, then in the next.

By stating my third commitment, I'm introducing a few ideas that I'm not ready to explain yet. You may be comfortable with them. If you are not, I ask your forbearance until I can expand on these ideas.

Think of three personal attributes and score them on the worst-to-best scale. Are you where you want to be? Are you willing to improve your standing? How? What steps would be required?

Sensing Energies

~ Four or Five Physical Senses, or Nine ~

"A sense is a physiological capacity of organisms that provides data for perception."

wikipedia.org "Sense"[18]

Up until the time I studied human anatomy and physiology at the Canadian School of Natural Nutrition in Vancouver in 2010 (having previously studied human anatomy during physiotherapy training in the 1960s), I believed that humans have five senses—seeing, hearing, smelling, tasting, and touching. But Marieb's *Essentials of Human Anatomy & Physiology* explains that we have just four "special senses"—seeing, hearing, smelling, and tasting—and that the sense we call "touching" is a combination of the "general senses" of perceiving temperature, pressure, pain, balance, and position.[19]

[18]Accessed November 1, 2014.

[19]Elaine N. Marieb, R.N., Ph.D, *Essentials of Human Anatomy & Physiology*, 8th edition (Old Tappan, NJ: Pearson Higher Education, 2009).

Since having a fractured hip replaced in 2014, I absolutely know that the ball-and-socket hip joint provides the rest of the body with information about balance and body position. I know this because twice since the surgery I have righted myself only moments short of falling. My artificial hip joint does not provide my brain with the information regarding balance that my original hip used to provide.

I realize what this greater vulnerability implies: that every other joint and muscle and tendon is also constantly providing information that my brain takes and interprets to keep me safe. Isn't that impressive? If you agree, you probably share my normal state of awe toward the human body, actually toward every animal's body, every tree, every plant, shell, feather, leaf, and perfect drop of water.

When we "lose" something, like a hip joint, and we "gain" something else, like an artificial hip joint, we also gain a new way of seeing and perceiving ourselves.

Have you lost any part of your body in your life? What did you gain in its place? How do the loss and the gain affect your perception of yourself? Physically? Sensorily? Emotionally? Mentally?

~ *Listening to Others* ~

"Children who are read to early and regularly quickly acquire
the skill of listening and the desire to hear stories.
They understand the immense pleasures waiting for them in books
and develop the ability to concentrate and relax."

Mem Fox[20]

Listening is an active skill, unlike the passive capacity to hear and the unthinking and unthinkable habit of not hearing or ignoring. Concentration is required for listening, as is a willingness to put aside the desire to

[20]Mem Fox, *Reading Magic* (Harcourt, Inc., 2001), p. 33.

respond, at least for long enough to register what the other person says. "Not hearing" seems to be on one end of a spectrum that extends through "listening" and "hearing with our ears" to finally "hearing with our heart."

not hearing | listening | hearing with our ears | hearing with our heart

If someone wants an answer and they announce their wish, in the more recent way of saying, "Question!" before asking what they want to know, we listen. It is a good idea to announce, "Question!" It means "Listen up!"

Another way people draw attention to the fact that they want us to listen to them is by speaking more loudly than us. Have you ever observed a conversation between two people in which the listener wants to interject with comments and the speaker "maintains the floor" by speaking more loudly? It's a style of conversation that shuts down dialogue, because it becomes a one-way conversation, a monologue rather than a dialogue. Maybe it should be called a "duelogue," because of its combative nature!

Active listening is suggested by following "heard me" with "out"; if "He heard me out" then he not only heard me speak to him but also paid attention until my message was complete. Such listening can pick up the emotions that energize a speaker's words.

Developing active listening skills yields wonderful results. I'm not talking about listening to a television program or a radio interview—though that requires its own kind of skill. I'm talking about listening to our loved ones, our colleagues, the people we interact with daily.

There are many aspects to attending to others' speech—we can pay attention to the actual words, the tone with which the words are being said, the body language that accompanies them, the timing, the speed, where those particular words sit within the whole conversation. Children and the elderly and people whose words go unheard often repeat themselves, in the hope that someone will finally listen and hear them with heart.

We cannot understand each other until we truly learn to listen. And, as Mem Fox implies, listening requires both concentration and relaxation. It requires being in the Now, something of a Zen state.

Are you listening to those around you? Are you listening to just their words or to the emotions that energize them? Are you so eager to get your own view across that you don't give others the attention that listening and hearing with heart requires?

~ *Honey to Hide the Bitter Taste* ~

"Give her the penicillin powder in a teaspoon of honey."

Emrys Williams, M.D.[21]

When I was a girl, I must have been rather uncoordinated, because I was often scraping my knees on the asphalt school playground. There came a time when I had fallen so frequently that I had what Dr. Emrys (a Welsh given name pronounced 'em-riss) called "septic knees." He prescribed the antibiotic penicillin, which was still being dispensed in powder form to take orally. It was so bitter that I gagged, unable to swallow it. So our family doctor advised my mum to stir the powder into a teaspoon of honey and I was finally able to swallow enough of it to reverse the infection in the skin over my knees.

Honey, however, then became a food that caused me to gag. The smell of it was enough to activate my gag reflex—our sense of smell interacts with our sense of taste—and my tongue would curl up, sensing that bitter penicillin hid inside. There was no way I would willingly eat honey.

Eventually, sometime in my forties, I set about reversing my conditioning around honey. I did this through conscious choice, by concentrating very hard on the actual flavours and aromas of the honey, again and again, and not on the anticipated bitterness. Nowadays, I love honey.

[21]Dr. Williams's advice to my mother about administering penicillin to me in 1954.

What we sense physically is so wrapped up in our emotions, thoughts, and memories that we have great trouble distinguishing result from cause. Mostly, our emotions and our sensations are so entangled that we perceive the result as truth. And we don't see that this "truth" is only our own take on the world as we know it at that moment.

Are you also tasting an inaccurate flavour—a flavour that isn't there? What flavours do you prefer? Salty? Savoury? Sweet? Which do you avoid? Pungent, bitter, sour, and metallic? What combinations do you like? Sweet and sour? Salty and pungent as in a curry? Bitter as in coffee and black tea? Are any of your other special senses providing you with information about something that isn't even there?

~ *Seeing Myself in a Mirror* ~

"Mirror, mirror, on the wall, who is the fairest of us all?"

"Snow White"

I do a lot of community theatre. Preparing and playing a role always requires that I learn something new while examining my own behaviour and nature closely. If my acting holds emotional truth for me and the audience, the whole experience of studying, rehearsing, and performing becomes very fulfilling. Also, engaging with others in such vulnerable ways provides deep relationships and rich friendships.

Often the call time for a play is one hour before the curtain goes up. After changing into my costume for Act One, I apply my stage makeup; none of these things takes me long. While applying rouge and eyeliner and afterwards, I chat with the other women in the play. Usually, I am older than most of them.

How interesting it is to chat to a person twenty or thirty years younger when no mirrors are around and then to do it with a mirror in front of us both.

Without the mirror, I feel I am as young as they are; with the mirror, I know I am not. Where I once just had laugh lines, I now have many more. And when I am with my grandchildren, and look in a mirror, I feel yet older again.

The word "feel" is confusing, because it means both to register a personal emotion and to perceive the tactile features of something exterior to us. In the previous paragraph, it refers to emotions, along with a sort of interpretation of my inner sensory state. This is where life can become very complicated, because it's hard to differentiate between "how we feel" and what we feel about that! And our feelings—our emotions, our sensations, and our interpretations of our inner sensory state—are all going on, all the time.

Back to the mirror; there's more. When I look in a mirror, I can also see that I pull a lot of faces. I would never make a good poker player or a film actor, because my responses—mental and emotional—are visible for all to see on my face. It's partly from having grown up in the fifties and sixties in Great Britain—I think we brightened our lives by reacting strongly to everything. Now, it's a habit, a useful one for stage acting, less so for film.

Does your facial expression give away what you are thinking and feeling? What do you see, what do you notice, when you look at someone else? If seeing is a perception, one of our four physical senses, what do you choose to perceive? Do you look for certain things, or do you actually see what is there?

Chapter 2—Several Minds

The Subconscious Mind

~ *The Role of Memory* ~

"The unexamined life is not worth living."
Socrates[22]

It's hard to know where to start when writing about the mind, but I'll begin with the subconscious mind, because that's where we store all our automatic knowings and responses for living our daily lives. Our memories, for example, are stored in our subconscious mind, and we frequently live our lives from the perspective of memory.

Memory and its role in our lives is such a vast topic—and probably more the terrain for psychologists and psychiatrists, neither of which I am—that I might prefer to avoid it. But I will demonstrate how fickle and flexible and plastic (to use a medical term) our memory is. This will work best when you have a diary from, say, five years ago, or a journal of the same age or older, or a "Dear John" letter you wrote, or an essay. Retrieve it from wherever it is and check out its age to be sure it's old, but don't read it yet.

Now write out an event from that period of your life that you think is in the diary, journal, letter, or essay. Flesh it out as well as you can, with all the details you can muster, paying attention to all your senses: seeing, hearing, smelling, touching, tasting, listening, and discerning.

Once the event is down on paper to the best of your ability, read your historical record of the event and compare the two. In your retelling of this story, have you left anything out, perhaps even a major element, or what today seems like a major element? Have you introduced new

[22]At his trial for heresy in 399 BCE.

elements that you now realize were not part of the original story? Is the story not even in that year's journal?

Or, by chance, is your current-day description pretty much a blow-by-blow for the historic one?

I doubt it.

The difference between two records of the same event shows the fickle nature of memory and how adaptable it is. This lends credence to the idea that we can change our past; it is not carved in stone: After all, it is merely thoughts. We can re-carve it; we can rethink it. We can have different emotions about it.

I love to act in plays, musicals, and skits; and early on, I compiled a résumé that included a role from high school, as Cecily Cardew in Oscar Wilde's *The Importance of Being Earnest*. Years later, I attended my fortieth high school reunion and learned that our school had not presented such a play while I attended! I was shocked, disbelieving. We hadn't performed it? I can only think that we did such a good presentation of it during my English Literature classes that my memory had shifted it into a real event.

I removed "Cecily Cardew" from my résumé.

In our physical, transitory world, many manmade performances, events, creations, and items come to symbolize or represent items and events that happen naturally and that exist in nature. For instance, artistic endeavours are like life—art takes us to the next level if we let it. Art—in its broadest sense—says, "This is mimicking life. Can you see the comparison?" Art helps us to see nature with new eyes. For instance, a sketch, a painting, a collage, a mural, and a statue say, "Look at this more closely. What is it saying?" A poem and song lyrics say, "Hear this." Music says, "Listen with your heart." A play might say, "This is what growing old might be like. Which of these characters will you be?" Memory works interestingly with art, taking our reaction to being part of art or observing art deeper into our subconscious, allowing it to rest there and inform our lives in deeper, more holistic ways.

One line from my most recent play says it all: "Art is nothing if it does not make you feel."[23]

Manmade analogies are everywhere; they are ours to learn from, as warnings, as flags, as heralds, as koans, and as welcome signs. Give them words and ask them what they mean so they can come alive and imbue even greater meaning into their presence.

A Course in Miracles says that thoughts have no meaning.[24] Even so, I believe that before a thought becomes a memory, an emotion ties itself to the thought, making it a repeated thought imbued with emotion. I remember respecting the awesome power of the Bunsen burners in the chemistry lab at my high school—Howell's School in Llandaff (HSL), near Cardiff; I remember being repelled by the smell of the cadavers in the Gross Anatomy lab connected with Cardiff Royal Infirmary when I was training as a physiotherapist, and never wanting to eat lunch after those lectures; I remember the gruesomeness of having my nose cauterized and smelling burning flesh—my own flesh; I remember performing the part of Scrap in *Dear Octopus* (we really did perform that play!) and trying desperately to swallow a cough in one of the scenes; I remember picking bluebells with my parents and my sister and loving their delicate blue petals, their sweet scent, and their juicy, bitter-tasting stems; I remember the thrill of picking mushrooms with my father before dawn and anticipating the joy of eating them later for breakfast; they were growing around the edges of an enormous circle, a fairy circle.[25] No wonder I still love mushrooms.

Can you release the unpleasant emotions connected to a memory and just let the now-pleasant thought drift away? Do you have any memories that are not tied to an emotion? If you remember something, does that mean you *felt* something about that event? Do those memories have a bearing on your present life?

[23]Ronald Harwood, *Quartet*.

[24]Schucman, Helen, with William Thetford, *A Course in Miracles* (Foundation for Inner Peace, 1996), Lesson 4.

[25]The field mushrooms were popping up around the edges of the mycelium in a vast air field.

~ Speaking for the Body ~

"My feet are killing me. Nina, run upstairs and fetch me my slippers."
Vera McGregor[26]

Our bodies have the ability—by Divine design—to talk to us very clearly with wisdom through our own mouths. If we only could listen to this wisdom—our advice to ourselves—then we would progress by leaps and bounds in our own health and healing.

As I helped my 95-year-old mother out of her weekly bath in her walk-in tub during her last year on Earth, I looked at Mum's two bunions—one on each big toe—and her words came back to me from fifty years earlier: "My feet are killing me. Nina, run upstairs and fetch me my slippers." And what had she been wearing around town? The fashionable high heels of that era, beautiful to look at, but hell for her feet.

She was sporting the evidence of the "killing."

Okay, wearing shoes with pointed toes did not *kill* my mother, but it did damage her big toe joints, which, amazingly, she never complained about.

With our ears we hear,
and when we take what we hear to heart,
we sit on Earth
at the hearth of our own wisdom.

Often, we speak without thinking first. Probably, a great deal of conversation occurs without the speaker forming their speech beforehand. This leads to more honest outbursts, responses, more brutal frankness, more cut-to-the-chase truths. If, when we burst out with a statement, we could stand still and listen to what we just said, we might learn a great

---

[26]My mother's request to me all through the 1960s after shopping in town in fashionable high heels.

deal. Try listening next time you involuntarily come out with something that surprises you.

If the moment passes without listening, not to worry. If our bodies want us to know something, they keep giving us the message until we hear it and take it to heart. It is a message to us from our body via our subconscious.

Sometimes, we just laugh off what we say, and that's great. Laughter lightens up a mood through the release of endorphins, so it rightly has a reputation for being the best medicine. But after the laughter, take a moment and think back. What did I just say? Did my unconscious intend it for my ears? How can I learn from it? How can this body wisdom enable me to "whole myself"—that is, make friends with a part of me that I have rejected but, for complete vitality, cannot actually do without? What is my body saying?

~ *Doing Things Mostly by Rote* ~

"We are what we repeatedly do.
Excellence, then, is not an act, but a habit."
Aristotle

The most difficult thing to remember in playing bridge is who just dealt the cards: not, as you might expect, the order of the suits or the meaning of a bid or the way to score (though that can be tricky, given the many scoring methods), but who just dealt. It's because we do it by rote, both the watching and the doing.

We do a lot by rote—driving the car, having a shower, cleaning our teeth. I do my morning exercises almost by rote. Sometimes, I try to remember if I've already done a certain exercise that morning. It's my muscles that tell me yea or nay.

The reason we don't remember is that we are acting habitually, and habits are extremely useful. They help us avoid a myriad of decisions in the moment. For instance, when my husband and I go to our local Blenz café, my husband knows what to order for me. I've already decided a dark decaf mocha made with almond milk is my favourite beverage. It's become a habit.

When we face a decision for the first time, we take a while to weigh up the options the situation presents, for and against; we decide how to respond. The second time we face the same decision, it is a lot easier. The third and subsequent times, we can rely on the decisions we made previously. Gradually, that habit becomes the responsibility of our subconscious mind. We no longer have to think about it. It becomes invisible; we can no longer see that we have made the same choice out of a series of choices, again. We begin to think—especially in some situations—that our choice is the only possible choice.

We always have more choices.

It is said that a person takes twenty-one days to entrench a habit—three days to anchor habitual steps into each of the seven major chakras of the body. I've noticed that it can take even longer to break a habit. Questioning our habits and making new ones is an opportunity to live differently. We have to reprogram our subconscious mind, our hard drive. We have to wipe it clean and write a new program, consciously.

Have you ever questioned some of your habits? Some of the things you do by rote? By rite, because you've made a daily ritual out of them?

~ *Seeing an Inner Image* ~

"Close your eyes and think of a horse. No ... stop and really do this!
Notice you thought up a picture of a horse.
You didn't see the letters 'h-o-r-s-e' floating nowhere in space.
You saw a picture of a horse. Your brain thinks in pictures, not words."
Terry Small[27]

Barbara Brennan in *Hands of Light* says that the thoughts that answer our own inner questions come to us along with "pictures, feelings, general concepts, words or even smells."[28] She also makes a simpler claim that our thoughts—and what are answers if not thoughts?—first appear to us as images, sounds, feelings, and knowings.

There is good evidence in the two ebooks by ordained metaphysical minister, meditation facilitator, Reiki master, and Kundalini Yoga instructor Tim Doyle that he has spent much of his life examining his thoughts and improving them. He says that when we are asked a question, our brains go from hearing the question, to seeing an inner image of the subject of the question, to answering the question.

"For example, if I asked you the color of your car, you might answer automatically with the color of your car. What you might not realize is that there is an unconscious process you first go through of visualizing the car in your Mind's Eye Chakra to identify its color."[29]

We store these images in our minds as both stationary and moving images. For instance, as I think of my car, I see it parked in our underground parkade, in a street parking spot, or on a parking deck of a ferry to Vancouver Island; I see the inside of it with myself as the driver and as a passenger; I see it getting bigger as I walk toward it. What I don't see is my car on a racetrack or on the beach, because it's never been on

[27]"Brain Bulletin #7—How the Brain Remembers Names," terrysmall.com/bb_07.asp; accessed February 9, 2015.
[28]Barbara Brennan, *Hands of Light: A Guide to Healing through the Human Energy Field.* (Random House, 2011), p. 169
[29]Tim Doyle, *How to Play the Game of Life: Beginner's Version* (ThePathToOneness.com, 2013), p. 20.

a racetrack or a beach. I can imagine it on a racetrack, but it's more of a stretch; the first examples just require me to tap into existing memories. But oddly enough, now that I've imagined my car on a beach, I can see it there quite clearly. There's sand in the treads.

How do you recall something? Through visuals, feelings, or using other senses? Can you catch your mind going through the steps between hearing a question and supplying the answer?

The Collective and the Personal Unconscious and Collective Consciousness

~ *Cultural Differences* ~

"That Was The Week That Was.... *was unlike any television programme we had ever seen before: funny, raucous, and deliberately rough in style. But what took our breath away was its impudence and its brashness."*

John Cleese[30]

Cultural and societal norms are almost impossible to see until we start looking for them. They are the result of what French sociologist Émile Durkheim called the "collective consciousness." Other terms for the collective consciousness might be fashion or trend or culture. Alternatively, politics, beliefs held by the whole of society (e.g., the Earth is flat), our value system, and our laws comprise the collective consciousness. When I attended Simon Fraser University (SFU), I was fascinated to learn that laws change over time just to reflect the beliefs of the leaders of the period. And, of course, it was obvious once I looked at that clearly. But until then, I had not seen it.

---

[30]John Cleese, *So, Anyway...* (Doubleday Canada, 2014), p. 152.

Seeing what the majority accept as the norm, the vanguards of society challenge it, changing society and what is "fashionable" in the process. David Frost, the host of the satirical television show *That Was The Week That Was* (TW3), led the team that blew away Great Britain's cobwebs of stuffiness and self-satisfaction, launching what many call "the satirical sixties" in my homeland. Like John Cleese, I, too, grew up in the hormonally driven days of rock 'n' roll and jive and satire, sharing with my girlfriends on the bus the discovery of TW3 and The Beatles' rise to fame.

Is it possible to see what the collective consciousness holds dear today? It's very difficult. Whenever a group comes together, they start to create a body of shared thoughts.

When I moved from the capital city of Cardiff in Wales to the small town of Penticton in Canada in 1969, I could see clearly those of Canada's values that affected me—a slower, quieter pace of life accompanied by muted colours, gentle behaviour, and very little swearing; riding a bike became weird and changing clothes on the beach unseen. When I moved from Penticton to Douglas Lake Home Ranch, I soon appreciated a lifestyle dictated by the weather, the environment, and the habits of cattle and cattlemen. That's when I realized that the ranch's history was still tangible and I became interested in recording it in what became my first book, *Cattle Ranch*.

When I moved from Douglas Lake Ranch in Canada to a small sheep and cattle property in New South Wales, Australia in 1979, I could see Australia's values clearly—an endearing brashness, an unendearing chauvinism, and a drive to endure against all odds and perversities. When I returned to Canada in 1984, from sheep country to Victoria, BC's capital, once again I saw the values that were different from mine.

With that last move, it was my older children who paid the highest price—their Aussie hairstyles, clothes, accents, and morals didn't mesh with Victoria's high schools, where who was sleeping with whom and who had to have an abortion were topics shouted down school hallways.

The term "collective consciousness" can be applied to a country, a city, a school, an institution. Those who work in one industry share a mindset that differs from the mindset of another industry: compare mining with growing tomatoes in a greenhouse. When we first move into a new milieu, we notice what is different; then we start to accept and absorb those differences. We begin to fit in.

Can you name three things that differentiate your setting from another's? This work from that work? This neighbourhood from that neighbourhood? This sport from that sport?

~ *The Collective Unconscious* ~

"The collective unconscious comprises in itself the psychic life of our ancestors right back to the earliest beginnings."

Carl Jung[31]

Analytical psychologist Carl Jung coined the term "the collective unconscious" to refer to the inexplicable phenomenon that humanity shares common archetypal truths that predetermine our experiences without seeming cause. I like to think that the collective unconscious is layered. After all, who does not think the darkest of thoughts when in the depths of a hellish problem? And so the layer of the collective unconscious that they are tapping into—*aka* accepting *aka* thinking—is the lowest level of thinking, the hellish level.

Which begs some unanswerable questions, "Is Hell a place or a level or a collection of thoughtforms?"

"Am I thinking or am I being thought?" Current studies in the area of neuroscience in connection with the fact that the unconscious mind initiates some actions *prior* to the conscious mind *deciding* to act in that way

[31]C.G. Jung, *Collected Works* vol. 8, "The Significance of Constitution and Heredity in Psychology," (Princeton University Press, 1960). The paper was first published in 1929.

throw new light on what constitutes free will. This will be an intriguing area of research in the coming decades.

Tim Doyle's channellings from The Golden Ones offers this information: "When the conscious mind is concentrating or focusing on a subject, there is no interference from outside random thought interference. 'Outside random thought interference' comes from a variety of sources, such as discarnate souls, random thoughts from individuals in our immediate environment, observation or awareness of our surroundings ... fantasies triggered by our desire nature, our own thoughts in which we are judgmental of the way another soul dresses, walks, talks, expresses itself, its nationality or religion, and other observations that may cause us to make judgments."[32] Those judgmental thoughts arise from our undiscerning subconscious mind, the one storing all our previous habits and observations.

Let me continue with this idea of the collective unconscious being layered. There is a common route that individuals take when they decide "I need to follow my journey and align my actions more closely with my heart and spirit." This route involves making emotional choices that move us from thinking of ourselves as solely our physical bodies living in a physical environment to thinking of ourselves as embodied spirits. In that way, we start thinking far more palatable thoughts, more uplifted thoughts. In turn, these feed into our more spiritual emotions, the more highly aligned emotions of tolerance and acceptance. The next level moves up to conditional love and harmony and, later, to joy, bliss, and unconditional love.

These levels and layers remind me of the "Map of Consciousness"[33] in *Power vs. Force* by David R. Hawkins, M.D., Ph.D. This psychiatrist, lecturer, author, and deep thinker states: "The basis of this work is research done over a 20-year period, involving millions of calibrations

---

[32]Timothy J. Doyle, *How to Play the Game of Life: Intermediate Version* (ThePathToOneness.com, 2014), p. 63.
[33]David P. Hawkins, *Power vs. Force: The Hidden Determinations of Human Behavior* (Hay House, 1995), p. 68.

on thousands of test subjects of all ages and personality types, and from all walks of life."[34] He established these "millions of calibrations" using Applied Kinesiology (see the section in chapter four, "Alternative Healing Modalities"). Originally, I borrowed Dr. Hawkins's book from the Vancouver Public Library—my favourite Vancouver institution—but the knowledge Dr. Hawkins shares is so thought-provoking that I had to go out and buy it, not something I often do *after* reading a book.

Dr. Hawkins sorted his research—the millions of calibrated emotions and life views—into levels, creating a "Map of Consciousness." "Fear, grief, apathy, guilt," and "shame" log at a value of 100 or below. At 200, emotions begin moving in a positive direction with "courage" and "empowerment." "Love" is at 500, "joy" at 540, "peace" at 600, and "enlightenment" ranges from 700 up to 1,000.[35]

So, what is your level? Do you have courage? Do you accept the difficult challenges that life presents you? Do you have reverence for all life forms? What are the ideas and thoughts that fill your day? Are they the thoughts and ideas you actively think because you want to think them, or are they just the ones that permeate and drift up from the collective unconscious into your vulnerable mind unbidden, the "outside random thought interference" that Doyle describes?

Once we recognize that some of our thoughts are unbidden, arising from the collective unconscious, we can recognize the corollary, which is that we can bid our thoughts, we can control them, we can invite them in and become active thought-thinkers, rather than passive thought-hearers.

Are you willing to examine your thoughts and see if you can figure out whose they are?

[34]Ibid., page 55.
[35]Ibid., page 319.

~ *Watching and Hearing as Unconscious Triggers* ~

"Triggers give us lots to work with....
I see them all as personal growth opportunities."
Theo Fleury and Kim Barthel[36]

Living now in the twenty-first century, we all have a myriad of opportunities to watch and hear others perform, act, declaim, pronounce, and speak—on television; in plays, operas, YouTube videos, and DVDs; at concerts and the movies; in ceremonies, rituals, and services. We can even pick up our binoculars and opera glasses and watch people more closely.

These are multiple opportunities to be voyeurs, to analyze others' body language without having to respond appropriately. A response of our own usually arises, so that we can compare ourselves with those we watch.

I consider that the many opportunities we have to watch and hear these days can speed up our learning considerably, can speed up our alignment with our highest values, if we allow them to.

Barthel observes something that I have known deep down for decades: "Triggers give us lots to work with." I define a "trigger" as something, anything, that launches me back to an unresolved emotional place. Barthel continues: "[Triggers] happen during conversations, watching movies, observing the actions of others ... I think this is why I love watching movies so much—I see them all as personal growth opportunities."

For me, watching plays works the same, though for some reason the space is not as private as a movie hall.

Many years ago, I watched Vancouver Playhouse's production of Arthur Miller's play about the "witches" of Salem, *The Crucible*. For me, the story was incredibly painful, repulsive, and way too familiar. My emotions were so deep that I came away feeling certain that one of my

[36]Fleury and Barthel, *Conversations with a Rattlesnake*, p. 293.

past lives was as a woman perceived as a witch and killed for my abilities to heal.

Have you ever watched and heard a story that felt so personal you knew they were telling your story? What do we do with that knowing? What did you do with that knowing?

If watching and hearing something opens a portal up in your psyche, explore that wormhole and see where it leads. Perhaps you too will be able to heal a past-life pain and progress in this life. Perhaps you have already done so. What can you watch next?

~ *Naming and Labelling* ~

"As soon as one begins to divide things up, there are names.
Once there are names, one should also know when to stop;
knowing when to stop, one thereby avoids peril."

Lao Tzu[37]

When Gertrude Stein wrote, "A rose is a rose is a rose," which was afterward written as, "Rose is a rose is a rose is a rose," she was intending that we understand that the name of an object cannot ever truly stand for the object itself; she wrote that way, to bring the meaning of "rose" back to the object itself.

Even so, being caught in this material world, I find it satisfyingly good to name something, because then it's as though one has a file folder in which to put all the attributes of that something, as a more efficient way of identifying the thing and adding meaning to it.

I emailed a friend about such an example: "It is interesting that you raised the topic of Charles Bonnet syndrome [CBS]. In the 1990s, I had a prolonged period during which my eyes functioned separately because of an eye-muscle disease. In reading about CBS, I realized that is the

[37]Lao Tsu, *Tao Te Ching,* translation by Victor H. Mair (Bantam Books, 1990), Chapter 76.

term for several experiences I had during that time in which constantly moving geometric patterns swirled and evolved in colour before my eyes. I decided to actively enjoy the experiences, appreciating right away that they were no doubt the product of what was going on with my eyesight. Nice to have a name for such experiences."[38]

Those constantly moving, colourful geometric patterns swirling and evolving in front of my eyes were hypnotic; they came and went over the period of a couple of months. I remember one occasion when I was sitting in a friend's living room with others sitting opposite. I could see my friends through the swirls, like constantly shifting kaleidoscopic images. I knew I wasn't crazy and that the images were just some kind of manifestation of the eye-muscle disease. Realizing they were just an illusion of my vision enabled me to enjoy them.

And on the same topic of naming and labelling, I recently heard a CBC interview discuss something called "finger tutting" and had to look it up on YouTube to know what it is. It reminds me of dubstepping and beatboxing and rap songs and Michael Jackson's hat dancing and moon-walking. Each is its own separate and distinct category of body moves combined with music, some with words. In another decade, there'll be a whole new range of such terms and the ones here may have fallen into the shadows.

Agreeing on the name for something allows us to find common ground with another person. Then we can be sure we are talking about the same thing, even though our opinion and understanding of it may not be the same. That's how we become part of the collective consciousness.

Are you involved in any activity for which a name has recently been invented? Tweeting? Texting? Even emailing was barely known in the 1990s.

[38]Email to Karen Tyrell, Dementia Consultant and Educator, January 8, 2013.

The Conscious Mind

~ *Comparisons* ~

"The song that I came to sing remains unsung to this day.
I have spent my days in stringing and unstringing my instrument."
Rabindranath Tagore[39]

Life offers us metaphors constantly, where this stands for that, and that stands for this. Watching a television series entitled *Merlin,* I heard a metaphor that alerted me to something I should avoid: "fighting a battle on two fronts." The episode was the one in which Lady Morgana had tied a mandrake root under King Uther Pendragon's bed to weaken him and absorb his energy so that she and Lady Morgause could take over Camelot. And then, as soon as the besieged army at Camelot was fighting heroically against the marauding troops gathered by Morgause's ally, King Cenred, Lady Morgana used the energized mandrake root to bring life back to all the skeletons in the catacombs and tombs. So the Camelot soldiers were fighting on two fronts: against the armed troops scaling the walls and against the skeletons spreading throughout the castle itself.

Both "fighting on two fronts" and "confronting our skeletons" have metaphorical meanings. As soon as we are struggling on two fronts instead of one, we are working with a major handicap. And a skeleton, whether from a tomb or a closet, is a hard thing to face, because it has been with us for so long, like a bad habit.

The symbolic link between an item and the thing it stands for requires that we pull our awareness of it out from our subconscious.

Ocean Resort, a beautiful spa on the east coast of central Vancouver Island, has an outdoor labyrinth whose path is lined with driftwood. Walking a labyrinth can be meditative and definitely metaphorical on

---

[39]Rabindranath Tagore, *Gitanjali,* tagoreweb.in, Verse 13.

many levels. As I walked into the centre of this labyrinth, I felt I was turning more to the right than to the left; and as I walked back out, I felt I was turning more to the left. And this sparked in me a metaphor for life: for the first part of our lives (when we are walking into the centre), we are trying to do everything right—following the guidance of our parents, our teachers, our employers, and the expectations of society. Once we reach the centre of our lives in our forties or fifties—the centre of the labyrinth—we start to leave behind what is "right" and consider what might still be "left" to do and to be in our lives. Usually what is still left undone is connecting with ourselves through our own yearnings and longings and the call of our soul to complete the purpose we came to Earth to accomplish.

International leader, corporate executive, and author Belynda Lee tells a very powerful story of leaving behind what might have seemed right, when she "resigned from a very successful nine-year career without any Plan B." But as she says, "Walking away from something has nothing to do with weakness; it has everything to do with realizing our worth and value."[40]

The fable of the six blind men who describe an elephant is a great metaphor for our individual experiences of our own inner life force, our Divinity. In case you don't know the story, each man describes the part of the elephant he is closest to—one of the ears, the flank, the trunk, the tail, one of the legs, and the foot—and the range of those descriptions shows that each of us sees our inner Divine life quite differently. To me, that elephant-description metaphor also shows how each of us can be a wisdom-bearer for an infinitesimal part of the whole. For instance, in any group, each person would exhibit a different combination of Divine qualities, as well as a different combination of not-so-Divine qualities. Then, all of us together on Earth exhibit the full human range of life force, as well as the full range of not-such-Divine qualities.

---

[40]Lee, Belynda, *Five-Inch Heels: When Women Step into Power and Success* (North Vancouver, Influence Publishing, 2014), pp. 108-9.

Are you living your life from the perspective of what is right? Or are you considering what you still might have left to do? Are you moving into the wholeness of who you are, of being fully your Self?

~ *Choose Your Thoughts* ~

"Thoughts become things … choose the good ones."

Mike Dooley[41]

Reflective writers have said much in recent decades about positive thinking and visualizing. Mike Dooley has registered the copyright Totally Unique Thoughts from the Universe and built tut.com as a home for the writings and talks in which he advances his ideas on these topics. In his video *Thoughts Become Things,* Mike Dooley asks a Toastmasters audience whether they believe the old Chinese proverb about being careful what you wish for, because it might come true. "There's a principle at play in the Universe that turns wishes into reality."[42]

Dooley goes on to explain how powerful positive thinking and visualizing are. "Thoughts become things and I don't mean it figuratively, I mean it literally. Thoughts become things, not sometimes but all of the time. And not just our positive thoughts, but the other ones too. Because it's an immutable law as rigid and predictable as gravity…. Whatever it is that you most want, truly lies only a thought away."[43]

A small child, perhaps four years old, is standing in front of a display of colourful ice creams. She is dancing around, singing, pointing at the different buckets, and calling for her mama. What are her thoughts? Her dancing and her happiness make her thoughts clear to us: she wants an

---

[41]Mike Dooley, Thoughts from the Universe©, tut.com

[42]© Dooley, youtube.com/watch?v=8x4sVR67wCk; accessed April 11, 2014.

[43]Ibid.

ice cream cone. Everyone watching her would know that, including her mama. This thought by the four-year-old is a desire hanging in the air and it's about to become an ice cream cone in her hand. Her mama does not even have to ask, "Would you like an ice cream cone?" She just asks, "What flavour would you like?"

Barbara Brennan gives us a different example when she says, "A thought form can be built from constantly thinking of a fear like 'He's going to leave.'... The creator of the thought form will act as if it is going to happen. The energy field of the thought form will affect the field of the person it is about in a negative way. It will probably have the effect of pushing the person away."[44]

Intuitive consultant Michèle Bisson-Somerville, author of *Voodoo Shit for Men,* knew on her wedding day that she "would not be married to this man forever." This was not just wedding nerves. Through two decades of marriage, she couldn't shake this rock-solid knowing that her husband would die young, before his forty-fifth birthday. How does a woman tell her husband that he will die young? She can't. Michèle didn't. Yet, he knew, and he started telling his boys to take it easy on him or he'd die of a heart attack before the age of forty-five. Indeed, the prophecy bore fruit, but not in the way Michèle expected; I suggest you read *Voodoo Shit for Men* to know the rest of that story.

But it just goes to show that we bathe in thoughtforms, ours and others'. Thoughtforms inform our emotions; emotions inform our thoughts. Once thoughts, emotions, and words are at play, they feed upon each other, and it takes a conscious effort to break the cycle (if the cycle needs to be broken), to think new thoughts, and have the new thoughts create new emotions.

Mike Dooley encourages us to choose only good thoughts and to fire the rest.[45]

I always knew I would author another book, and in 2009, I started to write out pertinent thoughts, trying to find my topic. It was hit and miss.

---

[44]Brennan, *Hands of Light,* pp. 93-4.
[45]Dooley, tut.com

Then in October 2010, I encouraged myself by posting an illustration on the inside of my office door (so only someone inside the office with the door closed would see it) with the word "Author" written twice. In the place of the upper "t" is an image of a phoenix and in the place of the lower "t" is a fleur-de-lis, two inspiring symbols. I was using the Law of Attraction, a visual aid, and imaging together to inspire myself, a simple vision board.

My simple vision board displays a phoenix, a fleur-de-lis, and the word "author" twice

By seeing this image regularly, I dedicated more and more time to writing this book, though I didn't quite know where my writing would take me. I created at least a dozen working titles, and under each one, my manuscript morphed: the thoughts aligned with the title. Then, finally, I knew what I was writing about. Now, the material is writing itself.

This may sound strange, that only "finally, I knew what I was writing about." Some say that we talk to know what we know. We teach to learn about something better. We also write to know what we know and to learn more.

As I glanced at that illustration each day, I had the opportunity to think about being an author. For a while, I rejected the idea; I ignored it. I could have put off the writing forever.

But gradually, the words sank deeply into my subconscious, and at a conscious level, I accepted the idea of rising from the ashes of life and living through another cycle of writing a book.

Do you believe it's important to be careful what you wish for? How do you go about receiving or achieving what you desire? Does that mean you put energy into the thoughts of what you want to happen? Or do you put energy into the thoughts of the things you don't want to happen? Whatever we put our mind's energy into becomes substantial. It takes on substance. What will your legacy be?

~ *Speaking Up for Ourselves* ~

"You can do whatever you set out to do."

Kenneth Grant McGregor[46]

I remember two major reasons I decided to take a weeklong intensive course in Nanaimo called "Insite" in May 1999, although there may have been more influences during that stressful period. At the time, I was going through the trials of being off work because I could not read—the condition of my eye muscles prevented it. (And what good is a communications officer who is unable to read?) I speak of that condition as a "dis-ease" because my life was not easy then, and my condition manifested coincidentally. I created a mind map of my sources of stress at that time to show my brilliant doctor, who had by then become my surgeon. I felt a need to explain why I might have the dis-ease. He didn't buy it; it was too far out of his mechanistic view of the world.

Three family members had attended the Insite course and found it beneficial. As well, my son Grant encouraged me to go, saying, "Mum, you have to do this." So I signed up with Insite and booked in at a charming bed and breakfast with a quirky name—the Pepper Muffin Country Inn on Jingle Pot Road—and started looking forward to this week, not knowing what to expect.

It was—I learned—a co-dependency workshop, and I found out that I was definitely co-dependent. Had I always been co-dependent? I know I was under the illusion that I "needed" another person to make me whole. Co-dependency certainly explained my relationship with my first husband. Was it starting to describe my relationship with my second husband? I didn't want that to be the case.

I learned a lot that week: actually, in the first class. Seated in a circle, we took turns speaking of who we were and why we were there—as much as we knew. I learned that the facility was also a place where

[46]My father to me in the 1960s.

addicts could find their way off their addictions. Several of the people in the Insite workshop were spouses of those undergoing rehabilitation from their addiction and then there were others, like me, who were there because they were co-dependent.

That first morning, one of the participants who was a spouse of someone in the rehabilitation program broke down and began crying. Several of us started to interfere, trying to offer verbal support, to stop the person's pain in some way. A tissue? A glass of water? Very quickly and bluntly, our counsellor stopped us. "You're trying to stop her pain because watching it brings you pain. Don't interfere. Let them deal with their pain as they need to and just support them by holding the space."

Someone pushed the box of tissues closer to the crying participant. Even that wasn't allowed. To help each of us become stronger, we had to speak up for ourselves, to own our pain, to own our actions, and not wait for others to step in and "save" us.

Through the week, I started to wonder whether people I knew were alcoholics, whether I was an alcoholic. I decided no in each case, but it was a strange mind game of confusion. I started to understand how each of us can get very tied up in our behaviour toward and with others, accommodating our behaviour to fit their needs. I quickly learned what a poor behavioural choice that is.

During the week, we went through many useful exercises. I cried a lot and learned more and more about myself. Then in the evenings, I would go back to the Pepper Muffin bed and breakfast, enjoy a hot tub, and sit at a table in the garden doing the evening's homework. I'd occasionally take a walk down to the foot of the property, or up and down the road. I'm a walker; I need to stretch my legs.

It was while I was down at the foot of the property that I allowed myself to receive the biggest gift of the week and it was an awareness connected with my father. He always used to say to me, "You can do whatever you set out to do." In other words, he had a ton of faith in my ability to carve my own path. But then, when I was close to leaving school, he, in the most supportive manner possible, limited my horizon by taking me along to two or three work sites to help me decide "what I wanted to be, now that I had grown up." It was a choice of librarian, optometrist (how surprising that is, given the later eye-muscle affliction!), and physiotherapist. I chose physiotherapist, and read some books in the library, and started dutifully down that road.

As I stood in that field in Nanaimo, I realized that my father did me both a service and a disservice in limiting my panorama of choices to just three. And I had allowed him to do that. Throughout Great Britain at that time, similar well-meaning parents were limiting the choices for their children. These days, the choices are far broader and the task of making authentic choices actually becomes far more challenging.

Although previously I had never been able to verbalize or even recognize this, I knew that the pendulum of family life had swung completely when I raised my children. I had not influenced them consciously but rather allowed them to flounder as I had never been allowed to do. I let them try what they wanted, while listening and supporting their decisions.

And so, I came away from a week at Insite with some definite insight into my life, realizing that I had allowed and was still allowing others to influence my choices. I was ready now to make my own choices in this life and to walk down my own path, not one that anyone else wanted to stretch before me. I started to stand up straighter. I still keep that Insite emblem in my wallet. In fact, it's been there so long, I'd almost forgotten what it was. I just knew I had to keep it with my change—my coins—to re-mind me to "change" myself into who I am, not who others think I should be.

Do you allow others to shape you? Your future? To limit your future? Do you allow others to describe who you are? Or do you speak up for yourself, write for yourself? Do you make your own choices, even if they seem counterproductive?

~ Opposites ~

"In lexical semantics, opposites are words that
lie in an inherently incompatible binary relationship
as in the opposite pairs big : small, long : short, and precede : follow."
en.wikipedia.org/wiki/Opposite_(semantics)[47]

I used to think that love and hate were opposites. Recently, I have come to the conclusion that indifference is the opposite of love, whereas acceptance is the opposite of hate. What else has gone unchallenged in the world of opposites in my thinking?

I have also determined that most polarities are just the extreme ends of a continuum rather than being so black and white as to be opposite. Take black and white, for example. Grey is in the middle, and, as we all know, there are fifty shades of grey!

Alternatively, words that are deemed to be opposites are often just a sizeable distance along the continuum, more of a relative opposite, if you like. For instance, the adjectives "big" and "small" when describing suitcases denote quite a range. But think how much bigger the range is when describing mammals: a pygmy possum is the size of a man's thumb and weighs around 30 grams; compare that with a blue whale weighing about one hundred tons.

There are also pairs of words that appear to be the opposite of each other—such as flammable and inflammable—but which actually mean the same thing: "capable of catching fire and burning." Another pair is ravel and unravel, both meaning "to unwind into separate threads." While linguists may explain these seeming opposites as words that have become stronger through usage with the addition of prefixes, these examples can serve as reminders that words are merely labels, symbols for something, and therefore always questionable.

---

[47]Accessed December 1, 2014.

Continuing with developing an awareness of the words we use, I notice that some single words mean their own opposite, such as "outstanding," which—when describing a task, for instance—means both "a task not yet done" and "a task done excellently." The movie *Philomena* played with this double meaning of "outstanding" in its opening scene, when the character of Martin Sixsmith—a BBC reporter—is quite self-satisfied until he finds out that he has yet to provide his "outstanding stool sample" to his doctor.

Father Markus Dünzkofer, resident priest at St. Paul's Anglican Church in Vancouver's West End until 2012, first helped me realize that some opposites cannot exist without each other. He used the example of a coin. A coin has two sides: a head and a tail. We cannot look at the tail at the same time as we look at the head; we can only look at the one or the other, or at the rim of the coin that shows the distance between the two. But if we look at the head of the coin, the obverse side, and we were to try to slice off that part of the coin, would it not still have an obverse side? It might no longer display the image of the tail. But the obverse side would still be there, opposite the head. In the thickness of the rim of the coin, where does the head end and the tail begin? Can one exist without the other? Are they not continuously married together to create the whole? If the one is so essential to the existence of the other, do we always need to compare the two sides?

How could one side be better than the other?

How could one side be more important than the other?

This reasoning becomes a metaphor for how I perceive the differences between one person and the next or between myself and my neighbours. They say that in relationships, opposites attract. I've noticed that to be the case: a woman who is very attuned to her clairvoyant abilities marries a man who wouldn't know a clair if it bumped him in the face; a person who focuses on the details teams up with a person who sees the big picture; a gal who is five foot no inches tall goes out with a guy who is over six feet. Psychologists conjecture that the differences—either in personality or focus or modus operandi—between partners in a relationship balance each other out, making a complete whole. Married couple Donna Eden (energy worker) and David Feinstein (Ph.D., psychologist) write in *The Energies of Love* that it is the difference in energy that attracts the other.

Rather than appreciating only the qualities with which I am familiar, I am training myself to appreciate qualities that are different, foreign, and unexpected in others. The difference between two sets of qualities does not detract from either set: it actually enhances the uniqueness and the strong bond between the two. It's as though by being vastly different from me, another person frees me up and gives me more space in which to explore my own possible differences, my full and wondrous potential, my dormant and latent capabilities, which I might have kept hidden even from myself, had I not perceived how very different others are from me and I from them.

This allows me to enjoy my uniqueness and to grow into it in bigger and bigger ways.

As Marianne Williamson says in *A Return to Love*, "Your playing small does not serve the world."

Are you living into your full potential or are you trying to stay the same as your neighbours, your family of origin, those in your community?

Chapter 3—The Word and the Interpreter

Received and Heard

~ *Words in the Iceberg* ~

"The word is not just a sound or a written symbol.
The word is a force; it is the power you have to express and communicate,
to think, and thereby to create the events in your life."
Miguel Ruiz[48]

I think about thinking a lot—I'm a metathinker. As an editor of spiritual, inspirational, self-help, and biographical books (only some of the genres I edit), I read a variety of opinions that others hold about thinking. Some of these opinions cross my desk as manuscripts and some appear in my hands as books by authors seasoned as well as new. As I consider these opinions about thoughts, I feel as though I'm a brush being cleaned by another brush, a cloth by another cloth, like M. C. Escher's "Drawing Hands," in which the artist's hand paints itself, or like the Ouroboros, the dragon that eats its own tail.

I have already proposed an analogy that each of us is like an iceberg and that our emotion-created, image-created, and word-created subconscious mind—most of our self—is that part of the iceberg below the surface, unseen and ignored at our peril. It's the part we are often unaware of and which others can often see more easily than we can. We disclose what's above the surface of the water, but the rest is frequently hidden from ourselves.

We use words to describe ourselves to ourselves and to others, starting with our thoughts about ourselves. "Words in the Iceberg" casts light on

---

[48]Ruiz, Miguel, *The Four Agreements: A Practical Guide to Personal Freedom* (Amber-Allen Publishing, 1997), p. 26.

the many small and large ways we can change, bringing the depths of our soul with us for healing in the light.

We negotiate our way through our lives using words inspired by thoughts and emotions to interpret the situations, challenges, pitfalls, and successes we encounter along the way. Mostly, we don't question the meaning behind the thoughts and the words we assign to signs, symptoms, and sounds. We float through our world unquestioningly.

Developmental biologist Bruce Lipton, Ph.D., makes the intriguing declaration that we consciously choose to think only 5 percent of our thoughts; he says the rest arise from our subconscious mind, which already taps into the collective unconscious. It's that other 95 percent of our thoughts that interest me. How can they be *our* thoughts if we are not actively thinking them? Aren't they then our conscious mind's hearings and our subconscious mind's regurgitations rather than our thoughts? Are they the words that others chose to describe us when we were seven or fifteen or thirty? Do they describe us now? Lipton says they arise from our childhood programming.[49]

The only way we can utilize our thoughts and feelings and images is to put them into words. Once we know what these words are, we speak some of them aloud; we write, text, and Facebook some of them to share with others. We exchange more words when we hear others saying words, when we read words others have written, when we hear words in our entertainment, and when we see and barely notice words on billboards, teacups, and t-shirts.

These words that arise from the collective unconscious, our personal unconscious, our subconscious mind, and our conscious mind create us and the world we live in. We become so entrenched in our own lives that we no longer see our environment or question our thoughts, conscious or otherwise.

---

[49]Bruce Lipton, Ph.D. *The Biology of Belief: Unleashing the Power of Consciousness, Matter, & Miracles* (Hay House, 2011)

Which words are in your iceberg? What is the vibe that your words give off? Can you change what you choose to say about yourself, about your life, about your past? By describing yourself differently, will you change?

~ *The Medium Distorts the Message* ~

"The Medium Is the Message"

Marshall McLuhan

During my fifth decade, I went to university for the first time, as a mature student; I enrolled in communication studies at SFU in Greater Vancouver. Having already published a book, having written, edited, and printed newsletters, having acted in community theatre, having directed children in plays and adults in a music hall, having written poems, having sung classical and nostalgia music in public, I saw myself as a communicator and performer, both challenged and enabled through communication, especially communicating via the written word.

At SFU, for the first time, I learned communications theory, which states at its simplest that there are four parts to every form of communication: the person (or object) who is sending the communication, the person (or object) who is receiving the communication, the message being sent, and the medium through which the communication passes. In the case of a conversation between two people sitting together over coffee, the people are the senders and receivers (back and forth, ideally), the message could be about an investment in an apartment, while the medium is the spoken word through the public space of the coffee shop.

Take that conversation into a corridor outside an apartment after 11:00 p.m. at night and it changes into something quiet and even secretive. Take it onto a football field and it may have to be shouted. Take it into a private sitting room, onto the seawall, into the gym, and it continues to change, even when the content of the message remains the same.

Marshall McLuhan (1911-80), Canadian philosopher of communications theory, developed some intriguing beliefs, summed up in his most famous aphorism, "the medium is the message," which he subverted by willingly accepting a typographical error for the title of his second book as *The Medium is the Massage.*

Applying McLuhan's aphorism to the example of a person receiving her news from the newspaper, he is saying that if she received the same news from the television, from a theatre marquee, from a tabloid, from a recording saved by her telephone, or from a friend, the message would change, massaged into a different shape by the medium.

Struggling to understand and apply McLuhan's communications theory to interactions, I further developed the ability to think about my thoughts, appreciating that where I am, the mood I am in, who I am with, and how I express my thoughts and receive others' alters my comprehension of the messages I see and hear. My interpretation of the forms of communication that involve words (or lead to words) has strongly influenced the shape of this book, its order and its content. Our words can take us away from or align us closer with our soul.

For instance, if I hear the message that "God is love" in a church, I take it into my soul in a slightly different way from when I read one of Reverend Christina Lunden's daily angelic affirmations, such as "I recognize the strength and love I have flowing through me. I AM strong. I AM love. I AM loved," (June 26, 2014). This affirmation makes me feel part of the love. Hearing "God is love" distances me from the source of the love.

Another example. English novelist E. M. Forster wrote the novel *A Room with a View* in 1908. The story is about a young Victorian English woman on holiday with her older cousin and chaperone in Italy. At the Pensione Bertollini, the two women meet an English father and son who are from a "lower class" than theirs. The chaperone does not approve of the love that gradually blossoms between the young people. Right until the final chapters, their love seems doomed.

In 1985, the story was adapted for the big screen and, with a star-studded cast of Helena Bonham Carter, Maggie Smith, Denholm Elliott, Julian Sands, Daniel Day-Lewis, and Judi Dench, *A Room with a View*, the movie, won multiple awards. Many synopses of the story in both book and movie form can be found online.

For years, I have sung a song by Noël Coward called "A Room with a View." Originally set in his 1928 revue, *This Year of Grace*, the song takes the basic plot of Forster's book of the possibility that a young couple's love might develop into something. Coward strips the song of all misunderstandings and class distinctions. It is best accompanied on piano with a crisp elegance and sung with clear enunciation so the audience misses none of Coward's clever internal rhymes—"I've been cherishing through the perishing winter nights and days a funny little phrase ...."

At a five-day intensive arranged by jazz vocalist Karin Plato, I sang the song "A Room with a View" in more of a jazz style, accompanied by jazz trio Jillian Lebeck on piano, Adam Thomas on bass, and Bill Coon on guitar. That changed things up. In January this year, I played the "scabby old bat" Mrs. Richards in "Communication Problems," one episode of John Cleese and Connie Booth's *Fawlty Towers*. One of the many things that makes Mrs. Richards cranky is that she asked for a room with a view and the view they gave her wasn't good enough, because she'd have to use "a telescope to see the sea."

I've shown seven presentations of the simple phrase "a room with a view"—a book, a movie, online synopses, a song sung in revue style and as jazz, and as a request in a play that also appears as a TV comedy. These different ways changed the thoughts the phrase provokes in my mind. This phrase can also be represented as a painting, a cartoon, a poem, a lecture, an advertisement. And on and on. Each time, the medium changes the message, taking it from our innate ability to conjure mental images by reading about the story, to our visual ability to absorb a written story, to our heart involvement from hearing a song sung.

During the distressing period of my life when I was unable to read because of an eye-muscle dis-ease, I quit work and stayed at home painting miniature watercolours, knitting, and listening to talking books. One of the books I heard was *A Map of the World* by Jane Hamilton. Ten years later, my eyes back in good shape and gobbling up books by the truckload once more, I started reading a book that seemed quite new to me, until I reached one point in the story where I suddenly knew that I had heard/read it before. Sure enough, it was Hamilton's *A Map of the World*. The two media for Hamilton's book—a talking book that I heard and a book that I held in my hands and read—were so different that I had read a hundred pages before I clued in.

McLuhan was on to something when he said the medium is the message. What are your favourite media for gaining information, for communicating, for social connections?

~ *Words* ~

"I'm ***totally*** *going to take this to school tomorrow."*

A teenage school boy[50]

Language is constantly in motion, dropping the old, morphing into the present, formulating and becoming the new. As our language changes—both globally and personally—so we change.

Take the word "literally," for example. At one time, "literally" just referred to something that had actually happened. Now, it doesn't often mean that; it only approximates that meaning and is used to emphasize a point that someone might doubt or dispute. Does it have something to do with the word "literature"? The first six letters are the same; the pronunciation of those six is identical in both words. My etymological

[50]The boy was remarking to his friend about the broken-off neck of a guitar. I overheard this on a #72 bus in Sidney, BC, November 13, 2013. Bolding as heard.

dictionary—the one that explains the origins of words—says that "literal" used to mean "according to the letter."[51] As we know, its acquired meaning has quite different emotional weight.

Take the word "totally" that I heard on a bus. The boy who spoke it meant "definitely" and it has come to mean that. And yet, the original meaning of "totally" described something that is done completely.

Through our speech, we humans are constantly passing from one state to another as we make declarations (of love, of war, of independence, and of interdependence), make offerings, make suggestions, make decisions, make statements, make amends, make believe, make way, make out, make fun, make peace, make an apology, make a case, make a date, make a booking, make a joke, and make a mess. We are making and creating a new world for ourselves as we pass from one state to the next, all with words, either thought or decided upon or discerned or interpreted or misinterpreted or written or read or understood or spoken or shouted or whispered. Of course, we can move between some of these states without words, at least without spoken words, but it's hard to do that without at least some thought, fired by our emotions.

The majority of the time, we are using words to interpret our state back to ourselves, whether we're awake or asleep (ignoring being under anaesthetic). Actually, there is another whole realm—well, maybe several—that we experience during dreams, near-death experiences, spiritually transformative experiences, after-death communications, and other such trance states. After we have visited any one of those realms, it is difficult to understand what happened until we put the visions we saw and the ideas we glimpsed into thoughts and those thoughts become words in our mind and we speak those words to someone who can allow us to interpret our experience without overlaying it with their own meaning. There are multiple steps between having such an experience and understanding it. It took the mystic Mother Julian of Norwich twenty years to understand the sixteen spiritual revelations she had on May 8, 1373.

[51]Walter W. Skeat, The Rev., *A Concise Etymological Dictionary of the English Language* (G.P. Putnam's Sons, 1980), p. 298.

We each live in our own world of words—the ones we use to interpret for ourselves what is going on within and around us. My world is unique to me; your world is unique to you. Our words change our world; our words create our worlds. We co-create our world with our words.

Words are strongly connected with the era, the geography, the nation, the cultural group and subgroup, and even the families who speak them. Families have certain code words and groups of words that sound cryptic to others but are full of meaning to the family members themselves.

Three of my parental family's phrases were "She's chocolate," referring to my sister; "Mummy made it," because all went well when our mother organized something such as a holiday and she was willing to take full credit; and "It doesn't rain on the golf course," which demonstrates my father's favourite pastime regardless of the weather.

Some phrases that became widely applicable to many situations once I became a parent were "Where'd 'e go?" said with the wide-eyed innocence of a two-year-old; "Has anyone brushed my hair today?" and "A movable feast," the last referring to when I would be carrying a latched-on breastfeeding baby with me to answer the telephone in the days when phones were firmly attached to wires coming out of the wall.

When I was a youngster (there's a word that gives away my age and my British birth!), my favourite words included "mystery," "adventure," and "and." How amazing that the word "and" was a favourite of mine! But it was. That was the doing of Enid Blyton—one of Great Britain's most prolific and beloved children's authors. Blyton's "and" could take her eager reader into rabbit warrens of adventures that were eye-opening and heart-thumping and page-turning. Her "and" meant that there were more and more adventures coming up. "Invisible" was also a favourite word at that time. As Antoine de Saint-Exupéry says in *The Little Prince,* "And now here is my secret, a very simple secret: It is only with the heart that one can see rightly; what is essential is invisible to the eye."

To me as an older teenager, there was a special vibration in the words "boyfriend," "girlfriend," "what to do," and "marriage."

During some of my middle years, my favourites were "baby, children, song, singing, audition, music, invitation, skiing." Favourite words don't necessarily signify a person's favourite activities; they might signify favourite colours and favourite people and favourite places and favourite flavours.

These days, I have other favourite words: "wisdom, consciousness, microcosm, transformation, peace, spiritual growth, reincarnation, angels, sound, healing, holism, integration of body-mind-spirit, indigo, words, writing, author, family." Our favourite words tell us a lot about ourselves.

Make lists of ten of your favourite words for today, for five years ago, and for ten years ago. You'll start to see part of your path illuminated by the charm of attraction. Your clusters of favourite words become stepping stones along your path.

ॐ

~ *Not Knowing the Language* ~

"All of them were filled with the Holy Spirit and began to speak
in other tongues as the Spirit enabled them. Now there were staying
in Jerusalem God-fearing Jews from every nation under heaven.
When they heard this sound, a crowd came together in bewilderment,
because each one heard their own language being spoken."

Acts 2:4-6[52]

In the late 1960s, I went on a week's ski holiday to the tiny village of Alpbach in the Austrian Alps. It was the first time I had ever skied; I had a great time.

And because my best friend from high school days lived in Switzerland, about three hours away by train, and we hadn't seen each other for about a year, having spent every high school day in each other's pocket before

---

[52]Holy Bible, New International Version® (NIV®) (Colorado Springs: Biblica, Inc.™, 2011).

that, we arranged that I should visit her for the day. I remember nothing of our visit together; I'm sure it was wonderful.

What I do remember is the discomfort I felt at being on my own in two countries—Austria and Switzerland—where I didn't speak the languages around me. It was only for one day—I was back in Alpbach with the friends I was vacationing with by evening—and yet I had felt desperately alone as I travelled that day. Perhaps the fact that I had to change trains about three times in each direction had a bearing on my discomfort, but I wonder how I would fare if I were to move to a country where I had to learn a new language, as so many people do. I am in awe of others' abilities to be out of their depth linguistically, and to remain cheerful! As it happens, my husband is a fine example of this; he immigrated to Canada as a Bulgarian refugee from a camp in Austria—possibly in the same year that I visited Austria.

Nowadays, living in Vancouver's multicultural West End, I often find myself surrounded by languages other than English. In our favourite coffee shop, the hospitable servers speak Korean, Japanese, Mongolian, and English. The clientele might be speaking Russian and Czech. We buy our feta and Kashkaval cheeses in an Iranian market; they always have Iranian music playing and their walls boast posters of Iranian pop singers. Our Member of Parliament is Trinidad-born Hedy Fry, M.D.

When I visit with one of my sons and his family, they are more likely to be speaking French than English, as his wife is from the Midi-Pyrénées in southwest France. She, too, left her homeland to learn a foreign language. In my daughter's home, Hebrew alphabet characters adorn the fridge and the bedroom doors. She converted to Judaism, the religion of her husband and children.

On the feast day of Pentecost, the Holy Spirit—once known as "the Holy Ghost" and these days depicted as a feminine energy—descended upon Jesus' twelve apostles and more than a hundred of his followers. As they spread the Good News of Jesus the Christ's messages of forgiveness and love and loyalty to Spirit, the apostles were somehow understood by each person listening, as though they were speaking in their language.

"Parthians, Medes and Elamites; residents of Mesopotamia, Judea and Cappadocia, Pontus and Asia, Phrygia and Pamphylia, Egypt and the parts of Libya near Cyrene; visitors from Rome (both Jews and converts to Judaism); Cretans and Arabs—we hear them declaring the wonders of God in our own tongues!"[53]

Knowing a language also has to do with the lingo of an industry such as the printing industry, the vernacular of an institution like the Vancouver Public Library, and the jargon of people who share the same pastime like quilting. Each different language and subset of a language takes a while to master, and until we do, we're outsiders, not getting the nuances and subtleties that deepen meaning.

Nelson Mandela said, "If you talk to a man in a language he understands, that goes to his head. If you talk to him in his language, that goes to his heart." I have to wonder about that. Why is that? I am thinking that if we understand a language but it's not ours, we still have to work at understanding it, which is head work. But if we have known the language from birth or have spoken it for an extremely long time, we don't have to work at it; we just let it draw images in our mind, talk to our hearts, inspire our soul, and connect us with our spirit.

For that reason, I am even more in awe of the bravery of those people who choose to leave their motherland and mother tongue behind to move to where they must learn a second language. I am in awe, because they have chosen to challenge the movement of messages from head to spirit. They are out on a limb where they are surrounded by foreign words and meanings. I am too much of an "enlightened-one-wannabe" to give up that much ground.

Are you comfortable with the language you work in and every one of its subsets? How do you feel when you leave your milieu? Do you know many languages? How many can you call your own, so that their messages bypass your head and go straight to your heart?

[53]Holy Bible, NIV®, Acts 2:9-11, NIV®.

Spoken and Sung

~ *Lying* ~

"I think the biggest life-changing day for me on this spiritual path was the day that I decided never to lie again—never to tell a white lie or be false about anything.... This energy that we're moving into, ascending [into fifth-dimensional energy], there are no lies; there's honesty and integrity and humbleness."

Reverend Christina Lunden[54]

I was intrigued to hear the Reverend Christina Lunden say her life made a huge shift for the better when she decided never to lie again. Our culture condones white lies—what the British call "fibs"—with the excuse that sometimes our decision not to "tell the whole truth" will soften the blow of a hard reality for others. But not saying what we believe in our hearts can be every bit as damaging as saying it; probably more so, because the other person may still glimpse the truth and we are just hiding our truth from ourselves.

In the movie *Words and Music,* Clive Owen's character, Jack Marcus, is constantly giving the etymological source and hence the meaning of the words he and Miss Delsanto (Juliette Binoche) are using. The word "distortion" has *tort* at its centre, which is Latin for "a wrong, a harm, crooked, pain," and "to twist." That is what happens when we distort the truth, tell white lies, and are false about our thoughts, our actions, and our deeds—we twist the truth into a wrong.

The first agreement in Miguel Ángel Ruiz's *The Four Agreements* is "Be impeccable with your word." Ruiz explains that "impeccable" means "to be without sin," and he defines sin as "anything that you do which goes against yourself."[55] In my words, this agreement—which I can also try to make with myself—is to always speak well and accurately on my

[54]Christina Lunden, "'Light' Angel Soul Teaching" (BlogTalkRadio.com, December 12, 2011).
[55]Ruiz, *The Four Agreements*, p. 31.

own behalf. As Christina Lunden says, to speak a truth with honesty, integrity, and humbleness is to speak a truth that is not boastful and that tells a whole truth rather than a little piece of the truth, which might distort the real truth.

What is the real truth? Is it superreal truth or "the really real truth," as Timothy Doyle calls it? "There is a heartfelt discernment for knowing the difference between the 'real truth' and the 'really real truth.'"[56]

For instance, if someone says to me, "Are you an actor?" I say, "Yes," and I have to add "in community theatre," so that I don't give—and no one receives—an inflated view of my experience.

This whole discussion around truth and lying reminds me of the Edgar Cayce quote: "Criticize not unless ye wish to be criticized. For, with what measure ye mete it is measured to thee again."[57] I cannot, therefore, criticize or sin (see Ruiz's definition of "being impeccable" just above) against someone else without affecting myself detrimentally. Now, that's a challenge! And so, I'm back to not saying anything against anyone else, because I would like to test whether I can live my life without lying.

Ask yourself, "Am I completely honest in all situations? Do I say all that is in my heart? What am I withholding? Why am I withholding something?"

~ *Vowels Contrast with Consonants* ~

"Let the vowel carry the sound;
delay the ending consonant to the end of the note."
Elizabeth Taylor[58]

[56]Doyle, *How to Play the Game of Life: Intermediate Version*, p. 24.
[57]Cayce, Reading 2936-2
[58]Teaching from my singing teacher, Royal Conservatory of Music, Victoria, BC, 1985..

My teacher of classical singing during the second half of the 1980s—a vivacious blonde Elizabeth Taylor—explained that sung vowels resemble the pearls on a necklace and that consonants are the small knots between the pearls. It is thirty years since I began studying classical singing and first realized that vowel sounds carry the singing voice and that sound stops (even if only imperceptibly) each time a consonant is voiced. In other words, our consonants serve to stop the sound we sing, chopping sound up into bite-size pieces. The same thing happens when we speak, only faster.

Interestingly, the sounds we make involuntarily—when we emote (see the section in chapter one, "Voicing Emotions")—are all vowel sounds; our emotional cries include no consonants to stop our involuntary cry.

If vowels are sound carriers and consonants cut off that sound, that makes vowels the primary sounds and consonants the secondary sounds, sounds that humans have added to speech to create meanings that are easily understood by other humans of the same culture.

As soon as we accept that vowels are the primary sounds, we can start to create a group in which belong the words "vowels, feminine, yin, silence, valleys, planes," and "the oral tradition." Granted, it's an eclectic group, particularly when we see vowel sounds in the same group as "silence." It's a group of primary states, each of which is better understood as belonging to this group when contrasted with the state that comes second, the more culturally created collective, the opposite states (recognizing that opposites are just mutually exclusive pairs).

So, I claim that feminine is a primary state in contrast to masculine being a secondary state. This might seem, to literal readers of the biblical story of Adam and Eve, to be so feminist as to be heretical or even sacrilegious. Yet each of us, whether male or female, emerged from a female. The female was first, providing both the egg and the nest.

According to this line of reasoning, if vowels came first, they are feminine, the basis of sound. And that makes consonants masculine.

Yin is darkness, quietness, stillness, calm, and potential. From yin erupts yang, which is light, sound, movement, energy, and manifestation. Silence is also a yin energy and contrasts with sound.

In the beginning of Earth's formation during the creation of landmasses, valleys and planes came first before the land buckled upward into hills and mountains, and before men (almost always men) came along and built walls where natural barriers could not deter invasion.

The oral tradition of passing along memories around the campfire, at the hearth, and in the still of the evening is a group endeavour, a mediated and approved truth, an anonymous pursuit, a widely accepted construct. The written tradition is an individuated, solitary event, capturing one person's opinion with which others may disagree. Whereas history recorded through the oral tradition may shift and morph gradually over time, history that is written down jerks from one version to the next. A new idea written down is frequently initially mocked as being laughable, untrue. Only after others do their own research and write something similar does the laughing audience settle down and listen.

Languages were initially unwritten. It is intriguing to realize that Hebrew—the longest, continuously used language still spoken in the world today—is scripted in an alphabet that originally included no vowels. An unusual feature! No vowels; only consonants. How very masculine!

The result today of having an alphabet for which only the consonants are represented and written (some are termed "weak consonants" and they indicate vowels) is that we can only guess how some Hebrew words were pronounced; only the letters that punctuate sound—the consonants—stood for the whole sound of the word. A change came around three thousand years ago, when written Hebrew began adding diacritical marks that suggested the appropriate vowels for words.

In 2013, I attended Jonathan Goldman's annual Sound Healing Intensive in Loveland, Colorado, which brought together my appreciation of the additional contrasting pairs I offer above, pairs that are opposites, together creating the whole. There would be little meaning from vowels without the punctuation provided by consonants. There would be no more females without males. Hills would not be hills without the valleys below them. We would never appreciate stillness and silence if we hadn't first gone through chaos and movement and noise.

If you're a singer, can you prolong the sound of the vowel? Or are you eager to reach the consonant so that your audience—even if it's only the dog—understands what you are singing?

Do you notice how your world divides between primary and secondary states? Are you comfortable being in a primary state of stillness and unending peace? Or do you need to be stimulated through the movement of secondary states?

~ *Talking Aloud* ~

"'I'll often mutter to myself when searching for something in the refrigerator or supermarket shelves,' said researcher Gary Lupyan, a cognitive psychologist at the University of Wisconsin-Madison."

Charles Choi[59]

It's wonderful to talk aloud to oneself. I do it all the time, especially when I'm writing.

Are you talking to yourself? I hope so.

Between the left and right sides of the brain is the corpus callosum, a dense bundle of brain cells that is wider in women than in men. The left side of the brain corresponds with the right side of the body, and carries out logical, rational functioning and decision-making. The right side of the brain, which corresponds with the left side of the body, is more interested in creativity, and in finding and understanding patterns, as in art or music.

[59]Charles Choi, "Talk to Yourself? Why You're Not Crazy," livescience.com; accessed February 13, 2015.

When we talk aloud, we allow both sides of our brain to hear what we are saying, planning, imaging, imagining, thinking, learning, and making decisions about. We expand our understanding. We then make better decisions. Creativity becomes married to logic; pattern seeking and pattern finding marry rational thinking. When we just read something in our minds, for example, we deprive our ears from hearing the non-visual harmonies, rhymes, and alliterations—as in "a cycling psychic" or "wholly hopeful."

As a result, talking aloud is a great habit to cultivate when we want to understand something more deeply.

My method of learning my lines for a play is to speak them aloud while I am walking. Somehow, walking and talking my lines gets them into my body so that when I am onstage, I can progress my way through the script comfortably.

The best way to understand poetry is to recite it aloud; then we hear its rhythms, pauses, and unspoken meanings. The simplest way to learn it again is to recite it aloud, trying out different emphases on different lines until the piece makes the most sense to us. And then it will make the most sense when we recite it to others.

The best way for me to edit my own writing and to copyedit and proofread someone else's writing is to read the passages aloud (see the scene in chapter seven, "Observing the Deed and the Actor, Processes, ~ Reading Aloud ~").

Are you a writer? Do you speak your words aloud? Does that help you improve your writing? Does it help you make more sense of someone else's writing? Does it help you realize what your writing lacks?

~ *"Each Melodious Measure"* ~

"Now I teach my children
Each melodious measure.
Oft the tears are flowing,
Oft they flow from my memory's treasure."
"Songs My Mother Taught Me"[60]

There are "Kodak moments" and there are spontaneous song moments. I enjoyed a spontaneous song moment when I attended a Women of Wisdom (WOW) Foundation event in Seattle in 1999.

I immensely enjoyed many of the WOW events. In fact, there were so many appealing two-hour workshops to attend that I had a hard time choosing between the ones that overlapped. The freestyle vocalization event in a gymnasium was fun. Most of the women (these events are attended mostly by women) moved and vocalized in the centre of the room. I danced around the perimeter of the room, as a sheepdog circles the flock, and later I realized there was something very symbolic about that, because part of my role these days is to provide a framework for others to grow within.

At another workshop, we re-enacted traumatic events in the lives of some of the women attending. I remember one woman—I'll call her Lindsay—had had a very traumatic experience as a passenger in a car when she saw a fatal accident between two cars going in the opposite direction. I was part of the team re-enacting the event and we did such a good job that Lindsay broke down and wept, and released some of the anguish and helplessness she had felt that day. We became instant friends.

Between workshops, I walked around the stalls, looking at all the great things for sale—crystals, scarves, books, and hats. Yes, hats. Well, I always love trying on hats—my mum did, too—and these were beautiful hats, all

[60]Natalia Macfarren's anglicization of Adolf Heyduk's Czech poem as set to music by Antonín Leopold Dvořák in 1880.

made by the milliner (we don't hear that word often these days) who was in attendance. Her name is Melissa and these were her "lids."

Well, one of Melissa's lids absolutely captivated me and I admired myself in it from every angle, checked out the price, and left it behind. But in the next break between workshops, I went back to Melissa's hat stall and my favourite was still there. I tried it on again and spontaneously began to sing a rather tricky song by Dvořák, "Songs My Mother Taught Me." As you would expect, all the other hat shoppers stopped in their tracks to listen. I wasn't showing off—I was just captivated and I'm sure the hat sang the song!

And, you guessed it, I bought the hat. I still have it and will probably now wear it for the launch of this book. And maybe I'll sing "Songs My Mother Taught Me" again then, too.

Do you ever launch into song spontaneously? Where do you sing? I love singing in corridors, for some reason, and have been soundly told off by one condominium council for doing so! Where do you sing?

Read and Written

~ Recognizing Handwriting ~

"In handwriting analysis, attention is paid to the stops and starts in the formation of the letters, the pen-lifts."

"Rich Boy, Poor Boy"[61]

I used to be thrilled whenever a plump envelope arrived at Douglas Lake Post Office with my name written on it in my mother's generous hand. This was when I first moved to Canada and my parents still lived in Cardiff, Wales. I couldn't wait to sit down and read all the latest chat

[61] An episode in CBC's *The Murdoch Mysteries.*

from home. My mother always wrote as she spoke, in a very chatty, friendly style, putting a wonderful spin on everything and seeing the significance in it all. Mum's large, round handwriting was, and still is, familiar to me. Like people who match the "sunny" stereotype, the way it took up extra space was happy in some way. My father's writing in comparison was tall and slim and sloped forward: purposeful, consistent, and neat.

That's what handwriting meant in those days, even when we weren't handwriting experts; somehow, the person's handwriting symbolized that person for us. It was as recognizable as their voice over the phone.

If I ever receive a handwritten letter from one of my children, I'll wonder what is going on. After getting over the shock, I will have to work a bit to recognize them through their handwriting. That's a reflection of the fact that people don't write as many letters these days as they used to. As computer usage has risen, instances of handwriting have shrunk. Recent decades have given us multiple different ways of communicating, including new ways of capturing words.

Nowadays, I have an account with a company called "SendOutCards" through which I am able to write letters and cards to friends in a unique font that the company created from a sample of my handwriting. Of course, my characters in this font are far more regular than those that I would actually handwrite: every *c* is the same, every *y* is the same, every colon is the same, and so on: no variety. And probably my handwriting has changed since I filled out SendOutCards' handwriting font form, making it time to fill the form out again. But I'm pleased that the service enables me to send out letters at Christmas and other times "written" in my own hand.

Even now, I can receive a Christmas card in the mail and know which friend or relation it is from, just from their handwriting on the envelope. The whole persona of a friend demonstrates itself through her handwriting, like looking through a window into their life. It's a symbol, a signifier, a representation of them, taking me directly from my name written in their handwriting on the front of the envelope to my memory of the person herself. Part of the thrill at Christmas time, when cards and letters come from friends in the United Kingdom, Europe, the United States, and Australia, is recognizing the handwriting before looking at the sender's name or the return address.

I want to honour letter writing more by sending more letters, yet it's an effort. I don't handwrite much more than notes for myself, shopping lists, ideas, and the occasional card.

I have a theory that handwriting is connected to heart; typing, keyboarding, hunting and pecking, and texting are connected to mind. (Writing with my non-dominant hand, I find, connects heart and soul, so I can connect with spirit when I handwrite a question with my dominant hand and handwrite the answer with my non-dominant hand.) It is possible to type on a keyboard with heart, but only with a specific approach, and making the transition takes time. With practice, I believe I can now stay in my heart centre while I keyboard, feeling the joy of keyboard speed when my thoughts come too fast for handwriting.

But I'll always love handwriting with a good pen.

Do you handwrite these days? What pen do you prefer? What do you handwrite? Do you enjoy reading others' handwriting? Has your style changed over the years? Is your signature reflective of your personality? Has it changed over the years?

~ *Spelling* ~

"[An] interesting understanding embedded in our language
is the arrangement of letters to create words. We call this 'SPELLing,'
for we understand the power of words to cast spells,
or energetic effects, based on their vibrations."

Raamayan Ananda[62]

My Soul Realignment™ teacher Andrrea Hess says, "Spells behave much as curses do, but are placed with far more intention.... [T]hey involve actual ritual.... [A] spell can have severe consequences for the caster as well as for the receiver."[63]

Having worked with clients to release spells using Hess's meaning of the term, I was surprised to read Ananda's suggestion that the verb "spell" (that means to put one letter after the next in an agreed-upon order to create a word that has shared meaning for others) and the noun "spell" (that means influencing another person in a direction they had no intention of going through the magic of saying certain words) are related words. After all, "casting a spell" meant something altogether different to me from "spelling."

Did my etymological dictionary agree? Well, under the entry for the Anglo-Saxon word "spell" meaning "to tell the names of letters in a word" was the Middle English word "spel" meaning "a story" and "an incantation." So, somewhere between 450 A.D. and 1066 A.D., the Anglo-Saxons derived the verb from the noun, and since then, the two words have become rather separate, as though they mean two different things.

This playfully suggests to me that we have to be careful when we spell something; if not, a "sacred" event could make us "scared"; we might shift from being "creative" to being "reactive"; a "feast" might become a "fast"; "satin" might get a "stain"; and a "united" group might become "untied." And I recognize that through play we often reach great truths.

Do you have a scoff barometer, one that has "gullible" on one end and "cynical" on the other? It's a useful scale.

gullible | suggestible | accepting | open-minded | prejudiced | skeptical | cynical

I realize that astro-numerology might be high on someone's scoff barometer, but I have followed the work of astro-numerologist Tania Gabrielle for

[62]Raamayan Ananda, *Michael Jackson: The Man behind the Mirror* (North Vancouver: Influence Publishing, 2014), p. 6.
[63]Andrrea Hess, Soul Realignment™ Practitioner Training, Level I.

long enough to acknowledge that this modality can assist us in divining guidance. I also trust her integrity and spiritual wisdom. She has a lot to say about the impact of spelling on a person's life and offers a special reading called, "Is My Name Fortunate?" She says that many people have names that resonate to an unfortunate number, but that my name—Nina Shoroplova—is fortunate.

How fascinating! How delightful, because I've changed my name three times already and I don't intend to change it again. My husband is Bulgarian and in his country, women add an "a" to their married surname to denote their gender. Initially, when I married Christian here in Canada, I became Nina Shoroplov. But that did not feel quite right—I felt I was describing myself as male. So, soon after we married, I changed my name to Nina Shoroplova on my business cards and my bank account and when introducing myself and so on, and I felt much better, wonderful in fact. And according to Tania Gabrielle, I made a fortunate shift.

I heard about Tania from my Soul Realignment™ teacher, whose name when I started training with her was "Andrea Hess." After her reading with Tania, she learned that "Andrea Hess" was not as fortunate a name as the one she now calls herself: "Andrrea Hess."

Have you ever wondered about your name and how its spelling is casting your life for you? Our name is one of the first things we tell people about ourselves. How unfortunate it would be if we were to keep repeating a description of ourselves—our name—that didn't promote our best qualities.

As you can probably tell, I do believe that a rose would not smell as sweet if its name were "stink cabbage." How about you?

~ *Writing Is Like Capturing a Dream* ~

"When you write, you strive for unleashed creativity
and it's very difficult to achieve, but in dreams
that's the natural state, the place where you begin."

Randy Murray[64]

Sometimes, when I sit ready to write this book at the computer or the laptop sits on me, my mind jumps to another place, going blank. It's the same when I walk through the entrance to the supermarket or the grocery store—my mind goes blank and I forget my shopping list. I believe my brain suddenly becomes aware of all the possibilities and is overwhelmed. Because of this, I have to write out shopping lists and notes for myself. And I had to have a game plan for writing this book.

I can write better from my heart, or my Higher Self, when I don't look at the screen. I am a touch typist (as many of us are these days, even the thumb texters or the three-fingered typists), so I don't need to be looking at my fingers; but there's a huge temptation to look at the words piling up on the screen. The reason watching the screen while staying with the creative part of myself doesn't work is because I switch too easily from being the creator to being the editor, and this is not where I want to be when I am writing something out for the first time.

It's as though I can't "hear" what I want to say when I'm looking at the screen. I know better what I want to say when I'm watching people crossing the street or the branches moving in the breeze or the sun sparkling on the leaves and lights going on and off in the buildings across the street.

Usually by the time I sit down to write, I've already had a thought, a theory, a story I want to capture and develop. But sometimes, re-calling that thought with all its nuances—calling it back—is tricky. Re-membering it—putting my bodies (physical and subtle) back together—is elusive. Writing becomes like capturing a dream.

They say that the best way to capture a dream before it disappears into the ether is to draw pictures and symbols and signs; they're faster. And then, with the images on paper, our more intellectual side can create the logic that will re-present and represent our dream.

What's your process for capturing a dream? For capturing a story? Do you write it out? Blog it? Put it in your journal? Chat about it with a

[64]Randy Murray, "Writing Assignment: Capture a Dream," October 7, 2011, whowritesforyou.com; accessed March 2, 2015.

friend? Let it go? Do you think your ideas are important? Your dreams?

Do you want to knit your thoughts together in a book? Capture one thought, idea or powerful dream message now, and you've started.

~ *Diaries, Daytimers, Journals* ~

"I never travel without my diary.
One should always have something sensational to read in the train."
Oscar Wilde[65]

I have a pile of journals on top of the glass-fronted bookcase in which I keep my books of music. I also have a stack of daytimers in the tall boy of books. And I'm sure I have other collections of written material in the shelves beside my clothes hanging in the bedroom.

I overheard the server at a Starbucks in Vancouver's West End a year or so ago chatting with a customer—both women—about her long-time habit of journaling. She said that she had been writing journals since she was young and had a great number of them. But that her habit nowadays, at the end of each year, was to take all her journals for the year, go through them, and rewrite the highlights, the best bits, in yet another journal—would that be a "metajournal"? It sounded admirable, but arduous. She told the customer her goal was to be able to leave these metajournals (my word, not hers) for her children who at the time ranged between eight and twelve years old.

Daytimers, diaries, and calendars are great places to write appointments—for those of us who don't use some digital method. But why do we write in journals? Gwendolen Fairfax suggests in *The Importance of Being Earnest* that her diary is sensational. Was that because she wrote what she wanted to happen or what actually happened? How about you? Do you write truth or sensation in your journal?

[65]Oscar Wilde, *The Importance of Being Earnest* (Kindle edition), Act Two.

A personal journal can preserve much of the background of a daybook entry with its setting, its sounds and smells, its emotional impact. By writing something on paper, we can let it go, release it, and get on with the next thought. Alternatively, we can build, expand, and stretch the entry for an intended purpose or as raw material for creative later use.

If journals are chronological (and most are), they are also interesting from the point of view that one thought (or story or event) leads to the next: "This happened and I understood it this way and then that happened and I was able to understand it better than I would have, had I not understood the first event." If I hadn't recorded the first event, I would have to deal with both mentally and would not be able to make conclusions as quickly.

We grow through our journals, which is why many self-help books encourage us to journal our thoughts and our actions as we read.

But do we go back and look at our journals, years later? Having been born in scarce times (Wales after the Second World War), I am reluctant to throw away things that still have some life left in them. And in this age of identity theft, I would never throw away a journal; I'd have to shred it. Unlike Oscar Wilde's heroine who travels by carriage or train, I don't take my journals with me to read. So they sit at home, piling up, unread.

Yet, I'm sure they contain some gold. It's just I would have to pan them for days to find those little nuggets. One day I might.

Do you have some old journals? Old letters? Why do you keep them? What do they say to you? Are they a way of contrasting yourself then with yourself now? Can they be more?

Part II ~ The Mystery

Chapter 4—Mysterious Phenomena

Mysteries We Ignore

~ Life Itself ~

"It's called a flower ... because it represents the cycle of a fruit tree.
The fruit tree makes a little flower, which goes through a metamorphosis
and turns into a fruit—a cherry or an apple or something.
The fruit contains within it the seed, which falls to the ground,
then grows into another tree. So there's a cycle of tree to flower
to fruit to seed and back to a tree again, in these five steps.
This is an absolute miracle."

Drunvalo Melchizedek[66]

New Age movement author, speaker, and leader Drunvalo Melchizedek is one of the special people on our planet. His unique knowledge and wisdom make him an excellent teacher of the esoteric. His abilities to perceive associations and link one field of learning with another are rare and inspiring. But for now, let us view life itself in the simplest way.

It was my father who taught me about the life force that is packed inside a tiny seed. I don't know when or where we were when he did, but I know it was him. He was a gardener who, no matter where he lived, always grew a vegetable garden. Whenever I had space for a garden, I did the same.

Think about it. A giant oak grows from an acorn not much bigger than your thumb. A horse chestnut tree that can provide an entire playground with shade grew from a chestnut the size of a toonie. All that potential is

[66]Drunvalo Melchizedek, *The Ancient Secret of the Flower of Life,* Volumes I and II (Light Technology Publishing, 1998), p. 40.

packed inside a hard covering. And all that is needed for the seed to germinate is warm acidic soil, rain, and sunshine.

Rabindranath Tagore, the renowned Bengali polymath says in *Stray Birds*, "The mystery of creation is like the darkness of night—it is great. Delusions of knowledge are like the fog of the morning."

The first crop my father planted each year was radishes, because their seeds are so sturdy. Other plants are slower, and some take several growing seasons before they yield edible food. Three times our family moved house before my father could harvest the tender shoots of the asparagus he always planted.

Cutting into a seed to see where its germ of potential might be is just as unprofitable as killing the goose that laid the golden egg.

Every bit as incredible as the growth of an oak tree from an acorn is the growth of a giraffe after copulation between male and female giraffes. Or the growth of a human baby from sexual intercourse between a man and a woman. So much information is packed into a microscopic sperm and a small egg—enough information to create a baby who will grow into a six-foot-tall man.

Until I became pregnant myself, I viewed reproduction and the birth of a baby as something almost mechanical, mathematical. One plus two makes three. But once I became pregnant, the true wonder of this mystery started to impress me. Conception and birth are so commonplace that we no longer see them as mysteries, unless we are right in the middle of the process. I cannot speak from a man's point of view, but I know that the nine months of carrying each of my children and the tender months following their births brought me into a liminal space that is otherworldly. It is a state of being present and open to the mystery.

How do you view the potential of a seed? The miracle of procreation? The cyclical nature of growth and decay, seed to maturity?

~ *Where Is My Mind?* ~

"If quantum physics hasn't profoundly shocked you,
you haven't understood it yet."
Niels Bohr

I am not a scientist. I greatly admire the ability of scientific curiosity to take human understanding ever deeper, farther, and broader into our natural world. Lay understanding struggles to keep pace. I also greatly admire the ability of those within the scientific community to conjecture links between seemingly disparate theories, and then to create experiments to test the accuracy of those new theories.

When Einstein looked beyond the explanations of Newtonian physics to explain the physical world, he developed the theory of relativity. His world-famous equation $E = mc^2$ expresses the equivalence between energy and mass at the speed of light squared; the matter in something with mass carries a rest energy, a potential energy. In lay terms, an enormous amount of energy can be released from the conversion of matter into energy.

Following on from Einstein's theory of relativity, quantum theory emerged in its more modern form around 1935. Quantum theory concerns itself with what is happening to energy (or mass) at the level of the smallest perceptible unit involved in interactions. Through the double-slit experiment, quantum theory demonstrates that the energy of light behaves either as particles or as waves, but never as both at the same time. Experimentally, the behaviour of light depends on whether or not and how it is being observed and measured. Matter—the solid stuff of our macro world—also behaves at the micro level in some respects as waves.

Referring to wave-particle duality (*aka* wave-particle "complementarity"), Einstein wrote: "We have two contradictory pictures of reality; separately neither of them fully explains the phenomena of light, but together they do."[67]

These scientific theories tell us our solid, stable world is not the way it seems to be, but depends on how we perceive it. Lesson 130 in *A Course in Miracles* says, "It is impossible to see two worlds." While in Hell, we cannot see Heaven. We cannot love when we hate. We are in darkness when we are not in the light.

Taking quantum theory—perhaps inappropriately and controversially—from the micro level to the macro level, I draw your attention to the fact that we humans are both physical matter as bodies, and energy as mind, thought, and decision.

A photograph of a person taken at one moment in time seems to solidify that person. Another photograph of that same person taken several months later shows a different person, sometimes perceptibly different. Is it just time—aging—that has caused the difference? Or is it the energies in the body that have changed that person? I think you know my answer and I hope yours is the same: it is the change in energy.

I am going to use a term I thought I had coined until I came across a documentary movie by the same name: "quantum wisdom." It's a metaphor for that place, that state which Einstein could not measure and yet we know exists between waveform energy and particle form matter. That, for me, is where the Divine resides, neither as wave nor as particle, but as immeasurable Spirit. In an acorn, quantum wisdom is the Divine life force that manifests as a huge oak tree. In a human fetus, quantum wisdom is the embodied spirit, the soul, that has the potential to improve its nature through the senses and feelings it senses and feels, the thoughts it thinks, the words it says, the choices it makes, the actions it takes, the life it lives. Quantum wisdom is how we connect with Divine Mind, with our Divine Maker, where we choose to align with our divinity instead of our ego.

---

[67]David Harrison, "Complementarity and the Copenhagen Interpretation of Quantum Mechanics" (UPSCALE. Dept. of Physics, U. of Toronto, 2002), accessed May 8, 2015 in Wikipedia, en.wikipedia.org/wiki/Wave%E2%80%93particle_duality

Deepak Chopra, M.D. has been challenged for coining the term "quantum healing" when he wrote his book in 1989—*Quantum Healing: Exploring the Frontiers of Mind/Body Medicine.* For him, the term captured the phenomenon he saw in patients who chose to recover from "incurable" diseases. I too have recovered from life-threatening diseases—viral meningitis, liver fluke parasites, secondary tumours of melanoma cancer, and giant cell myositis in the small muscles of my eyes. I've also regained perfect health after four pregnancies and deliveries, five surgeries, and six broken bones. And so I understand the power of energy (positive thinking, affirmations, and prayer) over matter (the disease process).

During the worst days of experiencing giant cell myositis—a condition in which eye muscles become swollen, weak, and watery—I learned from my doctor that most cases of patients who contract this rare condition die because the disease spreads to their heart muscle. Some of these patients chose to have a heart transplant. And so I had to decide. Would I choose to have a heart transplant? I decided I would not, for two reasons. One, I am sufficiently fatalistic to know that when it is my time to go, it is my time to go. Two, I am fully aware that the heart organ—perhaps more than any other bodily organ—carries the energies, the vibrations of its owner. I only desire to live my life—not someone else's.

A human being comprises an integration of a myriad of different wavelengths (or particles), with her vertebrae vibrating at a much slower rate than the rate of her thoughts, and even her various thoughts vibrate at varying rates. As the physical body ages and renews itself less and less efficiently, the rates of vibration of bones and organs and skin veer away from their optimal rates. Bones become less solid, arteries become less flexible, skin becomes thinner, more papery. At some point, that part of mind infused by her soul ceases to integrate with the body, and the result is death of the physical body and the return of consciousness to the soul's spirit.

Brain disease causes another state. When a person's brain no longer provides the bridge between her Divine spirit and her physical body, that body is "just a vegetable." As a physiotherapist I have maintained the range of joints and cleared the lungs for patients in respiratory and neurology wards who were being kept alive on respirators until their consciousness returned—or not. A body without consciousness—without connection to Divine Source—is purely physical, functioning at a very basic autonomic nervous system level. A body with a functioning brain is able to perceive and think, to function intentionally—physically, mentally, and emotionally. A body with a mind is also able to function spiritually, to connect with Divine Mind. The soul of a human with a functioning mind integrates itself through the body's chakras working together and making their spiritual connection with Divine Mind at the crown chakra—another instance of quantum wisdom.

These days, it is acknowledged that "brain cells" (neurons comprising cell body, axon, and dendrites) exist in the intestinal tract and the heart, making both sites of "integrative neural activity" in addition to the brain.[68] This discovery implies that brain science provides us with only one part of the study of mind and that a person can achieve "mind over matter" with the tools of gut instinct and practice in heart-led living (Sue Dumais's term).

So, I ask myself, where is my mind? Am I of one mind? I digress before I answer.

In the scene "~ Bathing in our Mothers' Emotions ~" (chapter one), I introduce the idea of the mirror neurons through which babies learn their emotional palette by mirroring their caregivers' emotions. We continue to mirror emotions and actions into adulthood. And there's more. According to Vilayanur Ramachandran, a professor of neuroscience at the University of California, San Diego, we also mirror the perception of sensations.

---

[68]Dan Hurley, "Your Backup Brain" published in pyschologytoday.com on November 1, 2011, quoting Michael Gershon, professor and chair of pathology and cell biology at Columbia. See also my introduction.

Professor Ramachandran has given several excellent TED talks.[69] He explains how mirror neurons work with people who have lost a limb and suffer from phantom limb syndrome, a phenomenon in which the perception of sensation in a limb (an amputated hand, for instance) continues even after the limb is not there. He explains that when a person with an amputated hand with phantom limb syndrome observes two other people shaking hands, the amputee feels the physical sensations in his phantom limb. A functioning nerve supply would make it clear that the sensation does not belong to his limb; the absence of the functioning nerve supply allows him to sense something that is not happening to him.

From this, I realize that only my neurons make it clear to me what is me and what is everyone else. Without my neurons, without my brain, I would feel and sense that I am everyone else as well as myself.

Another digression. I find fantasy movies intriguing and, therefore, enjoyable. But I find the violence and the tension of the constant threat of danger exhausting. Why? Because, even though the violence and its constant threat are not happening to me, I experience them as mine. My body goes through the stages of fight, flight, fright, or freeze through my autonomic nervous system's inability to realize the events are not happening to me. I left the theatre exhausted by the final movie of *The Hobbit* trilogy. At times, I had fought and, at times, I had fled. My mind became enmeshed in the fantasy of the film.

Another approach. Through my mind, I am able to connect with the collective consciousness. And, if I am able to partake of the collective consciousness, I can be both a receiver and a giver. By being and doing, I influence the collective consciousness. I am an active part of it.

More and more people are realizing that one of the most important lessons while we are on Earth is to relate to others well. Theo Fleury says,

---

[69]Vilayanur Ramachandran, www.ted.com/talks/vilayanur_ramachandran_on_your_mind; www.ted.com/talks/vs_ramachandran_the_neurons_that_shaped_civilization; and blog.ted.com/2007/10/23/vilayanur_ramac/; accessed December 7, 2014.

"True spirituality is all about relationship." My publisher Julie Salisbury says in her book *Around the World in Seven Years* that the most important values are "love, compassion, happiness, spirituality, and community." And what is community if not an aggregate of relationships? Jesus' main spiritual teaching, the Golden Rule, is to act toward others as if they are exactly the same as us, however great the differences in appearance, class, nationality, and so on. The words in King John's English, "Do unto others what ye would have them do unto you," apply no limitations to the notion of "others."

And so, where is my mind? It connects with my brain in my physical body; it's in my relationships, my experiences, and my actions. It is everywhere I am and I am in many places.

Can you think of all the places you influence? Your mind is in those places. Can you think of all the people with whom you relate? With whom you're in relationship, not just "a relationship," but in any relationship? Your mind is in those relationships. Can you think of all the activities you partake in? Your mind is in those activities.

~ *If Phi, Then ...* ~

"A transcendental number in mathematics ... is a number that comes from another dimension.... One of them is the phi ratio."

Drunvalo Melchizedek[70]

The Greek symbol Φ (the twenty-first letter of the Greek alphabet—spelled *Phi*)—stands for a mystical sequence of numbers recognized and brought to prominence by Leonardo Pisano, the mathematician known as Fibonacci of Pisa, Italy. Although Fibonacci lived during the Crusades

[70]Melchizedek, *The Ancient Secret*, p. 156.

in the twelfth and thirteenth centuries (from 1170 to circa 1250), the wisdom for which he is remembered was in use as early as 200 BCE.

The Fibonacci Sequence of numbers is 0, 1, 1, 2, 3, 5, 8, 13, 21, 34, 55, 89, etc., in which each set of adjacent numbers adds up to the subsequent number, as exemplified in 5 + 8 = 13 and 8 + 13 = 21 and 13 + 21 = 34. Also, the divisional relationship of adjacent numbers is constant and twofold: 1) the smaller number always divides into its higher neighbour 1.618 times, e.g. 89 ÷ 55 = 1.618; and 2) the higher number always divides into its smaller neighbour 0.618 times, e.g. 55 ÷ 89 = 0.618. While these decimals are irrational numbers, their constancy does not stabilize until the neighbours are triple digits.[71] These divisional relationships are represented by phi, and are the proportions and ratios known as the "Golden Section," "Golden Mean," and "Golden Ratio."

Once we start looking for it, phi becomes ubiquitous throughout nature and the Universe as the Golden Ratio. Take for example the interior image of a nautilus shell cut in half, the unfurled head of a fern that's known as a fiddlehead, the spiral of petals in an opening rose, the swirl of a spiral galaxy, the position of branches coming off the trunk of a tree, the side view of a curled-up trunk of an elephant, the curl of a child's fingers and palm as she displays relaxed openness. In each case, there is a spiral that starts with a ratio measuring 1 to 1 and then 1 to 2, 2 to 3, 3 to 5, 5 to 8 and so on. This spiral is visible in many vegetables and flowers—Romanesque broccoli, pineapples, pine cones, roses, sunflowers, daisies, and cacti. Not only does Romanesque broccoli demonstrate this spiral, it also demonstrates its fractal nature in which similar flowerets recur smaller and smaller.

The golden ratios of 0.618 to 1 and 1 to 1.618 have become the classical standard of design in architecture and art, and in everyday items such as playing cards, books, and television and computer screens. The Parthenon was constructed, beginning in 447 BCE, using this ratio.

---

[71]For instance, whereas 5 divided by 8 is 0.625, and 55 divided by 89 is 0.617978, 144 divided by 233 is 0.618026.

NautilusCutaway LogarithmicSpiral.jpg originally uploaded to Wikipedia by User Chris 73

Fractal_broccoli.jpg originally uploaded to Wikipedia by User Chris 73 from pdphoto.org

When I was studying holistic nutrition in 2009, the knowledge that the Fibonacci number sequence and phi are seen throughout nature stimulated me to search for such a relationship between the three macronutrients of optimal nutrition: carbohydrates, fats, and proteins. Again and again, I found relationships that are close to Fibonacci relationships in recommendations made by nutritional experts such as Annemarie Colbin, Sally Fallon, and Paul Pitchford, and in the diets of aboriginal peoples.

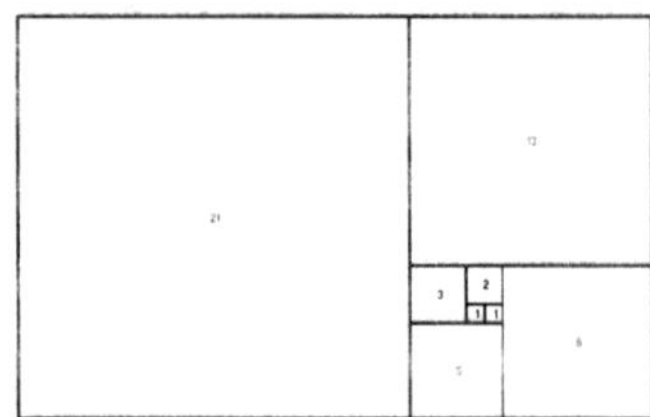

A floor-plan view of the phi ration in action

Understanding the recommended relationships between the three macronutrients—that we should eat mostly plant foods (carbohydrates), followed by fats, and then by proteins—I developed a Fibonacci Diet. Using phi, the percentage sequence goes from 100 percent of the diet in the following way: 100, 62, 38, 23.5, 14.5. Thus, of the complete diet, 62 percent comprises plant foods as carbohydrates and the combination of proteins and fats comprises the next number, 38 percent. Multiplying 38 by 0.618 I find that 23.5 percent should be proteins, leaving fats at 14.5 percent. So the final percentages in the Fibonacci Diet® become 62% + 23.5% + 14.5% = 100%.

The Fibonacci Diet® by Weight

Carbohydrates	62% of diet
Proteins	23.5% of diet
Fats	14.5% of diet
Total diet	100%

Because fats have a caloric value of 9 calories per gram, more than twice that of proteins and carbohydrates by weight of 4 calories per gram, and yet they weigh about the same, volume for volume, visually on the plate fats will appear to be an even smaller proportion, as in the pie chart. Thus, this creates a good visual of a perfectly balanced meal with 67 percent being leafy green and root vegetables, 26 percent being protein, and 7 percent being fat that is often on the protein (e.g. oily fish) or as butter or olive oil on the vegetables.

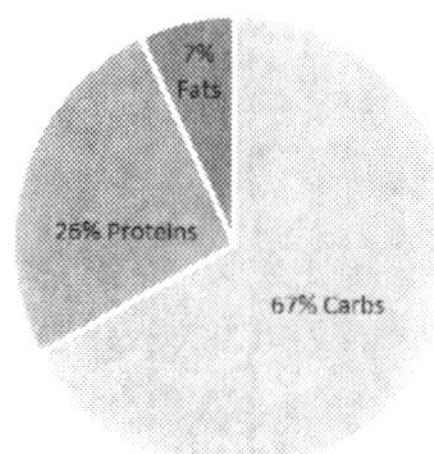

Visual of Fibonacci Diet on the Plate:
Carbs 67%, 26% Proteins, 7% Fats

I thought of yet another instance where two "things" are in close to a golden ratio—the twenty-four hour clock and the length of time we sleep. In fact, it's a bit off. Dividing 24 hours by 1.618 (or multiplying by 0.618) yields 14.8 hours—the hours that we are ideally awake. The balance is 9.2 hours—the hours that we could ideally be asleep. Interesting! Or should 14.8 to 9.2 be a ratio of active to resting hours?

My take on phi and the Fibonacci sequence is that IF it is so prevalent in nature and so mysterious at the same time and we can accept it, THEN we are already accepting the mystery into our lives without questioning it. And if we can accept the phi mystery, what else can we accept?

Is this an introduction to the Fibonacci number sequence for you? Or are you very familiar with the intriguing aspect of these numbers and the phi ratio in nature? Have you already noticed how the ancients relied on this property of nature to display pleasing proportions in their buildings, a proportion that we retain these days?

~ *Pi Goes to an Infinity of Decimal Places* ~

"It's beautiful to listen to the flow of numbers.
It's beautiful to see the concentration.
It's always amazing to be in front of one of the world's extraordinary persons."
Anonymous observer[72]

On March 14, 2004, Daniel Tammet—a man described as a "prodigious savant"—recited pi (π) to 22,514 digits from memory. It was International Pi Day. It began as 3.1415926, as it always does. Tammet ended after more than five hours of recitation. The feat has been done before and since to more digits. In fact, some authors have even written 10,000-word books using words of the length of the digits in order. I am in awe.

Another savant who works with pi—actually he draws pi—is Jason Padgett. Following a head injury in 2002, he saw the world differently; his doctors diagnosed him as having acquired savant syndrome. He became fascinated with space-time and pi, perceiving each thing and each event in single-frame geometrical terms. To learn how he sees the world, watch these YouTube videos and read or listen to his book.[73]

---

[72]"Count pi to 20thousands [sic] digit. See how by Daniel Tammet," YouTube video; accessed January 17, 2015.
[73]Jason Padgett and Maureen Ann Seaberg, *Struck by Genius: How a Brain Injury Made Me a Mathematical Marvel* (Amazon Books, 2014). Also accessed on May 21, 2015:
www.youtube.com/watch?v=VoMhyLJrz_M www.youtube.com/watch?v=11vLkP9WS9s
www.youtube.com/watch?v=bwRqWu0H61A

What I find truly fascinating, however, is the irrationality of pi—the fact that the ratio between the circumference of a circle to its diameter is constant as well as infinite in its solution. It's another "transcendental number," according to Drunvalo Melchizedek. Humanity, with our development of a system of numbers, is unable to "solve" this ratio. The answer goes on forever, beyond the capacity of the human brain. Just like the square root of some numbers, like 2 and 3. To me, this suggests that there is a far, far greater brain, a far greater mind, creating this brilliant Universe.

What does savantism suggest to you? How can a person memorize a string of numbers that long? How can someone draw pi? What does pi represent to you? Is it hard to imagine a number never resolving? How do you perceive infinity? What does all this say to you about the mystery?

~ *Reincarnation* ~

"I could well imagine that I might have lived in former centuries
and there encountered questions I was not yet able to answer;
that I had to be born again because I had not fulfilled
the task that was given to me. When I die,
my deeds will follow along with me—that is how I imagine it."

C.G. Jung[74]

Most people with whom I've ever discussed parenting believe that theirs was totally random, like the luck of the draw, the spin of the roulette wheel. I disagree. I believe that we choose our parents, just as we choose the demands inherent in our relationships with our parents. Such a belief goes hand in hand with my beliefs in reincarnation and our life between lives. Actually, having those beliefs completely changes things. Because

[74]Jung, *Memories, Dreams, Reflections*, p. 318.

as soon as we accept that we chose our parents intentionally before we incarnated into this life, we can take far more responsibility about those relationships. With far less delay than usual we start to learn the lessons those relationships present.

Also hand in hand goes the belief that the parent chooses the child and all the relationship challenges the child represents.

Jung says that people's belief in reincarnation does not make reincarnation so; "a belief proves to me only the phenomenon of belief, not the content of the belief."[75] Nevertheless, I am going to argue for my belief in reincarnation.

I believe a soul individuates from the organized energy of the Great Source to learn and understand through experience. That learning accumulates through many lives until that soul reaches an optimal level, at which point it returns to the organized energy of the Great Source as both an individual and as part of the One. Thus, I believe that when a person dies, it is merely the death of the physical shell that housed the soul. Freed from time, space, and physicality, the spirit returns to a state of consciousness, taking with it the ability to love and the learning gained through that life and all previous lives.

To me, child prodigies are proof of this set of beliefs. Take Mozart, for example. The younger child of a violinist in the court of the Prince-Archbishop of Salzburg, Mozart learned to play simple minuets on the harpsichord by the age of four, and by five, he was composing music that his father thought worthy to notate. His first piece was entitled "Andante in C" and was just ten bars long.[76] It comprised a simple theme presented in three ways with a conclusion, a format that he would have understood from the minuets his father taught him. By the age of six, he was performing in court.

How does a child aged four, five, and six accomplish such musical understanding, such creativity, such focus? I have to agree with Jung that in former

[75]Jung, *Memories, Dreams, Reflections*, p. 319.

[76]Accessed a midi of Mozart's first composition on April 13, 2015 at en.wikipedia.org/wiki/Nannerl_Notenbuch#Andante_in_C.2C_K._1a

lives we encountered a question we were unable to answer. I add, we return with our accumulated learning to try yet again to answer the question.

Do you believe in reincarnation? What skill did you have in your youth that seemed unusual for someone so young? What things were "on your mind" from a young age? Would it make a difference to you if you entertained the belief that you chose your parents? Or that you chose your children? Your grandparents? Your grandchildren? Or do you already know this? If the lesson you are learning by being the offspring of your parents had a name, what would it be?

Early Mysteries

~ Ayurveda—Dosha Typing ~

"By treating the underlying quantum mechanical body itself, Ayurveda can bring about changes far beyond the reach of conventional medicine, confined as it is to the level of gross physiology. This is because the power available at the quantum level is infinitely greater than that found at grosser levels."

Deepak Chopra[77]

Using the five elements of Hinduism—earth, water, fire, air (or wind), and ether (the void)—Ayurveda determines a person's body type and, as a result, their strengths and weaknesses, preferences and predilections. A person's Ayurvedic profile yields unique personal information and comprises a different approach to staying healthy. This profile is described in terms of the three *doshas*: *Vata* governs movement through air and ether; *Pitta* governs transformation through fire and water; *Kapha* governs fluid

[77]Chopra, Deepak, M.D., *Perfect Health: The Complete Mind/Body Guide* (Harmony Books, 1991), p. 8.

balance through water and earth. There are seven types: *Vata, Pitta, Kapha, Vata-Pitta, Vata-Kapha, Pitta-Kapha,* and the rare *Vata-Pitta-Kapha.*

My type is *Vata-Pitta.* What is yours? Deepak Chopra, M.D., the man who introduced Ayurveda to the West, includes an excellent test to establish one's *dosha* ratios in his book *Perfect Health.* Alternatively, you can take the test at doshaquiz.chopra.com. The most important aspect to Ayurveda that differentiates it from Western medicine is its ability to keep the body in balance and to work on the pre-cursors of disease, even before any Western medical tests would be able to determine that anything were amiss.

I first became interested in an Ayurvedic approach to health in 1998, when my daughter and I were on a cross-Canada rail-and-road trip. Struggling at the time to recover from the debilitating eye-muscle dis-ease that had been reluctant to respond to Western medicine, I was ready to invest time, energy, and faith in alternative healing methods. I found a copy of Dr. Chopra's book and filled pages of my travel journal with tallies of my readings and appropriate food lists.

On our return to Vancouver, I sought out an Ayurvedic doctor who confirmed my *dosha* type and used pulse diagnosis to establish which herbal medications, oils, foods, and behaviours would assist my recovery. I saw him every month for six months. Although slow and erratic, my recovery from the eye-muscle dis-ease can be attributed as much to my faith in Ayurveda as to Western medication and surgery. Had I worked with the principles of Ayurveda sooner, I might have avoided that "dark night of the soul"—that whole period of a year and a half. But then I wouldn't have benefitted from the gifts that such trials can deliver.

Only recently has Western medical equipment begun to demonstrate with any sensitivity—through the development of the superconducting quantum interference device (SQUID) in the early 1970s—the human body's ability to create bioelectromagnetic signals.[78] I believe that, as Western medicine improves its testing methods, it will respond to Eastern medical approaches

[78]Rollin McCraty, Ph.D., "The Energetic Heart: Bioelectromagnetic Interactions within and between People" (Boulder Creek, CA: Institute of HeartMath, 2003).

with greater acceptance and trust. That time can't come soon enough, as far as I'm concerned.

Have you ever experienced a dis-ease that is unresponsive to Western medicine? Do you know your *dosha* profile? Have you ever had an appointment with an Ayurvedic doctor? How do you reconcile the fact that traditional Chinese medicine works with five elements that are different from Hinduism's five elements?

~ *Numerology* ~

"Number 4 reminds us that honesty and respect are the building blocks of trust. Honor others by not interfering in their life, and don't allow them to interfere in yours. Strong boundaries will set you free."

Tania Gabrielle[79]

Chaldean Numerology, Pythagorean Numerology, and their cousins Greek and Hebrew Gematria are methods of assigning values and meanings to numbers, as well as assigning number values (and thereby meanings) to letters and words. Pythagorean Numerology is fairly straightforward—the English alphabet is lined up one letter at a time below the numbers 1 to 9, in three rows: A to I, J to R, and S to Z.

Pythagorean Numerology

1	2	3	4	5	6	7	8	9
A	B	C	D	E	F	G	H	I
J	K	L	M	N	O	P	Q	R
S	T	U	V	W	X	Y	Z	

[79]Tania Gabrielle, facebook.com/taniagabrielleofficial, December 4, 2014.

Chaldean Numerology
showing before and after

1	2	3	4	5	6	7	8
A	B	C	D	E			F
I		G		H			
J	K	L	M	N		O	P
Q	R	S	T		U		
Y				X	V	Z	
					W		

1	2	3	4	5	6	7	8
A	B	C	D	E	U	O	F
I	K	G	M	H	V	Z	P
J	R	L	T	N	W		
Q		S		X			
Y							

Gematria

Greek Gematria

1	2	3	4	5	6	7	8	9
A	B	G	D	E	VW	Z	E	Th
10	20	30	40	50	60	70	80	
I	K	L	M	N	X	O	P	Q
100	200	300	400	500	600	700	800	
R	S	T	YU	Ph	Ch	Ps	O	

Hebrew Gematria

1	2	3	4	5	6	7	8	9
A	B	G	D	H	V	Z	Ch	T
10	20	30	40	50	60	70	80	90
I	K	L	M	N	S	O	Ph	Tz
100	200	300	400	500	600	700	800	900
Q	R	Sh	Th	K	M	N	Ph	Tz

Values for last five letters in Hebrew Gematria - K M N Ph Tz - are for when these are final letters of words.

Pythagoras based his numerology on the much more complicated system developed by the Chaldeans, a race of people who lived at the mouth of the Tigris and Euphrates Rivers at the northwest end of the Persian Gulf where parts of Iraq and Kuwait lie today. I present the Chaldean Numerology in two ways, placing the letters of the alphabet in a row in an almost-recognizable way and then moving them up to leave no spaces.

The term *Gemaria*—also a scientific method of assigning numerical values to alphabetical letters—denotes something slightly different from Chaldean and Pythagorean numerology. Initially based on the Greek alphabet and converted to the Hebrew alphabet, the method has the letters actually standing for the numeric values in addition to standing for themselves. The numbers are equal to single digits, tens, and hundreds.

In zeroing in on my title for this book, I used Pythagorean numerology. *Trust the Mystery* is three words, symbolic of the trinity of Divine creative perfection. The phrase has two strong and three weak beats. Two signifies partnerships—you and me. Three signifies creativity. The title letters add up to 67, which in numerology reduces first to 13 and then to 4 (6 + 7 = 13; 1 + 3 = 4). The number four is symbolic of the Earth, structure, boundaries, and manifestation. And so *Trust the Mystery* symbolizes partnership, creativity, and manifestation.

My subtitle *Questions, Quotes, and Quantum Wisdom* is five words, the middle number of the range from 1 to 9. When we reach the middle of our lives, we start reviewing the past and wondering about the future. Five as a numeral—5—is a number that looks both backwards and forwards. In that way, 5 also stands for our media industry, travel, freedom, and being aware. These are intriguing energies for my book.

The phrase *Questions, Quotes, and Quantum Wisdom* is eight beats long or four strong beats alternating with four weak beats. Eight is the universal number for the year 2015, the year my book is published. Eight is aligned with infinity (turning the symbol 8 on its side reveals the symbol for infinity ∞). It is also the number for abundance and fulfillment. The letters in the subtitle add up to 130, which, just like the title, reduces to 4 (1 + 3 + 0 = 4). Tania Gabrielle says that the number zero "symbolizes the never-ending circle of life. 0 is nothing and everything." I also believe it provides Divine protection.

So together, the eight words in my book title and subtitle—*Trust the Mystery: Questions, Quotes, and Quantum Wisdom*—have a value of 8 (4 + 4), the universal number for this year and also the number for infinite abundance.

It also happens that there are some other significances in these words and numbers. So, one way and another, I'm very happy with my book title and subtitle, numerologically and word-wise!

Do you allow numerology to play a part in your life? Do you recognize the power of the number of your birth? Your birth name? Your current name?

~ *Divination* ~

"A physician without a knowledge of astrology
has no right to call himself a physician."
Hippocrates

Astrology and astronomy were originally combined as a method of studying the stars' relationship to events on Earth. During the Age of Reason, it was determined that astrology had no scientific value; it was separated from astronomy and downgraded. Nowadays, it is a method of interpreting a person's personality and the events of their life through an understanding of the position of the sun, moon, and stars at the time of their birth, and using that understanding to interpret their lives and make the best decisions for their future.

Astrology is a form of divination. So is numerology; crystal ball scrying; rune casting; throwing dice or coins; casting lots, bones, or stones; consulting the *I Ching* using yarrow stalks or coins; using a pendulum; pulling Tarot cards to read a spread.

The reason that most forms of divination work is because they help us tap into the Universal wisdom that is available to all of us; they actually connect us as individuals through our quantum wisdom to Divine Wisdom. In the same moment that we allow ourselves to trust the words written in the *I Ching* we become wiser. We make connections we could not make before. We see things differently. We see around and below and in front of the problem. We get answers to questions we hadn't yet voiced or even thought of. We become our own counsellors even as we listen to the voice of the person reading the *I Ching* for us. We have released our rational left brain from its role of keeping us within the parameters we accept as the ones that govern the world, and we have unleashed our playful right brain to search more widely and more deeply for patterns that help us understand ourselves and our lives in different ways, in new ways.

I have studied other forms of cartomancy (divination using a pack of cards). Card packs have proliferated in recent years from the traditional Rider-Waite Tarot cards to Doreen Virtue's Angel card decks to decks of animals, flowers, and fractal energy art.

I have given *I Ching* and tarot card readings to others. I often do card spreads for myself. (The *I Ching* is available in book and card form.) And each time, with an open mind and a gentle focus on the question at hand (or just the awareness that there is an unspoken question), answers come through. What a simple way to tap into our quantum wisdom and our own connection with Universal wisdom.

The term "fortune telling" doesn't equate with "divination"; it's more frivolous, more prone to doubt, more likely to be done with an audience present. Divination has greater respect for the result; in fact, part of the requirement is that advice that comes through from divining wisdom must be acted upon.

Have you ever had a tarot card reading? Have you done a spread for yourself, asking a question and looking for answers? Did you find answers? Did you allow the answers to help? Or did you dismiss them before you glimpsed their power to make your life easier?

~ *Beliefs and Belief Teaching* ~

"Thus do superior people consistently practice virtue and learn how to teach."

The Taoist I Ching[80]

The *I Ching*'s 29th hexagram that introduces this scene is called variously "Mastering Pitfalls" and "The Abysmal." It refers to studying the qualities of a virtuous life and then teaching what one has learned: students become teachers. Where might be the pitfall in this? We could follow the "wrong" teacher. We could dismiss a body of learning as having no value. We could declare ourselves unprepared for such ideas. We might decide we are not sufficiently "educated" to teach what we know.

Each of us is both a student and a teacher. What I have learned and incorporated into my belief system I now teach, not necessarily in a school or a university lecture hall; nor via an online seminar or a live call. I teach the beliefs I have embodied through the ways I live my life, through writing, editing, being, and loving.

Trust the Mystery is an argument for belief in the mystery of life; I build my argument on gentle persuasion. I begin in Part I explaining the basic tools with which we can use our physical and subtle bodies to negotiate and communicate our way through the lives we live. Then I offer some of the irrefutable mysteries. If there is just one—or just part of one—of these mysteries about which you can say, "Well, yes, I can accept that one," then the whole argument will have been worthwhile.

A statement can be proven false if there is just one small instance of proof (acceptance of possible existence) of an opposite. For example, "all clovers have only three leaves" can be proven false through the finding of just one four-leafed clover. I found one once preserved and dried between the pages of a small book belonging to one of my grandparents. Have you ever found one?

Three statements that many never challenge are "I am a human; I have no spirit; I am not Divine." Such people would have difficulty in accepting that they are part of the mystery.

I propose that a four-leafed clover can open the door to accepting and trusting the mystery for those people who previously lived their lives believing only in physicality, in what can be proven, and in separation

[80]Liu I-Ming, *The Taoist I Ching* translated by Thomas Cleary (Boston: Shambhala Books, 2005) from hexagram"29: Double Water," p. 264.

between themselves, their environment, and Divinity, which is the biggest mystery of all, the Infinite Omniscience. In all, I write this book to prove that each of us is a part, an example, a potential model of the essence of the Infinite Greatness, of Divine Source, of what many call "God," what the Kabbalah of Jewish mysticism calls *Ein Sof*, translating as "Nothingness" or "the Infinite."

The word "God" has become limiting and small through its patriarchal, casual, and profane use over time. Use of the word "God" anthropomorphizes the All That Is into a male entity. It suggests—as do many religions—an us-and-Him scenario, as though God were somewhere far away in the sky, only intervening in our lives at our request or for our punishment. My beliefs counter those. I believe, as do many these days, that each one of us embodies Divinity in each cell of our body, and that we are walking, talking physical embodiments of the Divine, here to experience life and to learn about Divinity through life. That is our purpose.

Each of us is one "chip off the old block" of the Infinite Omniscience of our Divine Source—unique in our physicality, emotional palette, mental processing, and gifts. Our gifts are the foundation of our potential. When we develop our gifts and our potential and thereby "follow our bliss," we come closer to the mystery. Our gratitude for life helps us to accept and trust the mystery.

We humans are inclined to sort statements into two piles: the ones we believe and the ones we don't believe. But we can't understand the Universe in terms of polar opposites like this, of divisions, but in terms of paradoxical truths—holding two or more seemingly contradictory views at once. This paradox only exists in our human minds where rules and ego reign; in the Universe, all is one. I ask you to suspend any remaining disbelief or reluctance to trust the mystery as you continue to read this book. Let the mystery insinuate itself into your belief systems and rest gently there, allowing your world to expand and your potential to grow.

What are you learning? What have you learned? What are you

teaching? How are you teaching your beliefs, the beliefs you trust in your deepest self?

~ *Sacred Geometry* ~

"[T]he five Platonic solids come from the first informational system of the Fruit of Life. Hidden within the lines of Metatron's cube are all five of these shapes."

Drunvalo Melchizedek[81]

Sacred geometry refers to the five three-dimensional Platonic solids—the tetrahedron, octahedron, icosahedron, cube (hexahedron), and dodecahedron. I present them in an atypical order for a reason that will be clear soon. With their rather daunting names (other than "cube"), these solids are made up of a number of equilateral triangular faces: four, eight, and twenty; six square faces; and twelve pentagonal faces. In each shape—triangles, squares, and pentagons—the edges are the same length and the angles are the same degree; if each shape were surrounded by a perfect sphere, each point would touch the surface.

According to classical Greek five-element symbology, the tetrahedron is viewed as fire, the octahedron as air, the icosahedron as water, the cube as earth (both "soil" and "Earth"), and the dodecahedron as ether, *aka* spirit. Perhaps my order is now clearer, because it took fire, air, and water (three 3s with triangular faces) to create physical life on Earth (a 4 that is square faced), and into that physical life came spirit (a 5 with a pentagonal face). I appreciate the logical order of 3 to 4 to 5 that appears in this elemental relationship with the Platonic solids.

Drunvalo Melchizedek claims that the Platonic solids were "thought to act as a template from which all life springs" and I now understand that claim.[82] His presentation of the codes and messages built into the

[81]Melchizedek, *The Ancient Secret*, p. 161.

design and positioning of the Egyptian pyramids (square pyramids rather than tetrahedral ones) and the Sphinx invites further exploration. He claims that the pyramid exemplifies spirit (symbolized by the triangle faces in this instance) descending into Earth (symbolized by the square base).

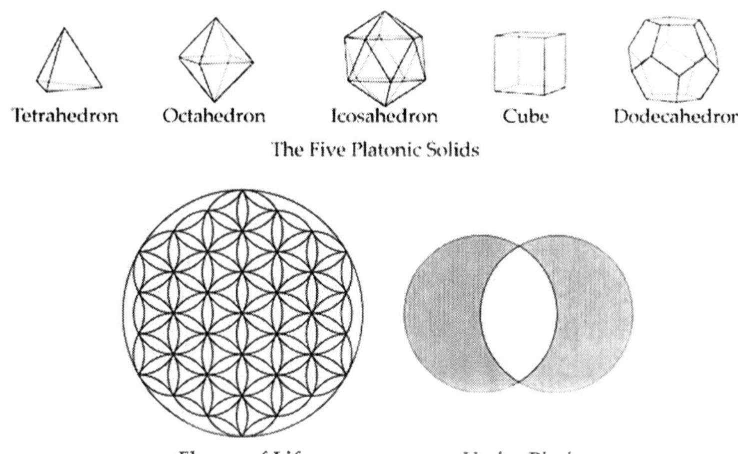

The Five Platonic Solids

Flower of Life

Vesica Piscis

Using the Flower of Life (in which the symbols for the Seed of Life, the Fruit of Life, the Tree of Life, and Metatron's Cube can be found) as the basis for his theory of humanity's Divinity, Drunvalo found examples of this informative pattern on the wall of Egyptian pyramids and in many other places throughout the world. The fascinating fact is that the five Platonic shapes are also hidden within the Flower of Life and Metatron's cube. So is the *vesica piscis* (a Latin term meaning "bladder of the fish"), a symbol that came to be used for Jesus the Christ, an example of perfect love on Earth.

The Tree of Life is identical with the Kabbalah of the Ten Sephirot, an esoteric teaching about life that's attributed to Judaism but is actually based in antiquity. The Flower of Life can also be overlaid with the Ten Sephirot.

Drunvalo has a great deal to teach us. Visit his School of Remembering at drunvalo.net and read his books, *The Ancient Secret of the Flower of Life,* Volumes I and II, for more about sacred geometry.

Can you find the various geometrical shapes in the image above? Do

[82]Credited to Drunvalo on numerous sites.

they have any meaning for you? Have you encountered the transformational, liminal space known as *vesica piscis* lying between two overlapping spheres? Have you worked with the wisdom of the Kabbalah? With the Platonic solids?

Alternative Healing Modalities

~ *Applied Kinesiology* ~

"A muscle moderately weak on testing often appeared to be associated with a weak viscera or organ. Evidence of a weak pancreas, stomach, liver, or kidney that could be measured by x-ray, biochemistry, or by some other accepted test, would correspond to a weakened muscle."
George J. Goodheart, Jr., D.C.[83]

Applied Kinesiology (AK) is a diagnostic tool—also called "biomechanics"—that uses the body itself as the instant messenger of its own state of health. Okay, the body is giving us messages all the time, in the form of aches, pains, warmth, coldness, tightness, and clicks. But these aren't always instant or clear.

George J. Goodheart, Jr., a Doctor of Chiropractic, first discovered AK (which he called "manual muscle testing") back in 1964 while searching for innovative ways to heal his more-challenging patients whose various conditions could not be cured by existing methods. Living up to his surname, Dr. Goodheart spent his working life as an alternative healer, standardizing muscle testing and expanding its clinical usefulness until his death in 2008.

Although Dr. Goodheart used AK to heal patients' longstanding physical complaints, following up his diagnoses with various palpations

[83]George J. Goodheart, Jr., D.C., *You'll Be Better, The Story of Applied Kinesiology* (AK Printing, 2000), Chapter One.

and remedies, my experience with the tool is in connection with mental and emotional discomfort.

Intriguingly, when we think of something negative, our physical strength diminishes. The way AK works is the body instantly responds to the client's thoughts and emotions with a weakened muscular response. An arm—more usually the non-dominant arm—is used for testing. The client is instructed to think of something negative or to repeat a negative word. Testing the deltoid muscle in its ability to hold the arm forward, the practitioner will instantly register a slight lowering of the arm as the client repeats the negative word or thought.

"The opportunity to use the body as an instrument of laboratory analysis is unparalleled in modern therapeutics, because the response of the body is unerring."[84]

It was AK that Dr. Hawkins used to create his "Map of Consciousness" for his book *Power vs. Force*. Practitioners of Three-in-One concepts, *aka* the One Brain® method, use AK to uncover the foundation of personal difficulties, relationship challenges, and circumstantial hurdles to provide integration between body, mind, and spirit.

Many non-traditional forms of medicine recognize the energetic subtle body—meridians, acupuncture points, Kundalini path, and chakras. Whereas traditional Chinese medicine utilizes the acupuncture points of the body to heal through acupuncture, acupressure, and auriculotherapy, Hinduism acknowledges the Kundalini path in Kundalini yoga and uses knowledge about the seven major chakras of the body to localize problems. Alternative therapists from acupuncturists to masseurs use crystals—quartz, lapis lazuli, coloured to correspond with the rainbow colours of the seven major chakras—as part of their healing modality. As the only inorganic matter that reproduces and grows, crystals can mediate healing between our bodies and our stressful environments. Donna Eden is one woman who has contributed clear understanding of the multiple energy systems of the human body through her nine books on energy medicine, each with the word "energy" in its title. Only now

[84]Goodheart, *You'll Be Better.*

is Western medicine recognizing the energetic nature of everything; by inference, this lays a foundation for a belief in every living thing having a subtle energetic body.

Alternative healing modalities recognize the potential of working with the energetic body. Emotional Freedom Technique is a specific style of physical tapping of acupuncture points for healing. Soul Realignment™ in part assigns abilities and proclivities to clients by recognizing which chakra they have the most affinity with. It does this through an Akashic Record Reading; *Akasha* is the Sanskrit word for "ether." A person's Akashic Record contains their entire history, through however many lifetimes they have lived on Earth and elsewhere. Akashic Record Reading work requires a leap of faith for its practitioners and avails its clients of Divine Wisdom; it solidifies their connection with quantum wisdom.

In what ways have you become aware that you have an energetic body, meridians, chakras? Have you ever proven to yourself through Applied Kinesiology the amazing effect on your body strength of feeling negative emotions, thinking negative thoughts, and imagining negative scenarios? What if you only ever thought positively?

~ *Naturopathy* ~

"Natural forces within us are the true healers of disease."

Hippocrates

Naturopathic doctors (N.D.s) are recognized and regulated in British Columbia, and each one provides his own eclectic mix of natural treatments to promote the body's innate healing abilities and return it to homeostasis (metabolic equilibrium). Naturopaths diagnose conditions and use herbs, supplements, nutrition, and homeopathic remedies to promote healing in their patients. Unlike Western medicine, which is most interested in diagnosing and treating current individual symptoms with medicines and surgery, naturopathic medicine is most interested in finding the actual source of illness and treating the whole person with natural methods.

I've been seeing a naturopath since attending the Canadian School of Natural Nutrition. Naturopathic doctor Keith Condliffe supports and improves my current health status, starting by taking a detailed history at each quarterly or half-yearly appointment. Then he tests my body with pulse diagnosis as developed by Paul Nogier, M.D., a Frenchman who created the original "map of the ear" to become known as the father of auriculotherapy and auricular medicine. Dr. Condliffe uniquely combines Nogier's pulse diagnosis with the Chinese five-element theory pertaining to fire, earth, metal, water, and wood.

When I saw Keith in mid-June 2014, I was recovering from having had a complete hip replacement that April and I was still grieving the loss of my mother. The ache of grief in my chest became unbearable at times. Keith recommended that I take a homeopathic dose of Ignatia, from the fruit of *Ignatia Amaris,* a Chinese climbing shrub. He said it would propel my grief to start moving in more healing ways. Once a week for the next three weeks, I let five pellets of Ignatia (each a mite larger than a mustard seed) melt under my tongue.

I digress momentarily. Homeopathy uses the Law of Similars to spur healing on the basis of "that which can cause can cure." From Latin, "homeopathy" means "similar suffering," whereby the catch phrase becomes "Like cures like." A homeopathic dose of red onion, for example, can cure a runny nose and eyes, the very condition it causes in kitchen preparation. The founder of homeopathy, medical doctor Samuel Hahnemann (1755-1843) discovered through experimentation on himself that a drug that was being used to cure symptoms of malaria brought out the very same symptoms when administered to healthy people.

I expect it is the dosage of homeopathic preparations that makes non-believers scoff at its efficacy. Hahnemann discovered that "repeated dilution and jarring shaking (succussion) of a substance"[85] removes any

[85]homeopathyplus.com.au/tutorial-3-potentisation

possible toxicity of the "cure" while also increasing its potency. Nowadays, the process is called "potentization." Dilutions can be done hundreds and thousands of times so that the remaining liquid carries only the energetic imprint of the original substance. The fact that homeopathy has cured animals as well as humans proves its virtues to me.

There are other ways in which the Law of Similars is utilized. For example, the two halves of a walnut are very similar in shape to the two hemispheres of the brain. And indeed, a walnut is great brain food. A pomegranate with its many seeds is associated with fertility. Tall leafy-green vegetables support spinal health because they carry Vitamin K1, one of the vitamins leading to bone health through calcium retention. The two halves of an avocado are somewhat similar in shape to a human heart and indeed avocado oil is very beneficial for healthy heart function.

Since the mid-1800s, the British Royal Family has been very much in favour of homeopathy and a holistic approach to health. These days, Peter Fisher, M.D., medical director of the Royal London Hospital for Integrative Medicine, is the Royal Homeopath.

Back to my experience with Ignatia. Three weeks after starting the homeopathic treatment, I attended a one-week prepare-to-perform jazz summit organized by musical artist Karin Plato. Each of the ten attendees prepared three songs to jazz up under Karin's sure guidance. I chose "Cheek to Cheek" by Irving Berlin, "A Room with a View" by Noël Coward, and "Can't Help Lovin' Dat Man" by Jerome Kern with lyrics by Oscar Hammerstein II. I've frequently sung these three songs as solos through the years. Well, somehow, Plato's more hearty and earthy style of singing jazz rendered me incapable of singing "Can't Help Lovin' Dat Man" while taking Ignatia, without dissolving into tears.

Homeopathy during that week of learning to sing familiar songs in a new-to-me way opened up new channels of healing. The people that I sang with that week probably thought I had always been a weepy creature. I tried to explain that my naturopath had me on some homeopathic remedy to help me with the loss of my mother, but I don't think it made much sense to them.

Do you have any experience with homeopathy? Are you willing to give it a try? Have you ever visited a naturopath? Do you believe that your physical symptoms could be connected to your emotional, mental, and spiritual bodies? Could you be open enough to visit a naturopath for a maintenance visit, even when everything seems to be going right?

~ *From Microcosm to Macrocosm* ~

"The microcosm of the ear was said to have energetic correspondence with the macrocosm of the whole body, and the microcosm of the whole body was said to have cosmic correspondence with the macrocosm of the universe."

Terry Oleson, Ph.D.[86]

I've always been intrigued with things containing their own miniature facsimiles—not for instance the Russian nesting matryoshka dolls (also known as babushkas), but more things like stamps carrying images of stamps, or plays describing the rehearsing and playing of a play while recognizing that "all the world's a stage," or a book about a writer writing a book, or a painting of an artist painting.

Our body contains a number of facsimiles of itself and our health status, in the palms of our hands, the soles of our feet, our ears, our eyes, our tongue, and our face as a whole. Using maps of correspondence, reflexologists mostly work on feet, but they could as easily work on our hands to influence various body parts. Each day, I end my morning exercise session by massaging every part of my hands with both reflexology and the meridian pathways in mind; I find that this practice wakes up my body.

Alternative medicine therapists who use auricular medicine—acupuncturists and some naturopaths—follow maps that designate particular parts of our ears to various organs and limbs of the body. Iridology

[86]Terry Oleson, *Auriculotherapy Manual: Chinese and Western Systems of Ear Acupuncture* (Elsevier Health Sciences, 2013), p. 5, referring to early Chinese texts on acupuncture.

is the study of the iris of the eye to determine a person's health. Using photographs of the patient's eyes, an iridologist uses this diagnostic tool to ascertain the health status of body organs and limbs by viewing the different segments of the eye.

The geography, colour, and size of the tongue are also used as visual diagnostic tools by practitioners of Ayurvedic medicine and traditional Chinese medicine.

The shape and prominence of our face and its features allow simple classification of our personality and behaviour styles to people who are trained in face reading.

In short, our physical body reflects itself in miniature in a number of places on itself. As we are in macrocosm, we sometimes are in microcosm.

Feng Shui, the Chinese system of arranging a living or working space in the most beneficial way, is another system of equivalence that recognizes that as we are within, so we are without; and vice versa. The system uses the *bagua* (pronounced 'ba-gwa), an octagon displaying eight areas surrounding a central ninth space allowing for the balance of yin and yang in the home, to assign meaning to each corner of the home.

The person whose thoughts are messy probably has a messy desk. The person who believes in celebrating life decorates their home with flowers and small treasures and incense. The person who has a fatalistic attitude toward life lives in a home that does not feel loved.

But Feng Shui is more than these simple reflections.

Feng Shui practitioner Mark Ainley has encouraged single adults who desire a loving relationship to hang pictures of happy couples and matching pairs of items in the marriage corner of the home—the far right corner from the home's or room's entrance—yielding great success. He encourages those who want success in their business to display tokens of fire—candles, red items, and stars—in the area that is opposite their office door. He had me display my various diplomas, plus an oil painting by my husband of a fiery red sky in my fame-and-reputation space, directly opposite the door to my office. And my business, which has gone from practising alternative healing methods to working with others who want to share their knowledge of such arts with the world through writing, has gone from success to success.

Does your home reflect your beliefs, your inclinations? Or is it a reflection of someone else's beliefs? Have you ever consulted a Feng Shui specialist? Have you ever considered the basics of Feng Shui?

~ *Laying On of Hands* ~

"At sunset, the people brought to Jesus all who had various kinds of sickness and, laying his hands on each one, he healed them."

Luke 4:40[87]

The laying on of hands has been practised since ancient times, as gestures above the body, as massage of skin and muscles, and as localized deep palpation of specific problems like muscle knots. Nowadays, practitioners use many different techniques to move energy and encourage healing.

An early memory for me is falling down on the asphalt in my Grade One playground. It isn't the pain in my hands and knees that I remember; it's the shock and the loss of equilibrium, the loss of the feeling of safety. Another slightly bigger girl came and took me by the hand to one of the teachers who attended to me. By holding my hand, by paying attention to my slight injury, they shared their physical healing loving energy with me and thereby stimulated my self-healing.

Paramahansa Yogananda, author of the spiritual classic *Autobiography of a Yogi,* was the first Hindu Swami to establish long-term residency in the United States, starting in 1920, for the purpose of introducing the ancient wisdom of the East to the West. Having heard his book (narrated by Ben Kingsley), for having sung his music and been initiated into Kriya

---

[87]Holy Bible, NIV®.

Yoga, the yogic discipline he espoused, I feel very close to Yoganandaji. I consider him one of the greatest teachers of the last century.

He taught a healing technique that begins with rubbing our hands together for ten to twenty seconds to gather energy and combines other arm movements with prayer for self-healing and sharing healing with others. The Self-Realization Fellowship that he founded in 1920 describes this healing technique at yogananda-srf.org.[88]

Current alternative healing modalities that involve the laying on of hands in various ways include Energy Healing; Healing Touch as developed by Janet Mentgen, R.N., BSN; Therapeutic Touch as developed by Dora Kunz and Dolores Krieger; Faith Healing as an extension of the ability of Jesus the Christ; Reconnective Healing as developed by chiropractor Eric Pearl; Emotional Freedom Technique as developed by Gary Craig; and Emotional Stress Release, developed as part of Touch for Health.

Reiki is a very specific pattern of the laying on of hands to direct Divine energy to the seven main chakras of the human body for health maintenance, relaxation, renewal of energy, and relief from maladies. Its founder Mikao Usui, a Doctor of Theology, adapted the Five Reiki Precepts from writings by Emperor Meiji:

"At least for today:
Do not be angry;
Do not worry;
Be grateful;
Work with diligence;
Be kind to people."

What parent does not cover their child's injury with his hands? Have you used your hands to heal yourself? To heal others? Have you received healing from the hands of others?

[88] Yogananda Paramahansa, www.yogananda-srf.org/prayer/Worldwide_Prayer_Circle/Healing_Technique_Taught_by_Paramahansa_Yogananda.aspx#.VQSnDeHzt-w

~ *Sound Healing* ~

"The power of sound can encompass so many things
from working on resonating and changing vibratory rates
in the physical body ... to working with the chakras,
and changing the vibratory rate of the subtle bodies."
Jonathan Goldman[89]

Sound healers use their voices plus the sound of resonant instruments—crystal bowls, seven-metal Tibetan singing bowls, Tibetan temple tingshaws (pairs of small cymbals connected by a leather thong), large cymbals, and gongs—to heal themselves and others. They work with the knowledge that every one of the fifty trillion cells in our bodies is in constant vibration; vibrations create wave forms, some of which are in the audible range, and others of which are merely palpable. Even inaudible wave forms affect our aura, our subtle body. As the wave forms created by the healer create audible sounds and inaudible effects, these forms combine with the wave forms being made by the client's own body, and the two align. As the perfect and whole sound and intentions of the healer and her instruments continue, wholing and healing occur in the client. All through sound.

When I attended Jonathan Goldman's 2013 Sound Healing Intensive I knew a lot about music. As a result, my music theory knowledge almost held me back from benefitting from the nine-day workshop. Gradually I let go of intellectualizing what I was hearing and opened myself up to a wide range of healing. In the process, I found some music that I can't analyze—sounds created by Tibetan and crystal singing bowls, tingshaws, gongs, and synthesizers. These are healing sounds that speak directly to my heart; I can listen to them and hear them with my whole body as they *whole* and heal me.

---

[89]Jonathan Goldman, interviewed by Lane Badger (healingsounds.com), "Chant and Sacred Sound Master."

I celebrate life with Jonathan and Andi Goldman
at their 2013 Sound Healing Intensive.

At home I display four singing bowls (*aka* standing bells) that, when struck one by one, sing out a major arpeggio—do, mi, so, do. Okay, I couldn't keep musical theory out of my engagement with sound healing forever!

Jonathan has a very useful belief: "Frequency plus Intention equals Healing." And so, I apply this to the sounds made by my four bowls and my knowledge of the seven major chakras of the body. Using solfège syllables, my "do" bowl is for my root chakra; "mi" is for my sacral chakras and spiritual heart; "so" is for my heart and high heart chakras; and the high "do" is for my throat chakra. Wonderful.

Have you experienced any form of healing through sound? Can you imagine that each of your organs sings its own note as it vibrates optimally? Do you find singing healing? What instruments do you play?

~ *Hypnosis* ~

"Contrary to popular belief, hypnosis is not a state of sleep,
or a state in which you are unconscious or not aware.
Hypnosis is actually a heightened state of mind in which you are deeply relaxed
yet have a much higher level of suggestibility and focused awareness."
Newsletter@NaturalHypnosis.com[90]

After completing high school in South Wales in the late 1960s, I trained as a physiotherapist at Cardiff's main hospital, the Cardiff Royal Infirmary. We were a small group of perhaps twenty women—only women trained as physiotherapists in those days.

During our first year of the three-year course, one of the most interesting classes we attended was given by an obstetrician who was experimenting with delivering the pregnant women in his care through natural childbirth using hypnosis for pain reduction. He showed us movies of childbirth with and without hypnosis. The reduced decibels of the hypnotized mothers was impressive! It was still a fairly experimental procedure, but it looked very helpful. The field is now called "Natal Hypnotherapy" and is a very solid movement.

During subsequent lunch hours, being a curious bunch, we physio students followed the process the doctor had demonstrated, and found that some of us "could be hypnotized" and some of us "could not"; some of us "could hypnotize others" and some of us "could not." We realized that our success at being hypnotized had to do with being willing, and I think the word "impressionable" was bandied about.

We did some interesting experiments ourselves, especially with post-hypnotic suggestions. I remember distinctly on one occasion when we found Ann Toulouse (as her name was then) sitting very quietly in a corner, trying not to attract our attention as she ate some orange peel. That had been the post-hypnotic suggestion one of us had given her. It had evidently worked, but Ann wasn't keen on our knowing how

[90]Part 2 of the "Essential Guide to Hypnosis" mini-series.

successful the suggestion had been, so she chewed on the bitter peel as secretly as possible in a room filled with thirty female physiotherapy students!

Later, in the early 1990s, I had some sessions with a psychologist who often ended our time together with hypnosis. The most successful occasion was when she invited me, under hypnosis, to consider the problem that was on my mind at the time, a sadness triggered by attending a wedding, suggesting I return to a previous time in my life when an event might have occurred that would provide meaning for the current situation. And I went straight back to a time when I had been about twenty and had attended a wedding that ended in my returning an engagement ring to my fiancé of the time. Suddenly, the current sadness made sense, and I was able to see parallels that had previously been hidden from me. My sadness dissolved with the new awareness that the hypnotic session revealed.

I realize that some people are very distrustful of hypnosis, fearing the power over us that it seems to give another person. But I think much of that supposed transfer of power is due to how well hypnotism's sensational aspects show on-screen. Movies and television have played a big part in sensationalizing hypnotism.

A year and a half ago, trusting the process of hypnotism myself and feeling enormously curious about a particular meditative state that can only be reached through hypnosis, I had a life-between-lives (LBL) hypnotherapy session. Michael Newton, Ph.D., founder of the Newton Institute, developed this field of hypnotherapy that takes us to the time when we are in Spirit; not so much to past lives as to the time between one past life and the next one. Newton has written three books about his findings—*Journey of Souls, Destiny of Souls, Life between Lives*—and has edited a book written by thirty-two LBL practitioners and entitled *Memories of the Afterlife*.

I searched online for an LBL practitioner to whom I was willing to entrust myself and selected Margarett Mae Monzo Ruthford in

Arlington, Washington, several hundred kilometres away from where I live in Vancouver, Canada. Her gentle online presence reassured me I would be in good hands; I also felt safe when I spoke to her on the phone. I made an appointment for January 2012, optimistically hoping for good road conditions in the middle of winter.

I enjoyed the drive down to Arlington, setting off from home before dawn and watching the sun gradually rise above the horizon, lighting up the sky with beautiful reds, oranges, and yellows. The day turned out clear and crisp, only a little cooler than I had expected. I found her clinic quite easily; I was early.

Arlington is a small town—I walked up and down the main street looking in all the shop windows in less than fifteen minutes. And then my appointment time arrived.

Looking a little thinner than her online image, Margarett Mae ushered me into her small room. We chatted a bit (to comfort me, I'm sure), she covered me with a blanket, we turned on a recording device, and then the morning session began.

Explaining that all hypnotism is only effective because it is actually self-hypnosis, Margarett Mae took me in the morning to my early childhood and then to a past life. In the three-hour afternoon session, she took me through my early childhood to my birth, and into my mother's womb. She asked, "Can you influence your mother's emotional state if she is under stress?" to which I surprised myself by answering, "Yes." Then she took me back to my immediate past life.

I answered questions such as, "What is your name in that lifetime?" with ease and assurance. How astonishing! How amazing! And this is information that is always available to me and to each of us any time we want to access it. In almost the same way that I can Google online information by entering words I want to know more about, I can ask myself both closed-ended and open-ended questions, and get answers that resonate deeply.

Interestingly, in order to write this scene, I listened to the recording of the afternoon session for the first time since the event, and the information that I felt and knew at the time but did not verbalize was elicited once more, just by listening again. In fact, I was able to write down the unvocalized information quite confidently, for future reference. In other words, I went back to that hypnotic state quite easily.

What's your opinion of hypnotism? Have you ever been hypnotized? What was the occasion? What did you remember, realize, reveal to yourself that you had forgotten, not known, and not seen previously? Have you ever hypnotized yourself? Have you ever hypnotized someone else?

Chapter 5—Everyday Paranormal

The Clairs and Intuition

~ Olfactory ~

"Angels use rose scents as physical signs of their spiritual presence with people. [S]ince roses have powerful energy fields that vibrate at a high electrical frequency —the highest of any flower on Earth—and since angelic energy also vibrates at a high rate, angels can connect easier with roses than with other flowers that have lower vibrational rates."

Whitney Hopler[91]

Images, physical sensations (such as shivers or a feeling of pressure), sounds, knowings, and smells that seem without foundation comprise information that comes from our paranormal senses. When we "get an idea," we seldom wonder where or how it comes to us. My view of life is that each of us is psychic to the extent that we all "get ideas" from time to time, and those ideas come to us through our paranormal senses, our six "clairs."

Images are visions that we see with our third eye chakra; the ability to see them is known in the West as "clairvoyance." If we hear sounds and voices that are not coming from the physical world, we may be "clairaudient." "Clairsentience" is clear sensing and feeling without using the body's regular neural pathways. Some people are able to taste something without it being in their mouth; they have the ability known as "clairgustance." Smells of scents from sources that are not actually there are impressions we gain through our throat chakra, using our "clairolfactory" ability known as "clairscence."

---

[91]Whitney Hopler, "Sacred Roses: The Spiritual Symbolism of the Rose," angels.about.com

Often authors who share knowledge about our sixth senses write about clairvoyance, clairaudience, clairsentience, and claircognizance. Seldom do they relate stories about the clairolfactory sense, but I clearly recall three experiences that could only be credited to my clair or intuitive sense of smell.

On one such occasion, I was having a three-in-one treatment with therapist Mark Ainley; we worked on an unsatisfactory relationship I had with a friend. Three-in-one work relies on memories stored in the body, accessed and tested through Applied Kinesiology (see the scene in chapter four, "Alternative Healing Modalities").

The treatment felt very successful. Mark gave me my homework—one of the cementing features of three-in-one work—and I took out my chequebook to pay him, when I suddenly smelled attar of roses, rose oil. I had been looking at an artificial red rose hanging on Mark's wall throughout the session, but now I could smell roses. I asked Mark if he had spilled rose perfume on his carpet. He assured me that he hadn't. I asked him three times before I could accept that I was smelling the scent of a rose that wasn't actually there. I finally accepted that I was experiencing a clairolfactory sensation, the sixth sense of smelling.

The scent of a rose.

Why a rose? I wondered.

When I returned home, I searched online for the significance of smelling roses when none are there. The thrilling explanation came from religious editor and journalist Whitney Hopler: "People regularly report smelling the fragrance of roses while communicating with angels in prayer or meditation."[92]

Margaret Starbird, in her 1993 discourse of research about Jesus' postulated marriage to Mary Magdalene (*The Woman with the Alabaster Jar*), suggests that Mary Magdalene was the Rose to Jesus' *Eros*, the name for the Greek god of love. I enjoy Starbird's play on words (*Eros* being

---

[92]Ibid.

an anagram of "Rose"), plus her brave ability to support the Magdalene Theory which was first promoted by Michael Baigent, Richard Leigh, and Henry Lincoln through their book, *The Holy Blood and the Holy Grail*; originally Starbird had intended to disprove the Magdalene Theory.

Starbird also suggests that many of the French troubadours' songs are filled with ideas of roses, and many of France's Gothic cathedrals are filled with rose-inspired windows, all in recognition of the myth or reality of Mary Magdalene's journey from the holy lands to the southern region of Provence-Alpes-Côte d'Azur in France. Arriving by boat, pregnant, and the widow of the recently crucified Jesus, Mary Magdalene is supposed to have landed at what-is-now called "Saintes-Maries-de-la-Mer," the coastal capital of the Camargue. The town, whose name in English means "Saint Marys of the Sea," gently boasts that it hosts the relics of the three Marys—Mary Magdalene, Mary Salome, and Mary Jacobé—the first witnesses of Jesus' resurrection from the tomb.

The second gift that Christian—my second husband—ever gave me was a dozen red roses. My parents came to stay that pre-Christmas weekend and when my mum heard that a work colleague had given me the roses, her eyebrows rose in that expectant way.

Did I just write "rose"?

Since then, I have saved all the dried petals from roses Christian has given me on Saint Valentine's Day, at birthdays, and so on. I keep them in a large vase in a display cabinet in our kitchen. Now, when I open that cabinet, it smells of roses.

The other day, I had a wonderful session with JZ Bown, my acupuncturist who also does ThetaHealing®, an alternative healing modality developed by Vianna Stibal to deal with physical, mental, emotional, and spiritual challenges. At some point when JZ was tuning into my energetic body, she saw me as a rose, which rather intrigued me. I told her that for a couple of decades I had not liked roses; in particular, I didn't like their thorns. I then realized that that was during my first marriage. JZ explained that the energy of that rose felt unprotected; the thorns were unable to carry out their regular function of protecting the plant. Perhaps during my first marriage, I needed to develop my own set of thorns.

I smelled something that wasn't there on two other occasions. Both happened in the home office of my highly gifted, spiritual friend Kelly Kiss. I can only label what I smelled as "purity." It smelled like Divinity; it was a "white" smell of absolute pureness.

Has life ever stretched you beyond your ability to know or say or describe what is happening? Have you ever had such "clair" moments preceding your thoughts and sending you grasping for concepts and thoughts and words? Which clair do you use most?

~ *Intuition* ~

"Our intuition is one of the most fantastic resources at our disposal.
When we are able to access this tool accurately and reliably,
it can save us time, money, energy, and a lot of frustration."
Andrea [later Andrrea] Hess[93]

I remember a time in my life—just moments before walking into a singing exam—when I realized that all the past months of vocal training and practising my exam repertoire were either going to pay off or I was going to let myself down and fail. What I felt in my body were "butterflies in my stomach"; it was the opposite of intuition—it was a hunch about not knowing rather than knowing an outcome.

The feeling was in my solar plexus chakra, which controls some of the organs of digestion, especially the stomach and the pancreas. If someone had suggested I eat when I was experiencing that kind of nervousness, I would have responded, "I'm too nervous to eat." Some people throw up when they are nervous in this way. Their digestion can't handle the chakra's imbalance.

---

[93] Andrea Hess [later Andrrea Hess], *Unlock Your Intuition* (Soul Star Publishing, 2007), p. 8.

The solar plexus chakra can also be experienced in a more positive way, through a gut knowing, an instinctual feeling that such and such a direction is the right direction to take. Businessmen frequently make decisions based on their gut feelings. They're operating from intuition, whether they realize it or not.

Daniel Kahneman received the 2002 Sveriges Riksbank Prize in Economic Sciences in Memory of Alfred Nobel for the collaborative work that he and Amos Tversky did on distinguishing intuition from reasoning. He explains in his Nobel Prize Lecture—"Maps of Bounded Rationality: A Perspective on Intuitive Judgment and Choice"—that intuitive operations generate impressions whereas reasoning results in explicit judgments. Intuition is fast and often lays the groundwork for later decisions that might also involve rationalization. Many of us function at an intuitive level in emotionally charged situations.

I wrote about triggers in chapter two, especially how watching *The Crucible* acted as a trigger to release some pain from my personal unconscious, the deepest part of my mind. I realize, all these years later, that seeing that play gave me an opportunity to forgive all those who punished women for the perceived wrongs of having supernatural and psychic gifts, or just for having different beliefs from the norm. I take that opportunity now. Men and women alike are still reluctant to own up to having gifts that others might deem supernatural. Some of this reluctance stems from those horrific centuries when witches were hanged or burned at the stake.

For a number of years, my business card and my website stated that I am a professional intuitive. To me this means that, although I did not display intuition from my youth, I have developed my intuition through specific training. I enabled myself to use that skill, which each of us is able to develop, to do Akashic Record readings and clearings for myself and others. I used this skill particularly to counsel others. We can also download wisdom when we write with a loving mind, a mindful heart, and a gentle spirit. And we can allow our intuition to create links between seemingly disparate items when we read a book, communicate with others, and walk through the world looking with "soft eyes," as much a mental as a visual skill.

Sometimes, I am still reluctant to profess this skill, watching whoever is listening to me with care lest they respond aggressively! Nonetheless, I am claiming this part of myself. This is progress.

Have you ever experienced nervous butterflies in your stomach? Have you ever sought and received spiritual information that you couldn't know in a "normal" way and you felt so good about it you moved forward with it? If not, what is stopping you?

~ *Clairvoyance, Clairaudience, and Clairsentience* ~

"Clairvoyance ... is the ability to observe the normally invisible spiritual process of life.
I was about three years old when my spiritual sight opened
to the beautiful world of auras. I began by seeing them
around people and things.... I remember taking trips into the country
and seeing the auras around trees and flowers
and thinking how beautiful life is. And how God must be everywhere."
Barbara Y. Martin and Dimitri Moraitis[94]

Along the way I have had many clairvoyant, clairaudient, and clairsentient awarenesses, building into a solid body of subtle communication of my connection with the Spirit world. It is the way I describe these events to myself that allows me to live a life that is strongly focused on my purpose and my spiritual path.

I have experienced clairaudience on a number of occasions. One was during a healing service at my church when we choir members continued

[94]Barbara Y. Martin and Dimitri Moraitis, *Change Your Aura, Change Your Life* (Spiritual Arts Institute, 2003) p. xiii

to chant, "Jesus, remember me, when you come into your kingdom," as we walked with other church members waiting for a blessing. As I chanted, I distinctly heard, "I have never forgotten you." No one was there. Tears came to my eyes. How affirming.

My clairsentience works consistently in confirming the truth of what others are saying and in confirming that a certain decision is the right choice to make and the right path to take, especially in conversation with others. I might be on the phone with a friend or with someone in person. What I experience is a tingling from my toes to my waist—what the French call *le frisson*.

The strongest instances of clairvoyance I have experienced are when I performed ThetaHealing® for my clients. Training in any alternative healing modality increases one or more of our paranormal senses. As soon as we pay something more attention, it improves, whether it is singing or our use of paranormal abilities. It is important to realize, though, that the clairs exist as pointers along the path rather than as destinations. I use them as signposts that I am on the right path.

Has clairvoyance been active in your life? Clairaudience? Clairsentience? What did these experiences affirm for you? How accepting of the situation were you? Which of the clairs have you experienced more than the others? When is a typical time for its appearance? Can you summon it at will? What is your process for doing so?

~ *Claircognizance* ~

"Thoughts are usually ego-based and want to protect you
from failure, embarrassment or disappointment.
Claircognizance transcends those fears
and comes from a place of wisdom."
Anna Sayce[95]

One of my early childhood views of religion was that the way heaven would present itself to someone depended on which faith or religion they followed: a devout Christian would meet Jesus Christ after death; a Buddhist would see Buddha, and so on. Of course, I couldn't have explained it this way, because I was far too young to explain such concepts. And the idea didn't come to me from my parents, because, as I was to learn over the years, my father was an atheist and my mother an agnostic. This belief was something I just knew deep down: a knowing, an instance of claircognizance.

Since then, I have read many books about near-death experiences and messages from souls who have crossed to the other side, and I have been on the lookout for an explanation of this childhood knowing I had. I have found such confirmation many times. I sense that this knowing was one that had not been erased when I came through the veil at birth. Even now, I can go to that deep inner place where I know this is true.

This type of knowing I now recognize as claircognizance, the intuition that most of us tune into without thinking about it.

When I trained as an intuitive with Andrrea Hess, the paranormal skill I developed was claircognizance; I learned to download pages of information about my clients. In the three years I worked in Soul Realignment™, I gave hundreds of readings, many of them startlingly accurate. For instance, I told one information technologist that he had lived a previous incarnation as a disheartened priest in the Mayan culture

[95]"How to Develop Claircognizance," annasayce.com

who had cursed himself; it turned out that he had focused on the Mesoamerican Mayan culture for his university archeology degree in this lifetime. His interest in that previous lifetime had not abated.

I told another client that she would blossom in a setting where, despite low pay, she could support older people less privileged than herself; she was thrilled to have recently started working in a seniors' home, much to the disapproval of her parents because of her low income.

We are each able to increase our psychic abilities, whether of claircognizance or clairvoyance or any other of the clairs.

Have you ever absolutely known something you could not know by regular means? Did you accept this knowing as claircognizance? Or did you refer to it as a visceral sense? A hunch? Women's intuition? A man's gut instinct? Or just a lucky guess?

~ *Mental Telepathy* ~

"The Lord of Amenti who had spoken telepathically to me remained by my side, while the other two [Lords of Amenti] moved to the opposite end of the wine cellar and waited, as if to receive instructions. The Spiritual being that stayed with me looked at me and I heard his thoughts. 'Now, we will demonstrate the power of thought.'"

Tim Doyle[96]

The term "mental telepathy" refers to the ability to know someone else's thoughts without hearing them speak, even though they might not be in the same room, city, or country as us. It's different from claircognizance, which is more about receiving wisdom from Spirit as thoughts.

---

[96]Doyle, *The Game of Life: Beginner's Version*, p. 3.

Tim Doyle, author of the quote above, has honed his abilities so that he realizes he is telepathic in some situations. I too have been telepathic at times, but never on command; more often as a side effect of being tuned in to whatever was happening. Telepathy for me results in being prepared for phone calls from a loved one, especially my mother when she was alive.

I remember experiencing telepathy at church one day. I was the healing minister that particular Sunday. I don't like to look directly at anyone as I wait for people to come for a healing prayer, because I don't want to influence them. I just wait quietly, eyes down, in the corner near the Lady Chapel. But I noticed one particular person and I instantly knew that, although she was not one of my regulars, she would come for a healing, not by any particular signal or visible emotion or even a glance. She took communion at the Lady Chapel beside me and then began returning to her seat in the church. I was surprised but didn't show it. Then she turned around and walked toward me for a prayer. As I'd known she would.

How did I "know" then? Normally I don't "know" so much.

I think when I prepare to be the healing minister, I open myself up in some way; I put my ego aside; I put my plans and goals aside; I am in the now, open and ready.

When and where have you been telepathic? Who with? What about? Can you expand that skill? Would it be useful?

Coincidence, Synchronicity, and Serendipity

~ *Singing "Vilia" for My Parents* ~

"There once was a Vilia, a witch of the wood,
A hunter beheld her alone as she stood,

The spell of her beauty upon him was laid;
He looked and he longed for the magical maid!"
Adrian Ross[97]

All my life, music has been of prime importance to me. As a child, I heard melodies rippling through my mind, like a brook that flows on and ever on to the sea. I would walk and run and skip to their rhythms and tunes. In the choir at Howell's, I longed to be selected to sing a solo, just one, and when looking back at my childhood, I wished that my parents had thought to send me for singing lessons. Regret is a good teacher. Finally, in my mid-thirties, pregnant for the fourth time, and living in Australia, I grew up (on this topic, anyway) and realized that it was never too late: I could take singing lessons as an adult.

My inquiries about teachers led me to a Mrs. Claire Keoghan living in Armidale on a street that bore my maternal grandmother's name, Jessie. Nana Jessie Rees has guided me from afar more than once. I phoned up Claire Keoghan and arranged to have a lesson to see whether I could actually sing after so many years away from choirs, being pregnant, and a mother.

Claire took me through some simple warm-up exercises, and then she established my vocal range. I remember her enthusiasm when she was able to take me comfortably up to a B flat, just below high C. Two good octaves! She assured me that I could sing and we quickly arranged that I would come into town for a singing lesson every couple of weeks.

As I drove away from that lesson, I was on an absolute high—it was a plateau. I felt as though as I had returned home. It was the warmest possible feeling of comfort. And there began some joyous times.

I learned Ivor Novello's songs first, because he was born in 1893 in Cardiff (half a century earlier than I was). Also, my grandmother Jessie Rees had known Novello's mother, Dame Clara Novello Davies (daughter

[97]Viktor Leon and Leo Stein (librettists), *The Merry Widow,* translated by Adrian Ross. Music by Franz Lehar. Sheet music, 1908 at www.amazon.com/Villa-Song-Musical-Merry-Widow/dp/B001157YMA

of Vincent Novello the musician and music publisher), a famous Welsh singer, teacher, and conductor; and the bus that had taken me daily to school went near Novello's birthplace on Cowbridge Road East.

I especially loved singing Novello's "I Can Give You the Starlight" and "Waltz of My Heart."

Waltz of My Heart

The lark is singing on high
The Sun's ashine in the blue
The Winter is driven away
And Spring is returning anew
Who cares what sorrow may bring
What storms may tear us apart
No sadness can kill the wonder and thrill
Of that waltz in my heart.

They're old-fashioned words and sentiments, but that's exactly how music made me feel, just like a lark that was singing on high. The song opens with a very unusual jump of the fifth from soh to re, a jump that feels like flying upward, as it should as a setting for such words.

Very soon, my singing teacher encouraged me to sing in public, so I assembled a simple program to present at the Armidale Ex-Services Memorial Club: "Waltz of My Heart," "I Can Give You the Starlight" and, to end with, "Yes, We Have No Bananas"! I was unbelievably nervous, but sang well, and at last, I had accomplished my first ever solo program.

During one lesson, Claire told me that a singer who was retiring was selling all her music. Claire suggested I take a look to see if anything appealed. Sure enough, this woman had stacks, literally, stacks of old music, which I leafed through, not quite knowing what to look for. Anyhow, I saw one old piece of music that jumped off the pile: Franz Lehar's "Vilia, O Vilia," from his opera *The Merry Widow*. It reminded me of something. Was it "Ophelia" in Shakespeare's *Hamlet*? Is that what I was remembering?

I bought the music and left.

For the next few lessons, Claire and I worked on "Vilia" until it was mine. Then, when my parents came for a visit for Ian's birth in November later that year, I told them I wanted them to hear something. And I proceeded to sing "Vilia" *a capella*. Both of them were in tears in no time, for different reasons. One reason they cried was because they had never heard me sing alone before, or perhaps not with so much confidence. It was as though they were learning something about me that I had always known was there and they had not. And it seems they liked what they heard.

My mother cried also because "Vilia" was one of her mother's—Jessie Rees's—favourite songs! So, once again, Nana, my maternal grandmother and sometimes my guide from the afterlife, had influenced me to do something that was distinctively me!

I had embodied and re-membered something from my early childhood—what age?—and yet I have no memory of ever hearing my grandmother singing. She was too ill by the time I was born. My mother told me she had had a lovely voice.

Have you ever embodied something that was cherished or even pivotal in an earlier generation? What are the coincidences in your life? I used to think that coincidences were just interesting phenomena. I recognize now that they are meaningful messengers. What's your view on coincidences?

~ *Synchronicity* ~

"It was divine synchronicity; when I called, she just happened to have a cancellation that day that fit perfectly into my schedule."

Sue Dumais[98]

[98]Dumais, *Heart Led Living*, p. 99.

As I wrote this chapter on everyday paranormal events, I knew I wanted to include an example of synchronicity—two events happening at the same time that seem coincidental but are in fact arranged by Spirit. I asked my angels to help me remember one. They did even better—they provided me with an example the very next day.

Some months earlier, I had been wondering who would edit this book. At Influence Publishing, I am the senior editor, so I knew I had to go outside the company to find someone. I thought back to 1979 when Douglas & McIntyre had published my first book—*Cattle Ranch*. Jim Douglas had been the structural editor and a young woman had done the rest of the editing. I couldn't remember her name until one day when I just decided I *would* remember her name (from thirty-five years earlier!). And so I did—Catherine Kerr.

I found Catherine online and emailed her (at an address she didn't often use); two months later, she responded. She'd been travelling. We discussed dates, editing parameters, and her fee. I slept on the decision, as I often do. And the next day, I received a one-off, unanticipated cheque in my mailbox for the full amount of her fee. I made my decision and I am very grateful that I did. That may sound like a coincidence, but for me it was more: synchronicity made me know she was the right choice as my editor.

Have you enjoyed synchronous moments in your life? In your research? In your friendships, relationships, collegial collaborations? Do you invite serendipity into your life?

~ *Taking a Divine Hint* ~

"Keep your head up. It's an amazing feeling and it will shift your energy.... Keep looking to God.... On the Earth plane there's more darkness right now and that's not where we need to keep our focus."

Reverend Christina Lunden[99]

[99]Christina Lunden, *"'Light' Angel Soul Teaching,"* BlogTalkRadio.com

Taking a Divine hint is like noticing the synchronicities in life. I've had three pieces of advice in the last couple of weeks to "look up" and listen. The first was from a friend I sing with, Trevor. He and his wife Toni have always encouraged their children and now their grandchildren to look up and listen to the birds around them. As a result, they can all identify many species.

The second was a book I edited—*Look Up! Birds and Other Natural Wonders Just Outside Your Window* by Woody Wheeler. This master birder's premise is multilayered—by looking up, we will see and enjoy birds and small creatures, plants and trees, fresh air and changing skies. Wheeler explains, "Looking at birds results in looking at the sky, which in turn, results in gathering light. But first you have to look up. You don't have to go anywhere special; your backyard or local park will do. If you have coastal areas, prairies, meadows, or wetlands nearby, so much the better. You will experience nature, gather light, and get exercise and fresh air—four uplifting sensations combined."[100] His term "gathering light" refers to the way Northerners can avoid suffering from seasonal affective disorder by absorbing as much sunlight as possible, even when clouds hide the sun.

Soon after, in June 2014, I listened to a rerun of Reverend Christina Lunden's "'Light' Angel Soul Teaching." I love this excerpt: "Keeping your head up will shift your energy."

And so, the next time I walked up to choir practice, I made a point of looking around, rather than thinking about or doing anything else. And I noticed perfect, cream-coloured dogwood blooms and beautiful catalpa blossoms. I spotted nasturtiums in oranges and yellows, and plants I can't name with pink and white fronds. I especially enjoyed walking under the catalpa trees that spread their huge canopies of branches over almost the entire road and the sidewalks here in the West End. Walking under them feels as though I'm entering a huge sacred chamber. And I certainly look up.

Raising my head to look up and listen up has me making a hopeful

---

[100]Woody Wheeler, *Look Up! Birds and Other Natural Wonders Just Outside Your Window* (North Vancouver: Influence Publishing, 2014), p. 31.

stance with my head. Try it and you'll see what I mean. Being hopeful is wonderful, no matter what we hope for. Hope can carry us forward.

Even before we're ready to connect with Ascended Masters, Guardian Angels, Angels, and Archangels, our Higher Self is sending us signs to help guide us. Are you noticing these signs?

Do you look up as you walk around? Or are you on your cell phone? Or looking at the sidewalk? The ground?

~ *Ahas, Epiphanies, and Eurekas* ~

"Thus it was only natural that Peter O'Reilly was the other person
whom Ward approached in January 1882 concerning the cattle venture.
'Long chat with Thomson & Ward in reference to the Cattle spec,'
noted O'Reilly in his ledger under the date 15 January,
'when it was agreed that we three should go in
with Van V., J.G., & J.D.P. at $5,000 each.'
"The 'Cattle spec' was finally underway."
Nina G. Woolliams[101]

I researched and wrote my first book, *Cattle Ranch: The Story of the Douglas Lake Cattle Company*, throughout the 1970s; it took me eight years. I was living at Douglas Lake at the time, the wife of the manager. That and raising Alun and Jessica kept me fully occupied. I learned that a syndicate of six influential BC men had purchased the land that became Douglas Lake Ranch. I wanted to show at the beginning of my book how these men were connected and how such a decision was made. I couldn't find proof.

---

[101]Woolliams, *Cattle Ranch*, p. 43.

I spent hours poring over records in twenty-two archival repositories in Canada and elsewhere, researching and compiling that history. Nearing the end of the research stage, I had just one man left to link to the other five syndicate members—Gold Commissioner Peter O'Reilly. I submitted a slip in the British Columbia Archives in Victoria, to request O'Reilly's journal for 1882. Suddenly, after an hour of reading, I found what I was looking for. I read it and reread it.

I remember exactly where I was sitting in the BC Archives reading room that day—two thirds of the way back on the left-hand side. This was such a huge find that it is embedded in my memory. My whole body wanted to shout "Eureka!" But I was in a cloistered, silent, historical sanctuary, and shouting aloud wasn't allowed. Nevertheless, I shouted "Eureka!" in my mind and rejoiced!

Words like "epiphany" (a problem-solving realization such as an awareness that one's consciousness can exist outside the body), "aha moment" (a small epiphany), and "Eureka!" (the interjection someone might shout when they find something they have been seeking) tend to be bandied about these days with little regard for their original meaning. I prefer to save them for the actual events, rather than dilute them.

What "aha!" moments have you experienced? Have you ever sung out "Eureka!"? Have you ever experienced a personal epiphany that truly changed your life? Gave you new direction? Can you list such moments?

Channelling

~ Hearing Melodies ~

"When I sing to make you dance, I truly know why
there is music in leaves, and why waves send
their chorus of voices to the heart of the listening Earth...."

Rabindranath Tagore[102]

---

[102]Tagore, *Gitanjali*, verse 62.

My first awareness that we choose our reality was realizing that, even as a child, I could switch on the ability to hear sweet melodies in my head. Recently, I have read about the idea of moving the dial on my own awareness receiver; that is exactly how it seemed to me as a child. I could move the dial over and in would come the music, the melodies. I knew they were there; I just had to be willing to hear them, and I was.

I can go back in my mind right now to when I was a little girl walking to school (on my own—how amazing that seems nowadays!) and listening to the rippling melodies. My little feet went tripping along at the same rate as the melody rippled over the streambed, the pebbles along the path. The melodies sped me along the walk to school and home again at the end of the day.

Early this century, I decided to move my receptive dial to my music channel again, and I started writing out music using a powerful yet easy software program, *Sibelius*®. For instance, I decided to write a piece for a recorder group a friend of mine led. A melody came to me as I was walking home from work down Robson Street one day, and so I called it just that: "Walking Home down Robson Street."

From hearing the original melody to writing out the piece in readiness for performance took a couple of months. During that time, my friend's group workshopped the piece several times so that I could refine it to make the most of the group's instruments, learning about differently voiced recorders' musical ranges as I went. Eventually, they performed it for an audience and I was there. What a thrill!

Here is how I described "Walking Home" online: "This is a challenging neoclassical piece for seven recorder parts (sopranino doubles with alto 2). What starts out as a simple melody and countermelody leads to canon writing with melody and countermelody (further developed) playing out together.... When the melody and countermelody return, they echo and move on from their original form."[103]

---

[103]www.scoreexchange.com/scores/28286.html

When I hear melodies in this way, I realize I am channelling music. Do you hear your own melodies? Or do you hear poetry? Or see images you want to paint?

~ *When I Get Out of My Own Way* ~

"I am a light house
of light and sound and healing
for all the seasons."
Nina Shoroplova[104]

Toward the end of the Sound Healing Intensive in 2013, I wrote this haiku poem. I had invoked the Spirit of Poetry at the opening ceremony to our day of silence, and many poems started writing themselves in my head.

Many times in the past, I have somehow geared myself into receiving poetry. Back in the early 1990s when I was suffering from the eye-muscle dis-ease, I focused on writing poetry and it was a way to help me navigate my discomfort. Here's one of them.

This Life

I've lived a life not all my own;
Sometimes I've lived it for others,
For others' ambitions, wants, and desires,
For the dreams long held by others.
The fault's my own. I understand.
But what is a great deal harder
Is learning the lesson I understand
And following my own dreams with ardour.
My dreams are buried under deep layers

[104]A poem I wrote on July 24, 2013, entitled "Healing Bees (Be's)."

Of pleasing, supportive placation.
I'm delving inside. I think. I dream.
What do I want? A vacation?
I've rested from work for two-and-a-half months
So as to regain my sight
And to see what's welling deep inside.
Who's Nina and where is her Light?
The things that inspire me, that give me Life
Are music and loving and caring
And singing and learning and beauty and peace
And words and joy and performing.
I've other goals, personal and close;
I'm already on a path that's right.
And the overarching path and goal
Is to regain and use fully my Sight.

I even started writing limericks—the Irish poems with verse lines of nine feet, nine feet, five feet, five feet, and nine feet, where the lines rhyme AABBA; i.e. lines one, two, and five rhyme, and lines three and four rhyme. I awoke one day around 3:00 a.m., a very prolific writing time for me (and others), and wrote about seven or eight limericks, one after the other. I must have been channelling an Irish poet! As is typical with limericks, these were rather bawdy, starting with something like, "There once was a woman from Wembley, who always came over all trembly, when ...." (You finish it!) I wish I could find those limericks and share them with you, though perhaps my memory of them enhances their perfection.

For a while, I wrote *haiku,* the Japanese 17-syllable form that in English becomes three lines, the first and third having five syllables each. Frequently, they mention something about weather, nature, or something else that can be just as fleeting. Often, their ideas are provocative or paradoxical. And there is always more to them than meets the eye.

Three days after writing my "light house" haiku that opens this scene, I wrote a more free-form poem that expanded on its ideas. I have presented it in full before this book's introduction.

A year and a half after I had these getting-out-of-my-own-way ideas, I received a manuscript by Kristina Sisu, which became a book entitled *How to Get Out of Your Own Way*. A coincidence? A synchronicity? Just another way for the Universe to get an important message heard. As a gifted healer, Sisu offers forty transformational techniques that help her readers "open space for miracles," perhaps even such miracles as seeing life metaphorically so strongly that they express themselves in poetry.

Can you turn your dial to your poetry channel? Which is your favourite of the poems you have written? What is your favourite poetry style? What do you learn from writing poetry?

~ *Channelling Wisdom* ~

"I knew I had no choice but to get up and begin to write.
My previous years of experience as a spiritual channel had taught me
how to distinguish between what was important and what was not."

Judy Satori[105]

Speaking as a gnostic, a spiritual seeker, and a non-medical specialist about the topic of consciousness, I see three ways in which our minds are creating things that can become thoughts:

- when we are awake, making conscious choices through ego;
- when we are passively dreaming during sleep, obeying expectations delivered by our subconscious; and

[105]Judy Satori, *Sunshine before the Dawn* (Satori Incorporated, 2011), p. 11.

- when we are actively listening to that still, small voice inside, *aka* the godspark, *aka* the god spot; this can happen when dreaming during sleep, daydreaming, or meditating intentionally.

When a spiritual counsellor advises a client, her mind is not creating things that become thoughts. She "gets out of her own way," opens herself up to receive, and transmits Divine wisdom for her client. Many times, the words I channelled for a client benefitted me too.

I am going to take the idea of receiving Divine wisdom even further. These days, many manuscripts come to me as channelled works. An author will say some version of, "I had no intention of writing a book, but this book came to me as a whole and so I had to write it." I heard a version of this from Judy Satori, Sue Dumais, Kristina Sisu, Tim Doyle, and others. To me, these authors are recognizing something that has been going on for decades, for centuries, for eons. Some of us who are inspired by channellings from Spirit choose to listen, to write, and to spread the messages we hear.

As a Soul Realignment Practitioner™, I was a very grounded light-worker; I would prepare lengthily for meeting with each client, creating three original documents to explain their soul journey to them:

- the knowledge I had intuited through the meditative process that Andrrea Hess teaches,
- the client's three weeks of transmutation homework (a very specific prayer), and
- a worksheet for clients to glean more about their soul as time went along.

And then the day of meeting with my client would arrive and, in the early days, I would be very nervous, wondering, "How can I possibly tell this person all about herself in this way?"

Yet, after the initial greeting and sitting the client down at my table, I would begin. And the words would flow out of my mouth. I was channelling the wisdom they needed to know. I was getting out of my own way.

What becomes clear for me is that we are telling each other's stories all the time, often without knowing it. Wisdom is all around us. Some of it comes from my mouth, some from TV shows, some from sermons, some from children, some from friends, some in the books I read, some from the aspiring and inspiring authors whose books I edit. We are all conduits to and from the same source of wisdom. We can be vessels when we choose to be: vessels, vehicles, and voices of Infinite Wisdom.

Do you accept that you can be a wisdom bearer? A wisdom revealer? Do you trust your advice? Is your advice coming from ego or from a selfless heart-full place? Have you allowed Divine wisdom to influence your path? Your goals?

~ *A Morning Routine* ~

"'On the 27th of June, I woke up and I started writing, and I wrote for like five months in a row, every single day, morning, noon and night. I just couldn't bring myself to stop writing,' [Dr. Wayne Dyer] said on a media conference call in December 2013."

elevatedexistence.com[106]

Elsewhere, Wayne Dyer, Doctor of Education, declared that his best time for writing is first thing in the morning when his brain is most rested from a good night's sleep. And in yet another place, Dr. Dyer claims that he wrote one particular book more easily after driving "35 miles east of where I live on Maui." He would then "hike over an incredible number

[106]elevatedexistence.com/blog/2014/03/01/dr-wayne-dyer-shares-insights-from-his-new-book

of rocks and through trees for about two hours. There's a place where a 50-foot waterfall drops into a pool, surrounded by guava trees covered with guava fruit. Here I would stay right under the waterfall and just let the water cascade down on my head. In the hours I spent there, everything I needed for my next chapter would appear."[107]

Many writers find that they can channel words first thing in the morning. They may be woken through the night or early in the morning with words flowing so quickly that they need to get right up and start typing or handwriting (or using shorthand, as Helen Schucman did with *A Course in Miracles*) before the whole message dissipates uncaptured. Some writers acknowledge that they are channelling; some call it inspiration; some call it automatic writing; some consider it the result of a good habit; others the result of working with a muse. On and on go the ways that writers credit the source of the words they write.

Author Bell Michel-Brown describes the process of channelling very well in her book *Message from the Gods*. "I was abruptly awakened from sleep in our hotel about three o'clock in the morning.... I quickly grasped that I had just experienced what seemed to be three unusual, vivid dreams. It felt important to jump out of bed and quickly write them down before their memory was lost. As I recalled and transcribed them, it strangely felt as though I were taking dictation. The writing flowed freely for lengthy pages, never hesitating [for me] to ponder nor change one single word."[108]

Important thoughts sometimes demand to be written down at night. I used to wake up all the time at 3:00 a.m. with an idea I didn't want to forget. Nowadays, I awake at other times.

It seems to me that an intention to write opens us up to wisdom, because frequently a writer does not know where their writing will take them until a session is over or a complete work has emerged.

---

[107]May 21, 2009, drwaynedyer.com/blog/heres-how-i-write

[108]Bell Michell-Brown, *Message from the Gods: Soul Secrets from 500 BC* (Cadbury Hill Publishing, 2007), p. 7.

I wrote my first book in the mornings, though not every morning, for eight years. For the first three years, I researched the topic, which required trips to the historical archives in Kamloops, seventy kilometres from home; trips to BC's provincial historical archives in the capital of Victoria four hundred kilometres away; and many trips to interview old-timers for source material. Then for three years, my first husband and I hired a sequence of *au pair* girls to look after our son and daughter, by then three and one, in the mornings, and that's when I wrote.

It's a common occurrence that inspiration for the same invention crops up all over the globe at the same time. This too is a kind of channelling. I know of a friend who suddenly realized there would be a market for different cell phone ringtones, because, when cell phones first came out, they all sounded the same. When a phone stays in one place, this uniformity poses no problem, but it does when several users are in the same space: whose phone is ringing? My friend didn't do anything about his idea; he missed an opportunity.

When I lived in Australia, I had an idea to create a board game that would be similar to Monopoly but with cattle stations and sheep properties, drought and flood, fire and pestilence. I thought about it, drafted it out, and selected player pieces, but didn't get my idea to market. Little did I know that there was already such a game on the market: *Squatter*, developed by Robert C. Lloyd in 1962. I picked up the idea rather too late!

The same sort of thing happens with medical discoveries and doctoral theses and television programs and book topics. As long as the development of the ideas gives each a "unique selling proposition," market success will favour all the innovators.

Do you have a routine for creating what it is you want to create? Do you make the time and space in your life to create the things that give you the greatest pleasure? If you're a writer, when do you write? Would other times or places be more effective?

~ *Prayers* ~

"Prayer is not asking. It is a longing of the soul.
It is daily admission of one's weakness....
It is better in prayer to have a heart without words
than words without a heart."
Mahatma Gandhi[109]

For a number of years, probably until I could maintain a constant realization that I am a spiritual being inhabiting a physical body in Earth school, I would repeat morning prayers in a ritual. They gradually evolved as I gained greater understanding, read other spiritual authors, accepted more ideas. I kept each new version of my prayers digitally, to track their evolution over time.

Author George Baxter-Holder, D.N.P. (Doctor of Nursing Practice), points out that ritual is part of the essence of spirituality. "Once you have truly started some kind of ritual practice you see that 'ritual' is at the heart of spiRITUAL-ity and it is in this place you are ready to dream big dreams."[110] Ideas can become habits that become rituals, and these can inform our spirituality in a very useful way.

Living Gandhi's words in my life, I am longing as I rise and I am grateful as I rest. He also says, "Prayer is the key of the morning and the [door] bolt of the evening," suggesting that we require protection in our lives on Earth.[111]

There are many prayers of protection—I have used Andrrea Hess's, Barbara Y. Martin's, Tim Doyle's, Christina Lunden's, Jonathan Goldman's (his Shamael Invocation), and others. They are very powerful, because of the intention we put into them and, because we are allowing Divine Source to give us the protection, we are open to receiving. They are statements of faith in the process.

---

[109]Mahatma Gandhi, *The Words of Gandhi,* selected by Sir Richard Attenborough (Newmarket Press, 1982), p. 76.
[110]George Baxter-Holder, *Drugs, Food, Sex and God* (North Vancouver: Influence Publishing, 2015), p. 102.
[111]*The Words of Gandhi.*

Over the years, I've dabbled as a director—directing a hat show at which all the models wore hats and sang songs about hats; directing plays at Douglas Lake Ranch, several of which I wrote or adapted from children's books; directing pageants in churches; and once, directing a concert in Vernon of Royal Conservatory of Toronto (RCT) music students, including myself. As I remember, there were several vocal students, several piano students, and one flute student.

Spontaneously I said the doxology with which I am most familiar at the Vernon RCT concert, to inspire each of us students to perform the best we knew how to perform for our families and friends filling the church: "Glory to God, whose power, working in us, can do infinitely more than we can ask or imagine. Glory to God from generation to generation, in the Church and in Christ Jesus, for ever and ever. Amen."[112]

The word "doxology" means "a prayer of praise to God" used during a church service. For me it means, "Help me to do that which You know I can do, for You enable me."

Always, that doxology helps me. It helps me realize that I am Divine within each cell of my being and, when I get out of my own way, Divinity can flow through me, making me into my better and best self, aligning me with my Higher Self.

These days, I am privileged to hold the position of Healing Minister at my church, as I've mentioned. One Sunday each month, I pray with whoever comes to my station. They tell me their name and what they would like me to pray for. The first few times I did this, I prepared myself by praying the doxology. Now, I just see myself as the vehicle, the channel for the right words to come through. I step aside from myself, open my mouth, and appropriate words come, without my intervention.

From the very first occasion, praying on behalf of someone else has felt as though I am receiving a gift from whoever requests the prayer. It is a gift of trust and faith in me. Quite often, after the session is complete, my eyes fill with tears of gratitude.

---

[112]Ephesians 3:20-21, as worded in the Anglican liturgy.

Does prayer have a place in your life? Do you pray with words or images or emotions? Do you open your heart to hold love for someone needing help? Or do you pray for specific solutions that might not be in that person's best interest? What do you pray for yourself?

~ *Predictions from Others* ~

"You will travel across waters to live far away, in green fields.
You will have three rings."
A Psychic[113]

Life is not fair, and that's because we each choose a particular path of challenges before our birth, to allow ourselves optimal soul growth in each incarnation. I believe we plan the major choice points in our lives prior to birth.

Before preparing our mother's ovum for our birth into this demanding physical experience, our spirit meets with our Spirit Guides and Guardian Angels and plans who our parents will be, our life's goal and purpose, our major and some minor life experiences, some exit points, and so on. And then we prepare our human body and settle into it before or at our birth.

Sometimes, the life we set for ourselves from the comfort of the other side is much harder than we could have known it would be. And so, having become human beings who may have forgotten that we are first and foremost spirits, we struggle in the yoke we have set for ourselves and wonder why life isn't fair.

Life is unfair, because each of us plays by different rules and for different goals. Are you one of the lucky golfers who enjoys your sport more and more because you have discovered that you are your only

[113]Substance of a reading I received in Cardiff, South Wales, in 1966.

competitor? In the same way, life is a great adventure once we realize that we set the conditions and rules ourselves, for our own growth, with the help of our Spirit Guides and Guardian Angels.

One of the ways that I know I am living the life I was meant to live this time is through the accuracy of the predictions of others. I can think of two such predictions: the first from a psychometrist (a psychic who read the past, present, and future of her clients by handling an object belonging to them), and the second from Vanga, a famous Bulgarian psychic.

A Psychometrist Who Lived on Cathedral Road

When I started studying physiotherapy in 1965, I was pleased to recognize two girls enrolled in the program who had also attended Howell's School: Penelope and Susan. Although I came to know all the girls in my year, we three quickly formed a bond that made the new world of studying a career very approachable. We soon shared our interest in things psychic, such as our dreams. For a while, we would record our dreams, discuss them, and try to figure out their meanings. I don't remember any of those dreams or their meanings any more, but I do remember that it was important to interpret them with my friends.

We also decided we would like to go and see a fortune-teller, which we did.

Either Penny or Sue had heard of a woman who lived on Cathedral Road in Cardiff on the ground floor of a rather forbidding Victorian three-storey house. If memory serves, it had a bell pull for the entrance buzzer rather than a push bell and the inside of the room where the psychic read our fortunes was covered in dark fabrics, with a heavy curtain attached to the door by a rod. I decided this was to keep the readings very, very secret, though it was probably to keep out drafts, since those big old houses were very expensive to heat. It was also the sort of place where you would expect black cats to come around a corner at any moment.

I seem to remember sitting on the edge of the seat, too nervous to relax and enjoy the event. My friends waited in the entrance corridor outside for their turn, eager eighteen-year-olds about to hear their future.

This psychic asked if she could hold something that I always wore—a ring or a watch or something. I took off a slim gold ring that had been one of the items I had received when my Great Aunt Nora had bequeathed her estate to my sister, me, and our cousins. I passed the psychic the ring and she started the reading.

It didn't take long; and it seemed rather vague at the time, but it was very accurate. From what I remember, she said I would travel across water to live far away in green fields. She also said I would have three rings. I don't remember any more.

Indeed, I did end up travelling across water to live far away in green fields, because in June 1969, less than four years later, I immigrated to Canada for six months, six months that became a lifetime (not counting late 1979 to mid-1984 in Australia). And a year after immigrating to Canada, I moved to Douglas Lake Cattle Ranch as the wife of the ranch manager. Okay, the fields weren't often very green, because Douglas Lake is classified as desert, but the fields that were irrigated for growing hay were definitely green.

And I did end up having three rings—an engagement ring from a man in my twenties, a wedding ring from Neil Woolliams in the 1970s, and another wedding ring from Christian Shoroplov in the 1990s. Could such a reading work for everyone? I don't think so. And anyway, the readings that my friends had were quite different from mine.

For the first time in my life, I had viewed an ethereal wisp of something I couldn't explain, and I was intrigued. I kept my mind open for the next wisp.

Vanga, the Bulgarian Intuitive

This is not so much my story as my second husband's or my second mother-in-law's. It began one day when the woman who later became my second mother-in-law, Stefka Shoroplova, was waiting to buy food in her home city of Sofia, the capital of Bulgaria. Waiting to buy food (bread, sugar, vegetables, and staples) was a daily event in Communist Bulgaria. Family members would take turns—Luben Shoroplov would get up early and wait for an hour or two. Then his boys, Orlin followed by Christian, would take their turns, and finally, once Luben had gone to work and the boys had gone to school, Stefka would take over.

But the event I'm now describing took place long after Christian had fled (his escape is another story), Orlin had married Raina, and their daughter Sylvie had been born. Stefka wondered whether she would ever again see her younger son, Christian. He seldom wrote to her and, without any news of her son, Stefka worried.

In addition to being a test of patience, waiting to buy food in Communist Bulgaria was also a social event, a time to chat to those around you in the line. On the particular day I'm writing about, Stefka was discussing what she regarded as Christian's thoughtlessness with the woman next to her in the line: "He never writes; I don't know how he's doing."

The other woman was very sympathetic with Stefka and she had some unusual advice: "Take a lump of sugar and put it under your pillow tonight and then send it to me at this address and I will ask my sister to tell you how your son is doing." As it turned out, the woman was the sister of Baba Vanga, a blind Bulgarian psychic of international renown, but Stefka did not know that at the time.

Strange as she thought the instructions were, Stefka followed them. Sometime later, she received a letter back: Vanga's words, transcribed by her sister. I don't have that letter, but I know its contents, because they became part of the Shoroplov family heritage. The gist was that Stefka need not worry about her son, because he was doing well in Canada. He would be having a serious operation soon and it would go well. And also, he would marry a woman named Nina and all would be well.

And here I am, Nina Shoroplova, the wife of Christian Shoroplov.

A postscript to that story occurred when the authorities finally allowed Christian to return to Bulgaria without recrimination for having defected years earlier. This was long after his father had died, a loss he had only been able to grieve from afar.

Staying with his mother in her Sofia apartment, Christian came out of the shower with a towel covering him from the waist down. The towel did not cover his chest, and the scar from the recent operation was clearly visible.

"Ah, you have had the operation," said Stefka.

"I didn't tell you I was going to have an operation," said her son, with some surprise.

"I know," said Stefka. "Vanga told me you would have an operation and that all would be well." And then she shared the whole story with her incredulous son. I was not in the picture at the time. Did he then start looking for a Nina to marry?

Do predictions by psychics become self-fulfilling prophecies for those who receive them? Have you had any predictions told about you, to you? Have you predicted the future for others?

Chapter 6—Ways to Engage with the Mystery

Time to Engage

~ *Through Placement* ~

"Many a morning and evening found Mother and me
meditating before an improvised shrine,
offering flowers dipped in fragrant sandalwood paste.
With frankincense and myrrh as well as our united devotions,
we honored the Divinity which had found full expression in Lahiri Mahasaya."
Paramahansa Yogananda[114]

The acts of creating an altar and paying attention and homage to that altar create a clear channel for recognizing our highest values. In his autobiography, Paramahansa Yogananda describes many different altars. One was at "the sacred Tarakeswar shrine" where "the altar contains nothing but a round stone."[115]

I have several personal altars in my home—one comprises a display of Tibetan singing bowls mixed with hand bells, tuning forks, and candles. This honours the power and pervasiveness of sound creating the Universe. Another is an eclectic mix of a conch shell, quartz crystals, a bagua-shaped mirror, an Inuit soapstone carving of a mother and child, a small Ganesha statue from India, and four dragons. Being Welsh myself, I perceive dragons as displaying bravery, the ability to surmount obstacles, and passionate, fiery, transformative energy. Two of my dragons are a mother and her baby just emerging from its egg. Divine Mother energy is particularly sacred to me, being a mother myself.

---

[114]Paramahansa Yogananda, *Autobiography of a Yogi* (www.gutenberg.org) Chapter 1: My Parents and Early Life.
[115]Ibid. Chapter 13: The Sleepless Saint.

Churches create altars to display the cross, flowers, candles, and such items as sacramental bread and wine.

Whereas an altar is usually created at eye level for when people are sitting or standing, a wheel is a sacred arrangement of objects more usually created on the ground.

Drunvalo Melchizedek describes the creation of several native medicine wheels in his *Ancient Secret of the Flower of Life* volumes. At the 2013 Sound Healing Intensive I attended, Jonathan and Andi Goldman created a wheel of crystal bowls, statues of gods and goddesses, and crystals arranged around an enormous bouquet of Easter lilies, lilies which gradually opened to their full glory as we attendees opened to the significance of sound's ability to heal. When I held a Sound Healing workshop on Earth Day in 2013 in Vancouver, I created a central wheel of shells, candles, and spiritual figurines.

The wheel at my Sound Healing workshop on Earth Day in 2013

When Tibetan monks painstakingly create an intricate mandala of different coloured dyed sands, they are seeking to represent "the enlightened mind and the ideal world."[116] I watched Tibetan monks building just such a mandala over the course of several days in a local church. (They built it at the church crossing, the place where time (*chronos*) and events (crises) intersect at the crux of life.[117]) At the end of their devotional labour, the monks swept the sands together and poured them away to signify how impermanent is our world compared to the unchanging qualities of the Divine.

Have you created a sacred altar in your home? Does it reflect your spiritual growth, your heart's desire and aspirations? If you don't have an altar yet, what might you put on your altar? Crystals? Flowers? A five-element display of fire, earth, metal, water, and wood?

~ *Through Movement* ~

"Namasté *is both a spoken Indian expression and a symbolic gesture*
that people use when greeting each other or in parting.
Pronounced 'na-ma-stay,' the term derives from Sanskrit
and literally means 'I bow to you.' It's more commonly translated
as 'the divine light in me honors the divine light in you'
or 'the God within me greets the God within you.'
Namasté *is the recognition that we are all equal and share a common divinity."*
chopra.com *"Namasté"*

Acknowledging, honouring, and celebrating the Divine within through specific ritualized movements also engage us in the mystery. Examples of such movement include performing temple dancing, moving through the nineteen positions of T'ai Chi, practising Zen walking meditation, Sufi

[116]gomang.org/mandala.html
[117]Jean Shinoda Bolen inspired these thoughts. I offer more of her wisdom in the Safe Circle scene in chapter seven.

whirling, QiGong, and dancing while singing sacred chants. There are many different schools of yoga, many still dedicated to the integration of the physical, subtle (mind, intelligence, and ego), and causal (soul or spirit) bodies. Paramahansa Yogananda practised Kriya Yoga throughout his life, a discipline that brought him and his followers closer to awareness of their Divinity.

I practise Divine movement in three ways—through a half hour of hatha yoga first thing each morning, when I follow the Crucifer who carries the cross into church each Sunday, and when I cross myself declaring either "I am as above, so below; as within, so without" or "Divine Source is within me through the power of the Holy Spirit" or at other times the more traditional "Father, Son, and Holy Spirit."

There is also a devotional element to practising Reiki, Reconnective Healing, and Energy Healing.

Placing our hands palms together with fingers pointing upward in front of the upper chest has several meanings, according to its cultural setting. In the West, it is a gesture used in prayer. In the East, particularly in India, it is a form of greeting between people, often accompanied by a bow and the word *Namasté*. The higher the hands are positioned—at the waist, at the chest, at the nose, above the crown—the higher is the sign of respect for the other. The hand *mudra* (position) of palms together above the head honours Divine Source.

In what ways do you move your body to recognize you are Divine? Is there a simple gesture you could add to your daily routine that would include this recognition? Do you see others moving in such ways?

~ Through Sound ~

"It's also been found that self-created sounds such as chanting will cause the left and right hemispheres of the brain to synchronize. Such chanting will also help oxygenate the brain, reduce our heart rate, [optimize] blood pressure and assist in creating calm brainwave activity."

Jonathan Goldman[118]

Almost every form of engaging with the mystery involves sound—ringing and striking bells, gongs, cymbals, and tingshaws; playing singing bowls, flutes, harps, and organs; singing chants, psalms, and hymns; chanting call and response; reading the Bible, the Torah, and the Quran aloud; proclaiming blessings and affirmations; listening deeply to one or more of these forms of sound.

Interacting with sound—whether we are its creators or its receivers—is one way we can influence our world and get involved in the mystery. One of the reasons I sing in a church choir is so that I can raise my voice in praise, and I find it interesting that hymn texts are often more in line with my spiritual beliefs than the liturgy is.

Another type of singing I enjoy is the call and response pattern of Kirtan, Indian devotional chanting in the Bhakti Yoga tradition. During his Sound Healing Intensives, Jonathan Goldman creates memorable evenings of singing and dancing to mantras that praise one or more of the myriad of gods of Hinduism.

A belief, if read silently, engages with our left cerebral hemisphere. A belief spoken aloud is heard by both our right and left cerebral hemispheres, allowing us to understand it both logically and playfully, rationally and passionately. We bring all of ourself to something we speak aloud with intention. And inherent in this is all the wisdom of proclaiming affirmations.

---

[118]Jonathan Goldman, interviewed by Vandana Mohata (healingsounds.com), "Mantras: An Interview with Jonathan Goldman."

St. Paul's Anglican Church Choir sings at the 11:00 a.m. service on March 8, 2015 during Bishop Melissa Skelton's visit.
Photograph by Sandra Vander Schaaf. Used with permission.

In what ways are you engaging with the mystery aloud? Do you play an instrument, sing, or chant in awe of something greater than yourself? Do you repeat affirmations, knowing that their repetition allows your subconscious to act on them as though they are commands? Do you recognize the opposite of this practice, which is to repeat negative statements about yourself and the world around you? Do you realize that this attracts such negativity to you through the same ability of your subconscious to follow statements as though they are commands, directions?

~ *Through Meditation* ~

"The saint and I entered the meditative state.[119]
After an hour, his gentle voice roused me.
"'You go often into the silence, but have you developed anubhava?'[120]
He was reminding me to love God more than meditation.
'Do not mistake the technique for the Goal.'"

Paramahansa Yogananda[121]

There are many meditative ways of perceiving God. Meditation is soul-led, when a person directs their ego to step aside and allows their observer to take charge. That observer is our constant self, our self who never changes, and is often as close as we can get to our Higher Self in this lifetime. And the aim of life is to align once more with our Divine nature, and thereby find the wisdom, peace, and love inherent in that state.

Spiritual leader and peace ambassador Sri Sri Ravi Shankar says,"[M]editation happens only when the mind settles down. How to settle this mind? By understanding the aim of life and having a clear focus. What is focus? Being fulfilled in the moment, being centered, looking to the highest and remaining in that space of peace is focus."[122]

I find it difficult to separate the practice of meditation from the use of a mantra. The first mantra I ever learned was the one I received when I was initiated into Transcendental Meditation (TM®) as developed by Maharishi Mahesh Yogi. That was the first time I had ever realized that I could think about thinking, could observe myself thinking. I had done it before, of course, but chanting a mantra and noticing all the thoughts ricocheting around in my head alongside the steady repetition of the mantra made me realize that I am the observer and I am the observed. And so, by reciting a mantra with one part of my mind, I can be the observer, the one Deepak

[119]Maharishi Bhaduri Mahasaya and Paramahansa Yogananda.
[120]"Actual perception of God." Footnote explaining Sanskrit word in original at gutenberg.org
[121]Yogananda, *Autobiography*, Chapter 7: The Levitating Saint
[122]"Demystifying the art of meditation," June 30, 2011, *The New Indian Express*.

Chopra calls "the witness," and not get involved with my thoughts. TM® proposes that thoughts just arise from the subconscious and that our continuous recitation of our mantra allows us to just observe the thoughts without attaching to them and entering into them.

I remember a moment in a Woody Allen movie in which the character Woody plays is on the phone in the background of the scene, calling his TM® instructor and saying, "I've forgotten my mantra." That struck me as especially funny because it had happened to members of my family, even after they had been working with their mantras for some time.

At one time, I practised TM® more or less regularly. I then went down other paths for a while. Soon after I returned to TM®, I stopped my practice completely because I began working with a colleague whose first name was almost identical to my one-word mantra. So, when I meditated, I thought of her. Needless to say, I could no longer use that mantra.

What to do?

I tried many others, but none of them had the supremacy of my TM® mantra. My ego got in the way: I always tried to improve on any self-created mantra.

Instead, I moved on to other types of meditation. Yet, for me, in regular meditation, the instruction just to observe my thoughts does not work. I become attached to my thoughts, enter them, and often need to write them down, because they have waited until that precise moment—when all other thoughts are less important—to come to mind.

Recently I reread Deepak Chopra's *Return of the Rishi* and I was attracted to one of the meaningful phrases—the mantras—he shares from his rich Indian heritage: *sat chit ananda,* which he says means "Eternal Divine Consciousness," but by simple translation means "being true consciousness bliss." The first two words—*sat chit*—flow in with an inbreath; *ananda*—meaning bliss and joy—flows out with an outbreath.

The website *Dharma Haven* calls mantras "enlightened sound," and suggests that, having "no intrinsic reality," they take us into "the union of Sound and Emptiness," where "our being is transformed into enlightened awareness."[123] A popular mantra is *Om mani padme hum,* about which Dharma Haven says, "The Mani mantra is the most widely used of all Buddhist mantras, and open to anyone who feels inspired to practice it—it does not require prior initiation by a lama."

Of course, the pure primary sacred sound of *Om*—said to be the sound of the Universe—is the simplest mantra of all. The Sanskrit symbol for *Om* follows each scene that does not end a chapter in this book.

Nowadays, I no longer feel that I need a specific mantra to meditate in order to get to a point of peaceful focus. I easily reach what Michèle Bisson-Somerville describes as "open-monitoring [OM] meditation," for instance, as I write this book.[124] She describes this process well—of gently focussing on an end goal without expectations and concerns. I can just let the ideas flow as I write.

Or I can walk and notice my breathing, or listen to the song of a singing bowl. I enjoy sitting in a visualization meditation, but I don't need a specific mantra to get me there.

Do you meditate? What style of meditation do you enjoy best? Do you use a mantra? What is the difference meditation makes in your life?

~ *Perseverance* ~

"Hope is that light at the end of the tunnel that drives us to persevere."

Carole Staveley[125]

One of the things we know about life is that we have the gift of time—the present. Let us be here and now with this gift; let our thoughts remain in

[123]With permission from www.dharma-haven.org/tibetan/meaning-of-om-mani-padme-hung.htm

[124]Michèle Bisson-Somerville, *Voodoo Shit for Men: Flex Your Intuitive Muscle* (North Vancouver, Influence Publishing, 2014), pp 33-4.

[125]Carole Staveley, *Conquer Your Pain in 9 Steps: Building the Mindset and Team You Need to Suffer Less and Achieve More* (North Vancouver: Influence Publishing, 2015), p. 131.

the present moment, rather than in the past or in the future. According to some, time is the only thing we have to spend that we can't get back. We can have "the time of our lives" with our life. Or we can spend the time in our lives meaningfully, joyfully.

Once we work out what it is we long for, what it is we long to express, we can pursue it and can persevere until we reach its expression through stamina, focus, and will power. Perseverance is a wonderful quality and when others credit me with it, I feel gratified.

Recently, I have admired the perseverance of many others, including all the authors whose books I edit. It seems that perseverance is a prerequisite for writing a book.

Me as Fanny Bovvington-Keye in Rebel Women by Joan Bryans.
Photograph by Nancy Caldwell, 2014.

Throughout October 2014, I had the welcome opportunity to perform in *Rebel Women*, a verbatim play about the suffragette movement in Great Britain compiled by Joan Bryans mostly from original reports and speeches. Before agreeing to take part, I had no idea what thousands of women and hundreds of men had endured over the course of eight years of militant action to gain the vote for women. Yes, "militant." At one point in 1910, over a thousand women were in prison, all of them following the lead of suffragette Marion Wallace-Dunlop and going on hunger strikes. After recognizing the power of this new action, Prime Minister William Ewart Gladstone spoke out in the House of Commons and it wasn't long before prison wardens were force-feeding the women, frequently in cruel ways.

Annie Kenney, Lancashire representative for 96,000 cotton workers, spoke out against force-feeding: "I urge that the operation is illegal, but I am seized and forced down on my bed. The scene which follows will haunt me with its horror all my life and is almost indescribable. Each time it happens I feel I cannot possibly live through it again."[126]

Thanks to the sufferance and perseverance of people like Suffragette leader Emmeline Pankhurst, her daughter Christabel Pankhurst, Lady Constance Lytton, Annie Kenney, and Marion Wallace-Dunlop, all women in Western countries have the vote, something we now take for granted. But it was only secured for us through the perseverance and long-suffering of many, many women and some men.

Interestingly, before Mohandas Gandhi left Oxford in 1914 (after which time he became better known as Mahatma Gandhi), he met with Lady Constance Lytton. They discussed the power of hunger strikes, something that Gandhi later used to huge advantage.

Ultra-endurance cyclist Leah Goldstein persevered through the Race Across America (RAAM), "the World's Toughest Bicycle Race," in 2011. She began suffering from Shermer's Neck less than halfway through what, for her, became an eleven-day, 3,000-mile race. Shermer's Neck is

[126]Joan Bryans, *Rebel Women*, Scene 12.

a painful condition (named for cyclist Michael Shermer, the first person afflicted with it) diagnosed in long-distance cyclists whose neck muscles weaken from the constant strain of holding up their head (and helmet) to view the route ahead.

Goldstein's team tried a variety of ways to fix her injury, from painkillers and neck braces to tensor bandages braided into her hair. Despite ongoing pain and near exhaustion, Goldstein completed RAAM so successfully that she swept the honours: Best Overall Female, Best in Age Group, Queen of the Mountains, Queen of the Prairies, and Rookie of the Year.[127]

Eugenea Couture, a Métis woman who was torn from her family as a young child, spent forty long years searching for her older brother Josh. Only through her persistence in chasing up every lead possible, including eventually the right one, was Eugenea able to be reunited with her brother in 2003. Through her book *Adoption Not an Option,* she now advocates for peace and an end to abuse in foster homes.

Author Julie Selby displayed perseverance against all odds during her five years of trying to conceive, first naturally and then through *in vitro* fertilization. Twice IVF was unsuccessful and Julie began questioning her own sanity as she tried everything from art classes to drinking an "evil liquid" of ground, boiled, and reduced Chinese herbs. Trying IVF for the third and last time, Julie and her husband Sam rewardingly became parents to twins, a boy and a girl. "Sam held them first and told me they were perfect. It wasn't until that moment that I knew it had all been worth it. George and Francis Dexter had finally arrived."[128]

In an entirely different endeavour, the European Space Agency's Rosetta mission began its ten-year journey in March 2004 to reach and land on Comet 67P/Churyumov-Gerasimenko. One of Rosetta's many historic achievements in December 2014 was to determine what Comet

[127]Leah Goldstein and contributor Lori Moger, M.Sc. *No Limits: The Powerful True Story of Leah Goldstein: World Kickboxing Champion, Israeli Undercover Police and Cycling Champion* (North Vancouver: Influence Publishing, 2015), p. 231.

[128]Julie Selby, *Infertility Insanity: When Sheer Hope (and Google) Are the Only Options Left* (North Vancouver, Influence Publishing, 2015), p. 168.

67P is made of. From such knowledge, much more will be known about our planet Earth. For me, though, the most fascinating part of cometary missions is the perseverance of many, many scientists pursuing one common goal, adding a small element to Earth's scientific knowledge base.

Is perseverance one of your qualities? Do you set yourself long-term goals and achieve them? How do you do it? What keeps driving you forward? Hope? Vision? Passion? If perseverance isn't one of your qualities, would you like to develop it? Why? For what purpose? What end goal?

Talent to Engage

~ *Varieties of Gifts* ~

"There are different kinds of gifts, but the same Spirit distributes them.
There are different kinds of service, but the same Lord....
Now to each one the manifestation of the Spirit is given for the common good.
To one there is given through the Spirit a message of wisdom,
to another a message of knowledge by means of the same Spirit,
to another faith by the same Spirit, to another gifts of healing
by that one Spirit, to another miraculous powers,
to another prophesy, to another distinguishing between spirits,
to another speaking in different kinds of tongues,
and to still another the interpretation of tongues.
All these are the work of one and the same Spirit,
and he distributes them to each one, just as he determines."

1 Corinthians 12:4-11[129]

[129]Holy Bible, NIV®.

I remember taking considerable time and effort many decades ago to fill in a questionnaire about my gifts—innate gifts that respond easily to being developed. It had been prepared by the church I was attending at the time.

What was so great about the questionnaire was that it revealed to me that my gifts from Spirit are mostly in connection with speaking, writing, and acting. These gifts both inspire and challenge me with wonderful opportunities. Many years later, I understood that my gifts are all communication gifts—fifth-chakra gifts. This was the very awareness that led me in my forties to attend university to study Communications.

Many of Spirit's gifts are gifts of communication: the utterance of wisdom and knowledge, prophecy, various kinds of tongues, the interpretation of tongues, describing visions, and interpreting dreams. And what is this book but an interpretation of the various ways we communicate about how we can inspire ourselves and others?

I found an online questionnaire to determine one's gifts from Spirit within the following categories: leadership, administration, teaching, knowledge, wisdom, prophesy, discernment, exhortation, shepherding, faith, evangelism, apostleship, service, mercy, giving, hospitality.[130]

There's a second place in the Bible describing innate gifts. In Romans 12:6-8, gifts from Divine Source are listed: "We have different gifts, according to the grace given to each of us. If your gift is **prophesying**, then prophesy in accordance with your faith; if it is **serving**, then serve; if it is **teaching**, then teach; if it is to **encourage**, then give encouragement; if it is **giving**, then give generously; if it is to **lead**, do it diligently; if it is to **show mercy**, do it cheerfully."[131]

Dorena Dellavecchio, Ph.D. and Bruce E. Winston, Ph.D. post an interesting working paper online that looks into these seven Divine gifts.

---

[130]lifeway.com/lwc/files/lwcF_PDF_Discover_Your_Spiritual_Gifts.pdf
[131]Holy Bible, NIV®, my bolding.

You can take part in their research by filling out your own "Motivational Gifts Survey" following the links at gifttest.org.[132]

I present the table below as my interpretation of the seven gifts from Romans and the broad deliverables and professions that utilize these gifts.

Name of Gifts in Romans 12	Translation of Term	Examples of Professions that Deliver
Prophesying	*aka* perceiving or prophesying, this comprises discerning and proclaiming truth	research, writing, speaking, presenting, blogging, doing readings for others
Serving	using available resources to accomplish a goal	workers in a wide variety of fields
Teaching	similar to prophesying, this comprises discerning, analyzing, and delivering information and truth	teachers, professors, teacher aides, lecturers, presenters
Encouraging	providing comfort, consolation, encouragement, and counsel to others	parents, daycare staff, counsellors, coaches, teachers, psychologists, psychiatrists
Giving	exercising generosity with time, talent, and treasure	benefactors, those who volunteer, philanthropists
Leading	*aka* ruling in such a way as to administer and manage activities, make decisions, and follow through so that workers can follow leadership	administrators, managers, directors
Showing mercy	assisting others who have physical, emotional, mental, and spiritual challenges	healers of every type: psychologists, psychiatrists, doctors, physiotherapists, naturopaths, chiropractors, nurses, church leaders, ministers, lay ministers, alternative healers

[132]Entitled "A Seven-Scale Instrument to Measure the Romans 12 Motivational Gifts and a Proposition that the Romans 12 gift Profiles Might Apply to Person-Job Fit Analysis." at www.regent.edu/acad/global/publications/working/DellaVecchio-Winston%20Romans%2012%20gift%20test%20and%20profiles%20manuscriptdv.pdf

Michael Walsh is someone who has the gift of leadership, which he uses as a visionary speaker and author, inspiring entrepreneurs to achieve and go beyond their growth goals by asking them questions and challenging their beliefs. In recapturing the growth of Louise Pasterfield's company Sponge UK in his book *Thinking Big Is Not Enough*, Michael asks, "What changed that allowed you and your team [Louise and Sponge UK] to generate these results in your business?"[133] Pasterfield became so excited about the options that revealed themselves that she began asking herself questions such as, "'What if the future was tomorrow or even the next hour and not just a big nebulous expanse of time ahead of me?'"[134]

Using this table and/or the questionnaire at gifttest.org, can you recognize some of your innate gifts? Does knowing your innate gifts move you forward? Do they feel appropriate, meaningful, and even God-given?

~ *Parables* ~

"For it will be like a man going on a journey,
who called his servants and entrusted to them his property.
To one he gave five talents, to another two, to another one,
to each according to his ability.
Then he went away."

Matthew 25:14-15[135]

In attempting to teach his disciples about the nature of the kingdom of heaven, Jesus told a series of parables, one being the parable of the talents. The word "talent" does triple duty in this story, meaning a weight of silver, money, and an innate ability.

[133]Michael Walsh, *Thinking Big is Not Enough: Moving Past the Myths and Misconceptions that Stop Business Growth* (North Vancouver: Influence Publishing, 2015), p. 23.
[134]Walsh, *Thinking Big*, p. 36.
[135]Holy Bible, English Standard Version.

It is certainly helpful in life to receive money, but it is far more helpful for us to discover our talents. Then we can develop them in pursuing our life's purpose. I believe our macro-purpose is to find Heaven on Earth—to love, to find joy, to experience, and to contribute in community; I believe our micro-purpose is to do the same by developing our own innate talents. So a person who has an innate musical talent will take part in the musical community that is a choir. The person who has an innate sense of direction and a feel for history will give historical tours of her city to visitors. The person who has a great aptitude for mathematics will share his love of numerical reasoning with students.

Jesus continues the parable of the talents after the man returned from journeying. "He also who had received the one talent came forward, saying, 'Master, I knew you to be a hard man, reaping where you did not sow, and gathering where you scattered no seed, so I was afraid, and I went and hid your talent in the ground. Here you have what is yours.' But his master answered him, 'You wicked and slothful servant! You knew that I reap where I have not sown and gather where I scattered no seed? Then you ought to have invested my money with the bankers, and at my coming, I should have received what was my own with interest.

"So take the talent from him and give it to him who has the ten talents. For to everyone who has will more be given, and he will have an abundance. But from the one who has not, even what he has will be taken away."[136]

When I was a child, this seemed a harsh judgment. I wanted the one-talent man to be allowed to keep his talent. But our talents will only lie dormant underground for so long; if we do not bring them to the light of day, their potential will decompose and disappear.

I don't think anyone could accuse me of not developing my minimal talents. I think I've taken each one as far as I can in this lifetime, to the point where often activities are competing with each other for time in my

[136]Holy Bible, English Standard Version, Matthew 25:24-29.

day: writing, singing, acting, editing. Each one has brought me closer to joy and community.

Making music with others brings me joy.

Do you have any undeveloped talents? Is it too late? What is holding you back from writing poetry? Climbing Mount Everest? Taking up T'ai Chi? Playing a saxophone? Learning Norwegian? Can you yet unearth an innate talent? Can you see this book as a parable of your personal hero story?

~ *We Are Not Our Linear Selves* ~

"Your Destiny Number Vibration is 94/13/4."

Tania Gabrielle[137]

[137]My "Personal Numerology Blueprint" created by Tania Gabrielle, Wealth Astro-Numerologist, 2014.

We humans are complex beings; we are not our linear selves; what understatements! We don't grow physically, mentally, emotionally, or spiritually in a linear way. If we could chart even our physical progress on a graph, it would rise and fall in jerks and spikes, erratically. More so our mental, emotional, and spiritual growth charts. Time, an Earthly construct, is not particularly helpful when it comes to viewing our path and our progress.

I find it useful to take a big-picture view of my life. Only then can I connect the dots and make sense of my path—our way is often obscured by brambles and thorns that we have to cut through to reach our goal, just like the Prince searching for Sleeping Beauty.

When I had an astro-numerological reading with Tania Gabrielle in 2014, she told me that my Destiny Number derived from the letters of my birth name "guarantees you are going through a major transformation all life long in order to help others transform their lives as well. It is a vibration of life, death, and rebirth." The number is 13. That is how it feels. I moved from Wales to England; England to Canada; Canada to Australia; Australia back to Canada. I suffered drought on a sheep and cattle property, went through a divorce and overcame cancer soon after, experienced financial losses and struggle before regaining firm footing, each time to start again: life, death, and rebirth.

A human life is not carved in stone. What we see of each other is just a snapshot in time. A human life is constantly re-interpretable. Different perspectives yield different stories; difference choices yield different lives. Even after a person dies, their life's story can be rewritten from a range of viewpoints.

What is the story of your life that you would like remembered? Is that the life you are living now? If not, why not? What's still on your bucket list? Who are you now? How did you get to where you are now? Who will you be? How will you get there?

~ Reaching an Agreement ~

"Have the courage to ask questions until you are clear as you can be,
and even then do not assume you know
all there is to know about a given situation.
Once you hear the answer, you will not have to make assumptions
because you will know the truth."
Miguel Ruiz[138]

I was feeling fully primed for my one o'clock interview with Julie Salisbury for contract work as an editor with her company, Influence Publishing. I had spent the morning sifting through my five decades of editing other people's writing in various ways, grouping and condensing the experiences into headings: newsletter publisher, government communications, developmental editor, manuscript editor, copyeditor, and so on. I had printed up the one page and folded it into an envelope. I mapped my route online, and set off early. I felt confident and I knew I was eager to fill this position and that I was capable of doing a wonderful job if it were offered to me.

The address was easy to find and I arrived with fifteen minutes to spare. I parked just a block away in a one-hour zone—that should be plenty of time—and walked to the building. I was still too early. Ahead of me was a T-junction with what-looked-like blackberry bushes on the far side of the road. It had been a great summer for berries. I had been picking blackberries each time I had visited my mum on Vancouver Island recently. So I crossed the road and ate some berries—they were ripe and juicy—feeling more confident with each one.

I returned to Julie's building and rang the buzzer for the office suite. She came out, smiling warmly. We greeted each other and she said, "Oh, you're English," with great delight in her Leicester-based accent.

[138]Ruiz, *The Four Agreements*, p. 72.

"Actually, I'm Welsh!"

"Wonderful," she said.

The other thing I had done that morning was listen to part of a free two-hour recording to promote the press she has founded.[139] As I listened to the recording, I knew she was English. No, wait! Was that some Aussie creeping in? Or South African? When I lived in Britain, I had been excellent at identifying accents. But now, having been away so long—I left in 1969—and having lived in Australia as well for five years—my ability to identify accents has diminished.

The delight in her voice was obvious and so was her heritage by her remark. She is English.

We kept establishing commonality—we both wanted some licorice tea. And we both love marmite. I'm sure there's some in my fridge even now.

The first hour of the interview, I felt as though I were interviewing her for the job of hiring me, because she was telling me about her company and its growth and its modus operandi and its authors and editors and on and on. I was loving this. While I listened to her attentively and with joy, the observer part of my brain was commenting on how well this was going, but that I had to state my case, put forward my strong points, my experiences, my skills. Bit by bit, I slid a few in, here and there, and the time just expanded.

An agreement—the moment that an agreement is reached—can sometimes be a rather nebulous thing. People don't necessarily say the decisive words: "you are hired," or "I would like to hire you," or "I would like you to do this job." I don't know at what point in our conversation—it was more a chat between two old friends than an interview—that we came to the agreement that I wanted the job and would be willing to work on contract for the sum of money discussed and that she would like to hire me. There was no one word that could be pointed to, to say "that was the moment." It was a gradual agreement.

[139] www.youtube.com/channel/UCc9Srbm1t5Et_gDLlZajksQ

Perhaps the agreement had started at the door when we both found we were from the UK, immigrants in a beautiful land. Perhaps it was over the licorice tea. Perhaps it was when she went to her storage cupboard for the second time to get something and was frustrated because she couldn't reach the book she wanted to show me because the closet was totally disorganized. And right away I contacted a colleague-friend of mine and described Julie as someone who needed help to move boxes and put up pictures and take display shelving down to her storage locker downstairs. And the friend I had phoned recommended Julie hire a certain professional organizer and Julie was thrilled. That was exactly whose help she needed.

Some years later, I attended Julie Salisbury's presentation and talk to the Bluewater Cruising Association about her circumnavigation of the globe, as captured in her book, *Around the World in Seven Years*. I edited Julie's book and she is publishing mine. Photograph by Lisa Halpern, February 2015

But when she said, "I'll start you with George's manuscript. His book launch is November 11," and she pointed to the wall chart and there was my first author's name—George West. Then I knew we had reached an agreement. I had been engaged as a contract editor with Influence Publishing—"Inspiring books that influence change." Julie and I confirmed and sealed our agreement with a hug when I parted.

It is as though an agreement is a plateau to be reached. At one moment, we are on opposite sides of a mesa, still climbing up. Then suddenly, we have reached the top and are there together. Perhaps we pave the way toward major agreements for weeks and years, accumulating all the small steps until finally we reach the height together. Then, any manner of great agreements can be reached, from agreements to work for someone to agreements to marry someone.

I think that sometimes one person reaches the plateau of the agreement before the other. I know this happens with one particular friend of mine. We will be discussing something and need to come to an agreement. I get there quite quickly, agreeing with all the details, but she has to continue the climb for some time before she can confirm for herself that we are in agreement. I wait for her patiently on the plateau.

Where is the healing in an agreement? An agreement requires two or more parties to move toward the same decision. Perhaps one begins with indifference and the other with high expectations; or one might be distrustful and the other have absolute faith that an agreement can be reached. It requires an alignment within each person with that decision and an expression of a desire to agree. An agreement happens when two people expand their viewpoints to reach an inclusive wholeness.

Contractual statements and letters bear huge weight and are frequently well remembered—by date and place, mood and weather. People often cite vivid details when recalling how a job was offered, or a proposal of marriage accepted, or a car purchase agreed upon. In my own life, recent contract-related events include a spoken agreement to sing at the induction service for the new minister at St. Paul's Anglican

Church; Alison Schamberger's phone call to offer me a part in Agatha Christie's *Murder on the Nile*; and an email from Trevor Ludski to say how glad he is I've agreed to perform (percussion and singing) with the 8 Enders—the group of ukulele and guitar players who perform at Stanley Park Lawn Bowling Club and occasionally other venues.

8 Enders at Stanley Park Lawn Bowling Club,
Nina, Judith, Trevor, Carrie, and Anne.

Have you reached an important agreement lately? Are you close to making one, or are you holding back? What agreement would you like to reach with someone? What is the purpose, the goal, the vision, the accomplishment that will be the result of the agreement? Are you ready to take the first step, with faith, knowing that by agreeing to begin you can reach your goal?

~ *Whispering* ~

"I came to discover that the horses would always cooperate with whatever the humans asked them to do if, and only if, the human could and would give clear energetic direction to the horse. We're talking about simple body language, which is nothing more than a product of our energy system....
[I]t's been my experience that we actually use words more often to avoid communicating with each other."

Wyatt Webb[140]

These days, I frequently hear about "whisperers," people who can calm others—babies and animals—through mutual consent with gentleness. The two parties come to an agreement without ever having to "say" anything. There are baby whisperers, dog whisperers, elephant whisperers, and even crocodile whisperers. Aren't all mothers baby whisperers? But, if we can believe Wyatt Webb in his quote for this scene, each of us can be a horse whisperer.

Webb's mission these days is to help others overcome their self-doubt and fear by working with his horses at Miraval Arizona Resort & Spa in what he calls the Equine Experience. Through the process, his clients end up accessing their deepest pains and releasing them. "A horse is consistent in his awareness—pure as he can be, totally sophisticated and always in the moment. A horse knows what to do every single time. It just depends how clear *you* are as a human being."[141]

Webb realized that individuals who aren't functioning well and are in pain are denying inner truths; they are being uncommunicative and inauthentic about their deepest problems. Webb's horses know this as soon as they work with these individuals. And the only successful way

---

[140]Wyatt Webb, with Cindy Pearlman, *It's Not About the Horse: It's About Overcoming Fear and Self-Doubt* (Hay House, 2002), p. 83.
[141]Webb and Pearlman, *It's Not About the Horse,* p. 101.

to communicate with Webb's horses requires a person to become authentic; that creates a healing.

A friend of mine explained what a powerful experience it was for her when she attended the Purple Sage Ranch at Miraval and worked with Wyatt Webb and one of his horses. She explained that she was able to have the horse turn around and come to her just by delivering clear energetic instructions. No words. No arm gestures. Just pure intention exemplifying the belief held by many that "God is the energy that connects all living things."

Imagine the large sphere that your physical and energetic bodies occupy. Imagine the large sphere that a horse and her energetic body would occupy. If those spheres came close enough to overlap, they would create a third shape, a *vesica piscis*.[142] In two dimensions, it is the same shape as an eye, an oval with points at each end. If we could imagine ourselves as spheres of energy, spheres of influence, spheres of communication, we would also see that where our sphere overlaps the sphere of another person is the space and time where we can find agreement; where we can share energy; where we can influence each other more easily. It's a shared space.

Theo Fleury, now retired from the National Hockey League and working as an advocate for trauma survivors and mental health, says, and I repeat, "True spirituality is all about relationship. Most addicts are traumatized in their family of origin situations, so what they really lose faith in is relationship.... The trauma causes emotional pain for which the best answer is spirituality."[143]

I see the relational and healing work that Webb is doing as spiritual because he is helping his clients find their souls, their true authentic selves, one person at a time, one-on-one with a horse.

I believe successful "whispering" is something to do with being in the present moment, finding that energetic space that is shared between us as verbal and pre-verbal humans or between humans and any other of God's creatures.

Are your intentions clear? Would a horse agree? How is your relationship

[142]See image in chapter four, Early Mysteries.
[143]Fleury and Barthel, *Conversations with a Rattlesnake*, p. 195.

with yourself? Are you living as your authentic self? Or are you hiding part of your talent or struggling to develop a talent? Are you living your life as a wallflower when in fact you are a sunflower? What inner struggle must you face before you can shed your inauthenticity?

Treasure to Engage

~ Daydreaming ~

"A daydreamer is a writer just waiting for pen and paper....
As I quietly stare off into space, eyes glazed over and brow thoughtfully taut,
know that I am going about my business. I am a storyteller.
Daydreaming is the best part of my job."
Richelle E. Goodrich[144]

Looking like a red-haired pixie who is just visiting this planet for the fun of it, children's book author Richelle E. Goodrich has all the right things to say about daydreaming. She sees it as one of the tools of the creative fiction trade—one of the arrows in the fiction writer's quiver—along with pen and paper and the time to capture the daydreams.

Goodrich's daydreaming for her might be close to the OM meditation technique that Bisson-Somerville describes and I adopt when I write this book.

Daydreaming—letting my mind wander aimlessly—is not something I do on a regular basis for creativity's sake. I have more of a non-fiction mind frame except when it comes to spiritual writing, and then it's more a case of meditating, of allowing ideas to come through, and accepting inspiration. And daydreams are usually not memorable for me, unless they

[144]goodreads.com/quotes/tag/richelle-goodrich

make it onto a list or a sticky note, or into my diary. But I do remember one episode of daydreaming that just about derailed me from my path.

At the age of eleven, I was sitting at a dark oak desk in a classroom in Howell's School, Llandaff (HSL), near my hometown of Cardiff in South Wales. It was the day of that year's school entrance exam, warm and sunny. I could see uniformed girls running and chatting in the schoolyard (it was at that time an all-girls' school). I started to dream about what it might be like to attend such a school. The teacher at the head of the classroom was droning on about something, but I was completely oblivious to what she was saying.

Later in the day, we girls who were potential HSL students were tested on the various things we had been taught during the day. You can probably imagine that I did not do very well on those tests, because I hadn't been listening. A few weeks later, the results of the entrance exams came in the mail: I had failed to gain a place into Howell's. I was deeply disappointed, because I had already set my sights on attending that school—it had a high academic reputation.

My lucky break came when I had a second chance to get in. In those days, an exam known as the Eleven Plus was administered to all eleven-year-olds throughout Great Britain during their last year of primary education. It was an intelligence test for problem solving in English and Arithmetic (the name we used then). I was fully prepared for that exam when it came along and, because it took place in the hall of my regular school, I was not distracted. I did not daydream, I performed well, and was granted a scholarship to my first choice—Howell's School. So I got there after all.

Perhaps that first failure curbed me of daydreaming and stopped me from becoming a fiction writer, making me more of a non-fiction writer. Who knows! That's something to daydream about.

Do you daydream? Is it a waste of time for you? Or is it productive? Do you daydream intentionally or just drift into the state? Can daydreaming be intentional?

~ *Money Is a Form of Energy* ~

"Who we are at Soul-level translates itself into business.
Time and time again, the evidence landed in my bank account,
and the bank accounts of my clients."

Andrrea Hess[145]

According to Charles Eisenstein, anti-consumerist activist, public speaker, and author, energy is first exchanged between humans as a gift, for instance between parent and child.[146] As we reach adulthood, money is the more usual means of exchanging energy. Through the eons, energy has been exchanged by gift, barter, trade, and battle. Slavery was a way for slaveholders to get energy "for free." It was theft of one person's energy by another.

It's helpful to remember that money is not the only way of exchanging energy. Staying alive requires us to exchange energy: we intake energy in the form of food, break down the food into its separate parts (proteins, carbohydrates, fats, minerals, vitamins, and water), and convert those separate parts into the building blocks we happen to need at the time. We can also exchange energy, and even encourage our life force energy to grow, through deep breathing, laughter, meditation, music, love, and through healing modalities such as Reiki, Healing Touch, and exercise. We can restore our energy by resting, sleeping, and meditating.

We incarnate into this world in a physical body with energy and time. How we spend our energy and our time is first determined by our family and our caregivers. If and when we become autonomous, we can decide how we use and spend our treasure of energy and time. While we cannot regain the time we have spent, we can regain our energy for life. If we realize we are spending our lives in an unproductive direction, we can redirect ourselves. It is literally never too late.

---

[145]empoweredsoul.com

[146]Charles Eisenstein, *Sacred Economics: Money, Gift, and Society in the Age of Transition* (Evolver Editions, 2011).

As adults, all humans except the most destitute are stewards of a triad of gifts—"time, talent, and treasure." How are you spending your time, talent, and treasure? In ways that deplete your energy or expand it? In ways that build separation and fear or that build community and love? Resisting or assisting? Criticizing or loving?

~ *Ideas* ~

"Be in awe of the immensity of our universe."

Wayne Dyer[147]

As a little girl of five or six, I grasped the universe's immensity more clearly than was perhaps usual for my age. Now and then, a thought would seize me: the already vast universe was getting bigger; it was spreading. My thinking started with small objects such as sand particles and shells and grew to trees, hills, towns, and countries. I would always reach a frightening place where I was so small in relation to everything else that I felt utterly insignificant. What strange thoughts for a small child!

There have been many theories about the Big Bang: possibly, matter throughout the universe has begun to fall back from a point of expansion; possibly, it is still moving farther and farther apart (today's accepted likelihood); or perhaps there is a myriad of universes, all overlaid, interconnected, one with the other.

Another childhood memory is of writing out my address as long as possible: Nina Grant McGregor, 59 Penylan Road, Penylan, Cardiff, Glamorganshire, South Wales, Great Britain, Earth, The Universe. That practice made me feel infinitesimally small, too, but somehow more in control. I saw something similar written by another child recently and

---

[147]Wayne Dyer, *There's a Spiritual Solution to Every Problem* (Harper, 2001), p. 238.

it reminded me of my childhood habit. Imagine how much smaller and less in control I might have felt had I known that our winter skies display Betelgeuse, a "red supergiant" that is more than "twice the size of earth's orbit around the sun."[148]

Where do such ideas come from? Are they true "ideas"? Could they be channellings? These days, some might call them "downloads"—gifts of awareness and wisdom from Spirit. Might my fear of the vastness of the universe have prepared me to tackle some of the weightier conundrums of life, just as a reading of James Hillman's best-selling *The Soul's Code: In Search of Character and Calling* might suggest?

I can be thinking about a problem, a situation, a dilemma I have, and a solution arrives in my mind before I have even had time to put words to the question. And when that happens, I say to myself aloud, "That's a good idea." And such ideas continue to come. By saying "That's a good idea" and acting upon the idea right away—or noting it for future action—I am showing gratitude for the download, the channelling, the idea. I sense that my gratitude encourages such ideas to continue coming.

In her book *One Thousands Gifts*, Ann Voskamp explains her certainty that giving thanks is the path to grace and joy; that giving thanks (she uses the Greek word *Eucharisteo*) during difficulties precedes the gifts of grace and joy rather than the reverse. Perhaps in that same way, my gratitude for current gifts allows more to come.

My solution to my fearful path of childish thoughts was to forbid myself from going there. After several failed attempts, I was able to accomplish the blockage, rather like children who stop seeing psychic phenomena. And I am also willing to entertain the thought that this realization of the vastness of the universe was a leftover piece of spirit knowledge from beyond the veil, too much for my immature human brain to handle. Nowadays, I am willing to entertain such thoughts again.

I had a lovely discussion with one of my granddaughters recently. It was about fairies. She was rationalizing about which of her fairy statues—

[148]Ann *Voskamp, One Thousand Gifts: A Dare to Live Fully Right Where You Are* (Zondervan Books, 2011), p. 31.

collectibles—were real and which weren't. She had a system based on the sparkliness of their wings. It sounded good to me.

Writing about early awarenesses that I chose to hide from myself makes me realize that we lower the veil between this world and the afterlife ourselves. "The veil" could be translated as "the physical body"; it could be seen as a cloak hiding the portal back to our true home. From our physical human perspective, the veil works as a filter, allowing in only a portion of Divine mind, stopping us from being fully aware of our Divinity, and shielding us from Infinite Wisdom. It also seals off—sometimes more efficiently and sometimes less—our memories of past lives and our life between physical lives. The brain works like a step-down transformer that allows only a portion of our Divine energy (a predetermined percentage) into the body. We don't want to blow our brains out by bringing in too much energy! But gradually, we re-mind ourselves of our Spiritual selves.

Are you grateful for the ideas you get? Do you remember some of your childhood ideas? Were they more advanced than you now imagine a child of that age could entertain? Why is that? How do you think the veil works? The brain?

~ *Adaptability* ~

"All failure is failure to adapt, all success is successful adaptation."

Max McKeown[149]

One of the skills I most admired in my mother was her adaptability. It gave her supreme strength. It allowed her to make the best of whatever situation she encountered. I remember a holiday in West Wales in a rented cottage that turned out to be still under construction. In no time, my mum had moved an orange box to be the bottom step to the open

[149]Max McKeown, *Adaptability: The Art of Winning in an Age of Uncertainty* (Kogan Page, 2012), p. 19.

stairway, then placed two more boxes on top of each other to be a temporary table with a tablecloth. She soon jollied us all into enjoying tea out of the landlord's still-warm teapot from his own table.

I remember sitting in a Spanish airport departure lounge waiting for a delayed flight and watching my mother unpack small parcels of leftover groceries she had removed from the fridge where we'd been staying. She found enough to feed our group of six comfortably.

I remember my parents' arrival in Australia to live in the shearers' cottage at Riverglade, our sheep and cattle property. From the bottom of one of her suitcases, my mum pulled out a large white decal appropriate for decorating the space above a Victorian mantelpiece. And she installed it above the fireplace where an earlier hired man had treated the home far less appreciatively: he had burned one end of a six-foot-long log in that fireplace; as the burning end shortened, he gradually pushed the log further into the fire. My mother and father transformed that shearers' quarters into a British home.

My parents married during the first week of the Second World War, aged twenty-one and twenty-five. They rented a flat in Cardiff. While my father served in Europe, my mother used his war pay and a bank mortgage to buy a home. When the war ended, my father returned to his own house; few young men returned to such stability!

Adaptability is a huge talent. Which of us does not find ourselves in situations that are less than ideal? We can spend our time and energy on complaining, blaming, and resisting the situation. Or we can seek out the good features and benefits of the change from what was, and allow the goodness to expand and grow, transforming our lives in previously impossible ways.

If I had not had to stop working because of the eye muscle dis-ease I had, I would never have taken the time to examine my life. If my first husband had not been so self-directed, I might never have found my own voice. If I had not lost money in various ways, I might never have understood its real value—to pave the path to what truly matters.

How adaptable are you? When a bad situation comes along, how do you greet it? Do you see it as a new challenge, a hurdle that you will climb to get to the next level of life, or as a door you'll never open? What are the personal qualities you can hone that will allow you to be more adaptable?

~ *Jesus and the Mayans and the Chakra System* ~

"If you love me, keep my commands. And I will ask the Father,
and he will give you another advocate to help you and be with you forever
—the Spirit of truth. The world cannot accept him,
because it neither sees him nor knows him.
But you know him, for he lives with you and will be in you....
But the Advocate, the Holy Spirit, whom the Father will send in my name,
will teach you all things and will remind you of everything I have said to you.
Peace I leave with you; my peace I give you.
I do not give to you as the world gives.
Do not let your hearts be troubled and do not be afraid."

John 14: 15-17, 26-27[150]

Using the chakra system as a lens on history, I am going to introduce an idea that may seem obvious once I offer it. The New Testament of the Bible explains that Jesus brought the message of love with him when he came to Earth as an Ascended Master. This gift of love—Divine Love—is the full realization of the fourth chakra, the heart chakra, awakened by Jesus' mission on Earth.

Toward the end of his life, Jesus promised his disciples the gift of the Holy Spirit, a time coinciding with Pentecost (see the scene in chapter three, "~ Not Knowing the Language ~"). The biblical book

[150]Holy Bible, NIV®.

known as Acts (Acts of the Apostles) says, "All of them were filled with the Holy Spirit and began to speak in other tongues as the Spirit enabled them."[151] So, while Jesus gave the gift of heart chakra connection, the Holy Spirit brought the gift of throat chakra connection, the ability to communicate one's own truth and to align with Divine Truth through the throat chakra. To teach, to encourage others.

These days, in the second decade of the 21st century, we are living through a time of consciousness-raising. A New-Age tenet is that human consciousness-raising is accompanied by the raising of the consciousness of our homeland planet, Mother Earth. As we reached December 21, 2012, the end of the Mayan calendar, there was curiosity and some foreboding about what this date might have implied, for good or bad.

I choose to view the consciousness-raising heralded by December 21, 2012 through the lens of the seven major chakras, saying that our sixth chakra has been opening to superconsciousness, to Higher Consciousness, to Spirit since that time.

How do you view this time in history? Do you see it as an end time and a beginning time? Do you see yourself as part of the consciousness-raising movement or as resistance to that movement? Are you living at the level of the sixth chakra? Or are you still caught up in the physical struggles of the second and third chakras—in healing your relationships and in seeking your own integrity? Do you just wish things were different? Or are you making things better yourself?

[151]Holy Bible, NIV®, Acts 2:4.

Part III ~ The Results

Chapter 7—Observing the Doer and the Deed

People

~ Your Team ~

"No man is an island entire of itself;
every man is a piece of the continent, a part of the main."
John Donne[152]

I have a medical team: a medical doctor, a naturopath, an acupuncturist, a chiropractor, and a dentist; I have a business team: an accountant, a financial advisor, an estate lawyer, and two banks; I have a work team: a publisher with whom I contract, and work colleagues who are editors, media communication specialists, and administrators.

Most of the endeavours I get involved in are team sports, not literally but figuratively. Responsibilities and talents dovetail in ways that are rewarding to think about, and I recommend mapping your teams as a self-reflective exercise.

I can cite community theatre as an example. It requires a director, a producer, set and lighting designers, set decorators, wardrobe and props mistresses, a stage manager and her assistant, a publicist, a cast, and a fully staffed theatre. And, most important of all, an audience comprising individuals who respond as a whole. Audiences vary from one night to the next. One night's audience might relish one particular scene; on another night, another scene solicits applause in the moment. One night's audience splits its sides over an exchange between two characters; another night, the chase through the garden captivates the audience.

[152]John Donne (1572-1631), *Devotions upon Emergent Occasions, and Severall Steps in My Sicknes*, "Meditation XVII." Published 1624.

Being a member of a choir also means being part of a team that comprises a director, a librarian, sopranos, altos, tenors, basses, instrumentalists, venue organizers, and an audience or a congregation.

Getting this book to market requires me as the author to work with a publisher, an editor, a proofreader, a typesetter, artists, a publicist, bookstore managers, librarians, and readers. Someone "has my back" as a writer—and my sides, top, and toes. Such solidity feels good.

One way of listing the teams you are on is by drawing three, four, or more interconnecting, overlapping circles. You will be in the middle of all the circles and team members who are in more than one of your teams—for example, my publisher is also the person I do contract editing for—will occupy the overlapping area between two different teams.

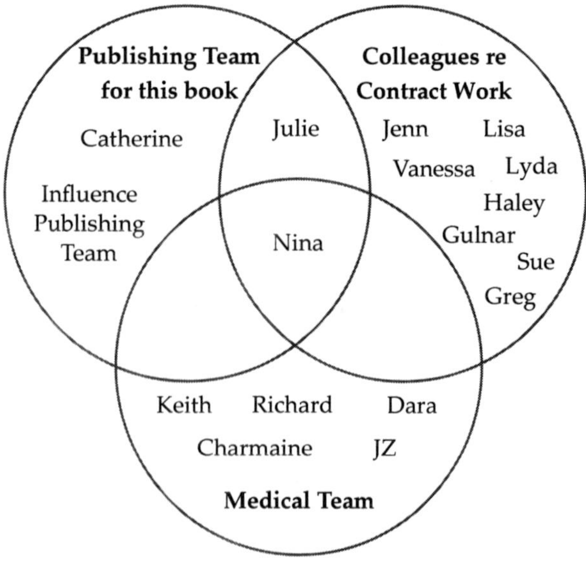

Some of my teams

There are many models for similar introspective exercises online providing opportunities to recognize who is in your circles of influence (can influence, cannot influence, can be influenced by, and cannot be influenced by) and your circles of relationship (intimate loved ones, other relations, friends, colleagues, acquaintances, teachers). The word "teacher" can be used here in the broadest sense to include people—dead or alive—whose knowledge or behaviour you admire and try to emulate as well as actual teachers in teaching institutions.

Who is on your team? Whose team are you on? How many teams are you on? Are you working with the best? Are you leading or following? Leading from the front or from the centre? Following joyfully or reluctantly? What other teams do you want to join? Create?

~ *The "C" Form* ~

"No one came from the 'C' form except Clare."

Nina Shoroplova[153]

My first year at Howell's School, Llandaff (HSL) in South Wales, we were put into three classes: UIIIX, UIIIY, and UIIIZ, standing for Upper Third random groups X, Y, and Z. HSL organized us that way that first year because we had entered the school through two different systems: the eleven-plus exam and HSL's own entrance exam. That first year, we girls were not graded by our marks (read "examination results"). By the next year, we Lower Fourths (LIVs) were graded into an A form, a B form, and a C form. The predictable effect was that we tended to hang out only with the girls in our particular form.

A stigma was attached to how we were ranked, according to our marks on whatever subject teachers tested us. And test us they did. The stigma turned into an "astigmatism" through which we saw the C form girls as the dunces! How cruel children can be! The A form girls were the bright ones; nowadays, we would call them "nerds." They are the

[153]Describing my fortieth high school reunion at HSL to my mother.

ones who went to university, some of them to Oxford and Cambridge. Everyone knew they would go there. Most of them would be encouraged to apply for university; the rest of us wouldn't be. The B form girls were the middle-of-the-road girls—interested in doing fairly well at school but keener on meeting boys and having fun, too.

I was in the B form.

Working my way through school, I took pre-university courses in the Lower Sixth, not because I was planning to go to university but because I was planning to train as a physiotherapist and I had to wait until I turned eighteen to be admitted to that program. September was the month physiotherapy college began and I wouldn't be eighteen until the following January, so I had to wait a year, twiddle my thumbs, doing something rather mindlessly, attending Lower Sixth classes. Such arbitrary systems are mindless.

We British students took our "O" level exams in the Upper Fifth form. Everything was letter-based in those days. The "O" stood for General Certificate of Education Ordinary Level Examinations—leaving-school exams. We'd ask each other, "How many O levels do you have?"

Six or seven was a good number. I was proud because I gained nine, I think. That was because students in the A form—I had "risen" in the ranks from the B to the A form in the Lower Fifths—were allowed to take a couple of O-level exams one year early. That was lucky because we increased our standing without having to do so much swotting all at once. So the next year, I just did the standard number of seven.

And that's what I say—the arbitrary system of ranking and grading us at HSL was based on our marks in the areas they chose to examine us. If they'd examined us differently, our marks would have been different.

Howard Gardner, author of *Frames of Mind: The Theory of Multiple Intelligences,* describes a number of types of intelligence, the type being taught in schools being only one, known as Logical-Mathematical Intelligence. In others such as Musical Intelligence and Linguistic Intelligence I might score higher than in something like Bodily-Kinesthetic

Intelligence, though the amount of singing and acting that I've done has enhanced that form of intelligence. Interpersonal Intelligence and Emotional Intelligence are demonstrated well by my husband.

Returning to the arbitrary ranking system in my high school, the letter "C" attached to the C-form girls became such a put-down that they all adopted a view of themselves, and we of them, that excluded their getting ahead in life through academic attainment.

Fast forward to 2005 when several HSL girls came together to organize our fortieth high-school reunion. I decided to attend, and so did thirty-eight other women from the A and B forms. But only one girl came from the C form—Clare. She was great fun, laughing and cracking jokes with a totally infectious, hearty full-throated, full-body laugh. She had shaken off any possible stigma years earlier. Was it the stigma that held the others back?

It was years before I even went to university; I was a mature student aged 46! Really! That was how old I was before I lived down the belief that only the A form girls could benefit from university training. Even though I'd ended up in the A form, I felt I was still a B student at heart. Moving into the A form was just a fluke!

In what ways have you been ranked that changed the impression you had or still have of yourself? What letters have been arbitrarily assigned to you, putting you into a group where you tried to fit? Have you ever denied yourself something because of such an arbitrary assignment?

~ *A Safe Circle* ~

"The round room was a physical container
that separated us from ordinary life,
and being in a circle of people where it was safe to 'tell it as it is'
was another container that held what was said within.
We were in a temenos, which is a Greek word for 'sanctuary.'
No container formed by two or more human beings is perfect,
but those in which soul work is done are sacred sites."

Jean Shinoda Bolen, M.D.[154]

One particular step in my spiritual journey began in fall 1997, when I signed up for a Friday evening talk and an all-day Saturday workshop with Jean Shinoda Bolen. At the end of Dr. Bolen's talk at Christ Church Cathedral, this seminal psychiatrist, Jungian analyst, author, and activist suggested that someone in the audience might want to organize a *temenos* as a result of the talk.

"[T]he spiritual form taken by women's spirituality circles and support groups of all kinds ... have a spiritual center. A circle with a spiritual center makes meeting together a sanctuary for its members, a time that nourishes the soul."[155]

Someone did come forward at Christ Church Cathedral to organize that women's group. In itself, that might have been enough, because I signed up to attend the temenos and that started my relationship with a group of women that has shifted and evolved over the years but with whom I am still meeting to do soul work. By sharing my truth with them, I learn about myself.

An essential feature of the group is that whatever is offered is accepted and respected—not criticized or judged. We aim to allow equal airtime to each person. And we do not trample on each other's words.

---

[154]Jean Shinoda Bolen, M.D., "Winter Solstice," jeanbolen.com
[155]Ibid.

After Dr. Bolen's evening talk, I attended her all-day workshop and, following her direction, learned more about myself. For instance, she led us in a meditation in which I perceived myself being as strong and expansive as a huge, healthy tree with roots deep in the Earth and a crown as high as the sky, spreading wide to host singing birds.

At that workshop, I also met two more women—a community programmer and a clinical psychologist—with whom I continued to meet regularly for a number of years. I learned a great deal about the spiritual search through my friendship with them, and more about myself.

Do you have a group of like-minded people you meet with regularly to share your deepest thoughts and feelings? Can you hear others' opinions without having to share yours or trying to influence theirs? Do you feel you are in competition with others, or in union?

~ *Lumpers and Splitters* ~

"Are yuz gentry or do yuz scrape?"

Wainie Robertson[156]

"Are yuz gentry or do yuz scrape?" is a delightful Aussie-ism that decisively separates the upper crust from the crust. If the table is where "yuz scrape" the leftovers on the dishes you're clearing away, then "yuz" certainly aren't gentry. If "yuz gentry," then you carefully carry out the leftover-encrusted dishes to the kitchen (behind a swinging door, preferably), one or two at a time, and scrape in the kitchen.

It asks so much. Are you practical? Are you busy? Do you take yourself too seriously? Or are you like us? Because of course if we didn't scrape, we wouldn't ask. But us, we have chooks to feed, so we scrape the leftovers and then go out to the chicken coop and go, "chook, chook, chook!" until all the chickens come running out from wherever they've been

[156]A Walcha grazier and gardener, speaking in jest.

sitting on their eggs and start chowing down on our leftovers.

When I worked for Agriculture Canada, a federal agency, one co-worker held that in biological sciences, people are either "lumpers or splitters": the lumpers see nature as divided into several lumps: humans, animals, birds, insects, fish, plants, rocks, and so on. The splitters are the ones who specialize in researching the stickleback that lives on the underbelly of the lesser black-tailed mongoose.

Both these examples show that some people automatically sort others into two groups that they have prejudged: the group they belong to and the group that everyone else belongs to. Their attitude is "us-and-them."

Is it valid? Are there ever two groups? Perhaps there are millions of groups, or billions: people who have undergone in-vitro fertilization to have babies and those who haven't; blonds and non-blonds; marijuana users and those who have never tried pot; stamp collectors and non-philatelists; opera buffs and opera loathers.

Perhaps such a desire to split the world two ways just shows a person's leanings. A person leans one way, and they're surprised that not everyone else leans that way. But, of course, if we all leaned one way, the boat would tip over.

By the way, I'm a scraper, even though I no longer have chooks. What are you? But there again, aren't we all one? Just one group with a billion tiny differences?

Processes

~ *Plans and Goals* ~

"A goal without a plan is just a wish."

Anonymous proverb[157]

[157]Often misattributed to Antoine de Saint-Exupéry.

You may wish to move on to the next scene if you feel you need to read nothing further about SMART goals: those that are Specific, Measurable, Attainable, Realistic, and Timely. If you're new to the topic, I can offer you an illustrative example—the goal that I set for publishing this book in fall 2015, knowing that a book is 5 percent inspiration and 95 percent perspiration.

- **Specific**—Write the first draft of a book that will provoke my readers into greater self-awareness, acceptance, and trust of their involvement in the mystery.
- **Measurable**—I'll know I have finished writing this book manuscript when every scene has a title, a quote, a source for the quote, and something interesting to say about the topic.
- **Attainable**—It's now mid-July 2014 and I have created the order for the parts, chapters, sections, and scenes; the manuscript is almost 100,000 words; and I am writing and rewriting almost daily.
- **Realistic**—It's a realistic goal as I have already spoken to Julie Salisbury, founder and publisher at Influence Publishing, and we have agreed on the timeline for the book.
- **Timely**—If I finish writing this book manuscript by March 27, 2015, and send it to my editor, this will give Influence Publishing time to get it onto the publishing conveyor belt and into the bookstores in September 2015.

So, my goal is SMART, but it also requires a plan. After I had made a good start, I set out my plan for finishing the manuscript: to keep writing as ideas come, to complete unfinished scenes, to search out good quotes, to get permission to use some of the longer quotes from their owners, and to ask myself questions about each scene to ensure it is useful for a reader.

And there's more. When I met with Julie to discuss my book, she suggested a way to create a market for it ahead of publication by creating a dedicated website/a blog and to write regular posts.

As I thought about this goal with a plan, I realized I had to find time in the fall of 2014 to devote several hours each day to polishing the manuscript. I wanted it to include lively and unusual information, flow well, be free of repetition, and make only thoughtful assumptions of knowledge on behalf of the reader. My allocation of time had to be regular and ample: say Mondays, Wednesdays, and Fridays starting in October.

Now, that's a plan! Where's my daytimer?

Do you have a SMART goal you're working on? Do you have a plan to go with that objective? Are you following it? Where you digress from the plan, is the digression for a good reason?

~ *Mental Exercises* ~

"What I think about, I bring about."

Law of Attraction aphorism

We often assign ourselves mental tasks.

For example, Stevens, the butler and protagonist of *The Remains of the Day* by Kazuo Ishiguro, tried to develop his ability to "banter" with his American employer, Mr. Farraday, owner of Darlington Hall. Not accustomed to having to be witty with his previous employer, Lord Darlington, Stevens was building his mental muscles for wit, with mild success here and there.

A more personal example for me is learning to dowse. Dowsing is the initial form of gaining Divine information in Soul Realignment™. "Dowsing" refers here to using a pendulum. When I started learning how to use my pendulum, asking many closed-ended questions that I would develop very carefully, I asked my questions aloud. It was only through focus that I trained my conscious mind to ask questions in silence.

What irony! My mind is seldom silent, frequently commenting on what is going on, mostly in a critical way. And this is what makes asking questions silently so difficult, because, almost as fast as I ask the question, criticism and answers appear. Which is which? What can I rely on? I found that the greatest test for my psychic abilities was to trust in the answers I received; at the same time, I learned to recognize my egoic mind and its running commentary.

If the abilities to select and initiate actions are the greatest powers of the conscious mind (as claimed by Frederick Bailes, M.D.[158]), it seems to me that accepting or rejecting the results of the actions we initiate must come close behind. The only way that a student of dowsing can hope to make any progress is by accepting every answer she receives. Rejecting an answer does not build trust; in fact, it destroys the process.

What mental exercises are you engaging in? Creating a knitting pattern? Learning a style of singing? Practising the moves and countermoves you will employ in an upcoming kickboxing tournament? Learning to score in bridge? Conjugating verbs in Latin?

~ *Choosing* ~

"I choose to believe I am well regarded
and well received by every person I meet.
My talents and abilities are known and recognized by those I meet.
My efforts are well rewarded. My activities are fruitful.
Mentally I take my place among those who get what they go after."

Frederick Bailes, M.D.[159]

[158]Frederick Bailes, M.D., *Basic Principles of the Science of Mind,* a twelve lesson home study course, 1951.

[159]Bailes, *Basic Principles,* p. 27.

One way of looking at life is that it is no more than a series of choices. And, because we have free will, we can choose from all that is on offer, as well as choosing to ignore all those choices and instead creating our own.

When I lived in Australia, I became involved with The Armidale School (TAS), a boys' boarding school in the university town of Armidale some one hundred kilometres away from our sheep and cattle property. One of the teachers at the school was Jim Graham, who augmented his success in teaching English and Drama by serving as playwright and director for TAS's annual Queen Victoria Music Halls. Jim's claim to fame was that when any one of Queen Elizabeth's sons went away to Gordonstoun School in Scotland, Jim would be summoned to teach them. This was a responsibility he thoroughly enjoyed.

During the first half of the 1980s, it was announced that Prince Edward would be visiting Australia and making a formal visit to TAS to meet up with his old English master. This was Prince Edward's gap year between Gordonstoun and Cambridge. Jim Graham collaborated with David Reeves, music teacher, composer, conductor, and organist, in writing a musical for the Prince's visit; they called it *Choices*. It was a time in Prince Edward's life when he was choosing between involving himself further in the family business (represented in the musical by the son of a grazier deciding whether or not to go "on the land") or striking out on his own. I was thrilled to be there for the performance and in awe of Jim's and David's talents as I listened to vocal quartets that would have made Mozart proud.

Whether or not their musical helped Prince Edward make the best choices at the time, I will never know. All I know is we can make new choices in every moment. And so this raises the question—how do we ever manage to stay in a rut? Does that suggest rigid thinking?

Working in community health when she was diagnosed with MS in 1983, home care nurse Linda McGowan realized, "I only had two choices. One was to sit at home, moan, groan, and complain that life was not fair. The second option was to take the skills and strengths that I had and do the best that I could with them."[160] She purchased a wheelchair and set out to travel the Great Wall of China to fulfill a life-long ambition, disability or not, the beginning of many such adventures.

What choices are you making these days that are absolutely in your best interest? What choices could you offer someone else who feels they "have no choice"? Can you "Be the change that you wish to see in the world" that Mahatma Gandhi encourages us to be, by thinking new thoughts and opening your mind and body to the constant newness of life?

~ *Reading Aloud* ~

"One easy way to find the clunky language is to read the chapters aloud."

University of Iowa Press[161]

I copyedit books by reading them aloud. Such a practice reveals the awkward phrasing, the unintended *double entendres*, the repetitive words that don't help anything, the unfinished sentences, the dangling modifiers, the verb-noun disagreements. Reading a passage aloud is incredibly revealing.

I know of English teachers who insist their students read their essays aloud before handing them in. However, many journalists and authors clearly don't read their copy aloud before sending it off for publication. Neither do all self-published authors using the mechanism that was at one time called a "vanity press." It's a mistake not to.

On receiving the printer's proofs of my first book, *Cattle Ranch,* I read them aloud, alternating page by page with my mother. We sat on the sofa with our backs to the big bay window in the living room in the

[160]Linda McGowan, *Travelling the World with MS in a Wheelchair* (North Vancouver: Influence Publishing, 2014), p. 7.

[161]"Revising Humanities Dissertations for Publication," uiowapress.org

manager's house at Douglas Lake Home Ranch, my home at the time. Our Golden Labrador Taffy wandered around our feet until he settled. I can see us now in my mind's eye, reading the printer's sheets, spotting a plural verb here that should be singular and a misspelling there. The whole manuscript took us the better part of two days, as I remember. Memorable! And effective.

Do you read your emails aloud before you send them, ensuring they will not be misunderstood, having been sent in haste? Do you stand and pronounce your magazine article before firing it off to the magazine editor? Do you read the most recent chapter of your book to your dog to be sure it says what you want it to say?

Products

~ *Thought, Word, and Deed* ~

"In the beginning was the Word, and the Word was with God, and the Word was God."

John 1:1[162]

Many cultures, religions, and belief systems state that the Universe is no more than a thought that is, was, and will be created through words that are spoken or sung. These are sonic creationist stories that help humanity understand our ancient origins.

We are co-creators with God, with the Great Creator of All That Is, creating our world, this world, a slightly different world for each of us, depending on the words we use to describe it. In creating our worlds, we join with many others—with the ancient Egyptian god Thoth, God's messenger and scribe, who spoke himself into being; with

[162]Holy Bible, NIV®.

Spider Grandmother who, according to Navajo mythology, sang the song that created the stars; with the Australian aboriginal ancestors who sang the original songlines that created every rock and river, every billabong and bush by naming them; with Oduduwa, son of the Yoruba sky god Olorun, who, with the help of a five-toed chicken, fashioned Africa and its inhabitants from a handful of Earth and a germinated palm nut.

The indigenous people of the Pacific Northwest Coast of North America hold dear the story of Raven, the creator and trickster who coaxed the first people of Haida Gwaii out of their clamshell. One of Haida Gwaii's sons, sculptor Bill Reid, perpetuated and expanded on the creation of his people through his sculpture "Raven and the First Men."[163]

The Supreme Being Io of the Maoris of New Zealand created light from darkness by uttering words; and the Seal People of Greenland believed that the hare created light by speaking the word "day."[164] The Bible states that Adam named "all the wild animals and all the birds in the sky."[165]

Swami Sri Yukteswar in his book, *The Holy Science*, establishes the similarity between the Bible and Sanskrit wisdom by comparing various passages. He claims that "The Word, Amen (*Aum*)" is "*Pranava,* the Word, the manifestation of the omnipotent force."[166] From this came time, space, and the atom. He finds such a Sanskrit claim comparable with "In the beginning was the Word, and the Word was with God, and the Word was God.... Through him all things were made; without him nothing was made that has been made."[167]

In channelling The Golden Ones, Tim Doyle writes that we humans—you and I—are training to become Co-Creator Gods by learning how to manifest: "When we have a desire we wish were a reality, we visualize,

[163]See billreidfoundation.ca/banknote/raven.htm

[164]David Adams Leeming and Margaret Adams Leeming, *Encyclopedia of Creation Myths* (Oxford University Press, 1994).

[165]Holy Bible, NIV®, Genesis 2:19.

[166]Swami Sri Yukteswar, *The Holy Science* (Self-Realization Fellowship, 1984), p. 23.

[167]Holy Bible, NIV®, John 1:1-3.

feel, and **normally we verbalize what it is we will bring into manifestation**."[168] Tim also says, "A vision and a feeling will accompany all manifestations."[169] And so, that expands the basics of "thought, word, and deed" into "seeing, feeling, thinking, speaking," and "manifesting."

What do you desire? See your desire with your third eye—your inner vision. Recognize and acknowledge to yourself the feeling you have when you see your desire with your inner vision. Think about the object of your desire. Speak aloud about this object with others (but not to the point of dissipating your energy to work toward your desire). Manifest your desire through action.

I used this process in writing this book. I recognized my desire to write a book that would cause readers to become more self-aware and to move their lives in more desirable directions. The feeling that accompanied my desire to write this book has been a relentless longing—a knowing that my life would be incomplete without manifesting it. I have given much thought to this book: how, where, and when to write it; how to organize the material; what its title will be; who its audience will be; how to publish it; how to market it. I have spoken my intention aloud: "I am writing a book that I am calling *Trust the Mystery*." And my longing has manifested into the book that you hold in your hands.

What do you desire? See it, feel it, think about it, speak about it (but not too much), and manifest it. What world are you creating through the thoughts, words, and deeds you manifest?

[168] *How to Play the Game of Life: Intermediate Version*, p. 45, my bolding.
[169] Ibid.

~ *Autobiographical Material* ~

"As you entered this dimension through birth,
you had within your consciousness a heroic mission—a goal.
The nature of that goal is firmly written in the deepest recesses of
the inner you, and what you are today …
is actually a part of that goal in various stages of completion."
Stuart Wilde[170]

Each thought I have that leads to an idea I have that leads to a decision I make that leads to an action I take that leads to manifesting something in my life comprises "writing" my life to the plan that I made for myself before incarnating into my current body. As I move closer to the plan, I align myself more closely with what spiritual author Nanci Danison calls "Universal Knowledge" about the Divine Self within.

Tears of joy are indicators; they point to what matters. Sometimes as I write my life, tears spring unbidden to my eyes. You may have experienced this, too.

In the last year of his life, my father wrote out his life story, the life he had "written." Here—from "Ken McGregor's Memoirs"—is the reason he gave for doing so. "While confined to bed in Saanich Hospital in June 1993, so many interesting characters asked me questions, it suggested to me to write a brief survey of my rather varied career." His memoirs are as straightforward as he was, describing his life in the simplest of terms.

Always straightforward, gentle, reserved, modest, and unassuming, my father lived a full life. The eldest of seven, he wanted to train in agricultural stewardship. His father expected him to take over his drapery business in South Wales. Then, the Second World War intervened. When he returned to Wales after being overseas at war for five years, my father began an administrative career in South Wales liaising between Remploy (a company that re-employed disabled people) and its staff. His hobbies

[170]Stuart Wilde, *The Three Keys to Self-Empowerment: Miracles; "Life Was Never Meant to Be a Struggle"; Silent Power* (Hay House, 2004), p. 10.

were rising in rank at the Territorial Army (his final rank was Lieutenant Colonel), rifle shooting at Bisley, chess games in person and by mail, golf, and fishing. His passions were my mum, my sister, and me.

My sister Liz, my mother Vera, and I attend a wedding in 2007; my father Ken is in the inset.

In 1983, he and my mum emigrated to Australia to retire, joining me and my first husband on our sheep property. Then, when we decided to return to Canada, my parents emigrated to that country ahead of us.

My father died of kidney cancer soon after he finished his memoirs. By then, he knew he would. He didn't fuss. In fact, he had not made much fuss about the pains he'd been noticing for months, because my mother was also ill. By the time he spoke up about his level of pain, the first surgery revealed it was too late for the doctors to do anything. They just sewed him up.

What was the life he wrote for himself? It was one of service, loyalty, family, friendship, living life to the best of his ability, to the fullest capacity. Wherever he was, he lived life large. I am so grateful to my father for his straightforwardness and his love.

A friend came to visit me some months after my father had died; my father's plastic-ring-bound memoirs sat unprepossessingly on a bookshelf. The topic of the memoirs came up and my friend began to cry, unwillingly. She expressed disappointment that her own father had not written about his life before he died. He had had three heart arrhythmias, and all three happened within moments of each other when he was aboard his yacht. The shock had caused him to fall overboard and drown.

Your life is the product of the way you have "written" your life. Are you "writing" it in a way that pleases you? Are you also writing *about* your life? What are you learning about yourself as you write about your life?

~ *Contributions* ~

"It is not enough to just be; I want to contribute as well."

Mario[171]

Despite the reminder that we are "human beings" rather than "human doings," most of us want to contribute something to the communities

[171]Told to me by Mario, a Downtown Eastside Vancouver senior, January 2015.

we live in. Canada's Gross National Product (GNP) measures Canada's total economic output. That includes its roads and bridges, books and magazines, cabbages and cattle. It includes ticketed events like concerts and plays, and the use of spaces like hotel banquet and conference rooms. But I'm not just talking about roads and books, plays and hotel rooms.

Each day we live, we expend time and energy. Does our time and energy always equate to an output, to a product? What about Canada's total non-tangible output? For instance, a juggler who performs on the beach and passes the hat and doesn't declare his income: he has brought pleasure to his audience and money to his pocket, but GNP captures neither. A child who is giggling as she runs under a garden sprinkler brings joy to her parents. She has contributed. An audience that applauds a scene in a play brings a smile to the performers' faces; the audience has contributed beyond their ticket cost. A teenager who gives his seat to a white-haired person with a cane has demonstrated compassion.

What about volunteer positions? Not-for-profit organizations provide a range of services that are financially immeasurable. Private gatherings in someone's home may use gasoline for attendees to arrive and electricity to light the event. But even if food and beverages aren't factored in, the result of the gathering is always far more than the sum of the inputs. Homemade jam from blackberries growing wild is tastier than blackberry jam from the store. And, as a gift, it brings great pleasure to its recipient.

Community theatre survives on the willingness of its casts and crews to donate their time. I'm often asked whether I'm paid for the numerous acting roles I've performed and I must answer no. But there is huge recompense, because of the many reasons I act: to entertain, to try on another persona, to portray the human condition to others in larger-than-life ways.

Each of us is a contributing member of society. The question is, "Discounting financial value, what are we contributing? Discord? Towels? Joy? Peace? Flower arrangements? Noise? Paintings that never sell? Flair? Laughter?"

~ *Leaving a Legacy* ~

"It is suggested that before you write your eulogy, you should have a solemn, peaceful and quiet place for writing. Meditation rooms, cemeteries, or churches are all good locations for your own eulogy writing."

eulogyspeech.net[172]

When my mum was still alive and I visited her, we used to watch the television makeover series *Style by Jury*. I have always been a sucker for makeovers; they used to appear in magazines decades ago, when they were mostly about improving a person's hairstyle. There's no doubt that making us feel better about ourselves improves our self-confidence. And once we improve our self-confidence, our posture improves, whereby our breathing improves, whereby our whole body improves from our digestion to our skin, and we start to sparkle.

The *Style by Jury* episode that involved a woman writing her own eulogy introduced us to someone who had lost all self-confidence and all hope for a better life. She seemed to have given up completely. A psychologist instructed the woman to fast forward mentally to the end of her life and to think about what she would like to hear said as a eulogy at her funeral or memorial service.

This was a real challenge for her. At first, she couldn't think what nice words anyone would want to say about her. But then the psychologist encouraged her to think of the desires she still had, such as being a good mother, being a good friend, doing good work at her job, and travelling to places she would love to see.

This instruction turned the tables and in a mock memorial service the woman stood up and delivered her eulogy about herself to a small gathering of friends and family. From that point forward, the items in the eulogy that were highlights in her imagined life became goals in her real life. We, the television audience, could see the woman gain confidence and give up her poor-me attitude.

---

[172]Eulogyspeech.net, "How to Write Your Own Eulogy."

What is the legacy you are going to leave when you die? How would you like people to remember you? For something you have done? Or for something you died still wanting to do? Is anything holding you back?

Chapter 8—Incorporating the Mystery

Writing

~ A Pearl of Wisdom ~

"Mistakes are positive. Mistakes are positive!
You don't go out of your way to make them, but if they happen,
they are opportunities to learn from."
Joshua David Stone, Ph.D.[173]

Sometimes, when we learn a skill—such as playing the piano—we embody that there's a "right way" and a "wrong way" to do it. We learn what mistakes are and we try to avoid them. We learn the rules and the restrictions. And that can inhibit us from creating music with heart. An artist can be inhibited by too much knowledge of art criticism. A trained writer might find it harder to write from her heart. This was brought home to me recently.

A friend of ours, Jody McWhirter, lost her husband Duncan in 2010. Jody held a Celebration of Life at her home, and my husband and I attended. I talked to Pearl there, another friend of Jody's, and we got on to the subjects of working, attending university, and writing. She explained that she had started out as a nurse and then had gone back to university, first to get a bachelor's and then a master's degree in English, but that she doesn't write, because the focus in the university she attended was research rather than creativity. She had then used her English degree training people as medical transcriptionists. She had regrets that she does not write in any way such that her writing might be published.

I explained that I don't have any kind of degree in English (if you don't count Communications) and that I do write. In fact, I've earned the

[173]Joshua David Stone, Ph.D., *Soul Psychology: How to Clear Negative Emotions and Spiritualize Your Life* (Light Technology Publishing, 1994), p. 14.

majority of the money I've ever earned in my life from writing. I told her I was writing this book. She explained that she couldn't begin to write anything because she would be worried about the phrasing, the punctuation, the sentence structure, and the themes, and all of that would get in the way of the creative activity of writing. I sympathized with her.

Her story reminded me of my mother's sister, a scholar with a B.A. in English who never published anything and yet taught writing to others. Hers was the same pattern. And in thinking that, I thought what a blessing that my father had limited my career choices to physiotherapist, optometrist, and librarian, because I wasn't hampered with too much knowledge of sentence structure; I just took English and Latin grammar at high school, linguistics and communications at university. Okay, that's sounding like quite a bit of theory, but I got the point. I write (and these days edit) because no one has specifically told me *how* to write (and edit).

At times, I have done the "If only I had gone on to university and studied English" route when I thought back over my life. But now I can say, look at where it might NOT have got me!

Thanks, Pearl, for the pearl of wisdom.

Having viewed education from a critical perspective that suggests education might be inhibiting and unhelpful, I must now praise and support those who teach in ways that provide students with all the knowledge of the topic under discussion while also freeing them to experiment within their chosen medium.

I always find it interesting that I, for one, learn something about myself from talking to others. I explained a bit of my writing process to Pearl, explaining that I write the most freely at the computer with my eyes closed. I just write and write and can go deep into my memories, connecting the dots, staying with the story and the event, and not getting caught up in the surface of words, spelling, and punctuation. There will always be time to go back, correct, and refine. But at the beginning, I just want to do the work of getting onto the page the story themes and development ideas that would otherwise wake me up in the wee, small hours through the agency of my spirit guides. That's work enough. It's active meditation rather than the different approach of copyediting and substantive editing.

Since attending Insite in 1999, I have thought of my blind acceptance of my father's guidance into a career as something of a mistake on my part. I didn't give myself time to consider deep down what I wanted to do. But when I examine the possible truth in Joshua David Stone's view that "Mistakes are positive," I can see that my presumed mistake in becoming a physiotherapist is what brought me to the country in which I and my children have thrived. Canada needed physiotherapists when I applied to immigrate; another person with an English major wasn't needed.

I woke up early on the morning of July 30, 2010 having a conversation with my angels. It started with my envy of a friend who has a beautiful garden, a lovely two-storey house, and few financial worries. My angels piped up, "If you had a big garden, you'd garden; if you had a big house, you'd keep it clean, entertain, and have people to stay. You have a husband who supports you in all you want to do and who does most of the cooking and shopping. What more do you want? So we keep you poor and needing extra money so you write. We'll keep you broke if it kills us. So you'll write."

And then I thought, "You're my angels, you're not alive in the way that you can be 'killed' anyway." And they laughed! And I wondered to myself, "Did I have that conversation with myself, with my angels, really?"

In the end, does it matter? Because the result is the same. I write and edit to earn money, and I accept angelic conversations. Thanks, angels.

Do you have regrets—"mistakes" even—that, when you think about them deeply, are advantages? Are you doing now what you wanted to do decades ago? Are you doing something altogether different? Is there something else you'd like to be doing? What's holding you back? Don't wait for a diploma to qualify you to do a certain thing. And don't let a diploma hold you back from exercising that skill. Just do it. But there again, if a diploma is required to do what you want to do, what is holding you back from getting it?

~ *Inspired Writing* ~

"'In shallow men the fish of little thoughts cause much commotion.
In oceanic minds the whales of inspiration make hardly a ruffle.'
This observation from the Hindu scriptures is not without discerning humor."
Paramahansa Yogananda[174]

When I observe someone with excellent posture walking down the street, I am inspired to stand up a little taller. But, strange to say, I am almost equally inspired (or more) by observing someone with very poor posture, created perhaps by a spinal joint disease such as ankylosing spondylitis.

In the same way, I am as often inspired by bad writing as by good writing, since (although the good causes me to imagine and dream and think) bad writing inspires me to write: to realize that I can write as well as the next person and that, if I am willing to put in the 95 percent of perspiration to add to the 5 percent of inspiration that a book requires, I too can write a book, a good book.

Inspiration is all around us all the time, for us to notice and act upon. Recently, I asked Reverend Christina Lunden whether both writing and editing are my callings. She replied that spirit would take away the time to write or the time to edit, if I should not be doing them. Soon after that, I suddenly had the time to just write, which encouraged me to continue writing.

We can write in many ways—non-fiction, fiction, magazine articles, poetry, journaling, blog posts, emails, and letters. When an idea comes

[174]Yogananda, *Autobiography,* Chapter 12: Years in My Master's Hermitage.

along and begs to be recorded in words, it often carries its form with it. For instance, wonder about the power packed into a seed may beg to be expressed as a poem. A thought about how to fix an editorial process stirs me into creating a Word document with a table and emailing it to my colleagues.

Inspired writing is that writing which helps us move efficiently through our lives with acceptance of the mystery of our place in the Universe. Its format does not matter. What does matter is that we act upon our urgings to record something.

I first read about "Morning Pages"—three pages of handwriting done first thing in the morning—in Julia Cameron's *The Artist's Way*. She says, "They seem to have nothing to do with creativity, but what they do is clear your mind.... It's as though what you're writing down, in meditation terms, is cloud thoughts." She explains that they are a clearing exercise for the mind, to allow greater consciousness, greater awareness of those thoughts that are trying to get through the clutter.

I also see the discipline of writing Morning Pages as a way to flex one's creative writing muscles. Then, I call them a morning "down lode," to coin a term that shows how valuable they sometimes are.

Some people just know they have a book inside that's burning to get out. A friend recently told me that she did an exercise to discover what was important in her life and what revealed itself was the driving desire, the essential need to write what she has learned in her lifetime, to share it with others in book form. And, basically, she didn't know how to get going. My suggestion was to start, to start anywhere—the end, the beginning, the middle, with one particular story, with an overall shape, with a title, anywhere—and to make a habit to write at least half an hour a day. A burning desire combined with disciplined action appeals strongly to our conscious mind and helps us to reveal to ourselves what our book will be about and how we will reach our goal.

A while ago, I heard a story about a high school student who couldn't write any more than a few very mundane words in an essay until the subject she was asked to write about was shrunk down from generalities to specifics. In this student's case, she found her writing voice when her teacher assigned her to write about a brick, one particular brick in a certain wall in a certain street in her town. And that brick became for her a portal into her own originality, her own writing voice.

When we are first exercising our writing muscles, we often make the mistake of editing what we have written as we write. It helps to realize that being a writer is a very different role from being an editor. A writer has one set of goals and skills; an editor has a completely different set. My suggestion for when you start out would be to write, write, write, and don't read what you've written, the Morning Pages way, uncritically. Then, leave what you've written overnight or longer. When you do pick it up to reread it, you can edit it with a clearer mind.

What inspires you to write? The healing it will bring you? The memories you will find, reveal, dust off, and release? The improved organization it will bring to your day? The conclusions you will come to as you go from one idea to the next? The revelations that will arise as you write? What is your story? What was your story of yourself last year? What will it be next year? Are you changing as you write about yourself? Or someone else?

~ *Grievance Stories* ~

"[E]ach decision that you make is one between
a grievance and a miracle. Each grievance stands
like a dark shield of hate before the miracle it would conceal."

A Course in Miracles[175]

[175]Schucman, Helen, with William Thetford, *A Course in Miracles* (Foundation for Inner Peace, 1996), Lesson 78.

Fred Luskin, Ph.D., author of *Forgive for Good*, claims that three core components create a longstanding hurt, grudge, or grievance: the exaggerated taking of personal offense; the blaming of another person for one's feelings; and the creation of "a grievance story." Having deduced this, Luskin as Director of the Stanford University Forgiveness Project developed ways to transform offense, blame, and the desire to create false stories into forgiveness, hope, and optimism.

I find absolutely fascinating the idea that creating grievance stories explains to ourselves why we are where we are in our lives. As a soul counsellor, I know that we each walk around within a cloud of thoughtforms, some that we create and some that others create about us or for us and that we accept. Through my Akashic Record, I was able to clear myself of many of these thoughtforms, just through intention.

Sometimes people's personal stories are so visible that it seems as though they are walking around with a dark cloud above their heads. This reminds me of when Winnie the Pooh was *being* a "little black rain cloud," trying to deceive the bees from whom he was hoping to steal honey. He had a purpose for disguising himself. We too may have a purpose for disguising ourselves; but unfortunately, we tend to confuse ourselves with our disguises.

It can be difficult for us to see how false our own stories are. They are a combination of beliefs, misbeliefs, stories, myths, mysteries, and our own histories integrated into convenient, believable, shape-shifting explanations of why such and such in our lives is not working and why something else could.

How great it would be to look in a mirror and see our own little black rain clouds. For me, one route to do that is by examining the idea that the "other person" is to blame. In itself, this seems to require that we assign a benefit to the other person. Perhaps, if we could name this benefit, we could start to turn the whole event on its head and remove the other person from the equation. And then our own grievance story might dissolve.

Let's try.

A woman might create a grievance story about her husband leaving her for a younger woman. The story might contain such elements as the other woman's conniving nature, her youth, her blatant sexuality, her lack of morals. The story probably also contains elements describing the errant husband: his inability to commit to the marital relationship, his restlessness, his wandering eye, his lasciviousness. The woman creating the story might cast herself as the innocent female, the deserted wife, the hard-working housewife and mother, and even the daughter for whom male-female relationships were always difficult.

Where does the truth reside? Probably somewhere else, in a place not mentioned, in a time unrelated to the current events.

How can the deserted wife change the story? By naming the benefit to the other parties. She could say the other woman is gaining a lover. And she could wonder, "For how long?" She could say the other woman is gaining a companion. And she could wonder, "How good a companion?" She could say the other woman has found someone to help pay her bills. And she could wonder, "What extra bills will he create for her?"

The wife could try examining the benefits for the husband. She could say that he no longer had to be loyal to her. Yet she would realize that to benefit in any long-term relationship, we have to be loyal to our partner. She could say that he would be satisfying his roving eye. But she would realize that, if he has a roving eye, then this relationship might not last long, either. She could say that by moving on, he was filling his life with more excitement, and this, yet again, would demonstrate that the new woman in her husband's life was probably just one more in a string of new women.

I have a friend whose husband married and remarried about five times. She was number three, I think. At one time, they went for marital counselling and their psychologist said that her husband had never left his teenage years behind; he continued into his sixties to yearn for the adrenalin rush that accompanies the chase.

Our fictional deserted wife has now chipped away with her rock hammer of reasoning at the truth for the other parties involved. Perhaps she was hanging onto a false belief in the first place, the misbelief that she and her husband were together for their lifetimes. What about her own part in the story? Was she as loyal and reliable a partner as she could be? Are there other benefits to being single again? Now is the time for her to look carefully at those benefits. And at her hurt feelings, her exaggerated personal offense.

Let me describe a misbelief I had that I stopped from becoming a grievance story. My husband and I vacationed in New York in April 2014 and, on day four of our week visiting that fascinating city, I fell coming out of a subway station and broke my hip. One of the first thoughts I had (after we had found out that we did indeed have travel insurance!) was a memory of what a broken hip meant to older women in the 1960s. Frequently, they would die soon after.

Christian and I enjoy Central Park in New York, 2014.

Fortunately, soon after my emergency hip-replacement surgery, I learned that people today can make complete recoveries from hip surgery. I decided that I would be in the complete-recovery crowd. Being an actor and a physiotherapist, I have been mimicking gaits for decades, so I tried different styles of walking until I could completely disguise that I have an artificial hip. For a while it was easier to go downstairs than upstairs, but now it's all the same.

Even as I recovered from hip surgery, that old belief about dying from a hip fracture was still hovering around my subconscious, depressing me. My acupuncturist, JZ Bown, who is also a medical intuitive, gave me several ThetaHealing sessions, turning around that misbelief.

What irony that my vacation email responder while we were in New York said, "I am out of the office for a short spring break." Be careful what you wish for!

Are you cherishing a grievance story? What are its elements? Can you flesh out the grievance stories for the other parties involved? Does writing about the various grievance stories help to dispel the problem? See it differently? What misbeliefs are you holding onto? Are they holding you back?

~ *A Family Genealogy* ~

"My kids have often asked how they are related to the Morgans,
the McGregors, the Thomsons, and so on. I am preparing something
for Christmas (or as soon thereafter as I can get it done!)
for my offspring and Liz's offspring about our ancestors
and I wanted to add more names, dates, and places to what is on this table."

Nina Shoroplova[176]

[176]An email request for family information to my cousins, December 2012.

I recently completed a time-consuming self-assigned project of creating a family history: 165 pages of photos, facts, and opinions. An aunt of mine, Sheila Morgan, had created the bulk of the older genealogical material over many years; she was the family historian. So I took her carefully created family trees—about a dozen of them in all—and rekeyed the pertinent ones into MS Word tables showing the family lineage of my father's father's paternal line, my father's father's maternal line, my father's mother's paternal line.... You get the idea.

Then I proceeded to contact my first cousins—all twenty-seven of them—to ask if they were willing to share their birthdates, places, marriage dates, whether they'd had children, their children's names and dates, where everyone now lived, and what their passions were. What a wonderful project! Almost everyone responded warmly and co-operated, in some cases, to the extent of sending photographs.

At the same time, I was visiting my aging mother on a regular basis, and she had a large collection of old family photographs that she kept in a hollow footstool. So, bit by bit, one by one, we went through those photographs. And what a joy when Mum remembered the photo details, or when a date, location, or the names of the people in the photograph was written on the back.

At one time during the 1970s and 80s, I laboriously wrote on the back of every photograph I took. But when the era of digital photography came about, I didn't even print my photos. With the challenges and disappointments of digital photography becoming more obvious, for a while I returned to printing up some of our better pictures and putting them in binders.

Family histories are based on stories, mostly oral. Without words somehow attached to photos, without facts recorded—like the date someone emigrated from Wales to Canada—we have to rely on memory. And our memories are faulty, personal, adjustable.

Does it matter that our ancestors' names and stories are gone? What about our parents' stories? Our children's? Our own? How do you share your memories of your aunts and uncles and cousins with your children? Your memories of your parents and grandparents?

Righting

~ *Dialoguing* ~

"In the course of my life, I have often had to eat my words,
and I must confess that I have always found it a wholesome diet."
Sir Winston Churchill

When I started thinking about it, I identified so many styles of dialoguing that I had to list them as comparative pairs to clarify them for myself.

discussing versus arguing
sharing a point of view versus debating
interviewing versus cross-examining
questioning versus interrogating
directing versus ordering
reminding versus nagging
teasing versus bullying
joking versus bandying
consulting versus conferring
advising versus counselling
reciting versus lecturing
gossiping versus rumour-mongering
recounting versus bragging
describing versus exaggerating
instructing versus teaching

requesting versus challenging
explaining versus digressing

Your own list might easily be as long but different.

Each of these contrasting dialogue forms shows two particular styles of speaking, each with a different purpose and intent. As we consider each term, we know the amount of energy and preparation required, the tone of voice likely to be used, the bodily stance, and even the amount of engagement of the fight-and-flight system in each person. Sometimes, one form of talking can lead to the other, as for instance with "discussing versus arguing." How often we have all observed and/or been part of a discussion that turns into an argument!

Other pairs are divided more formally: "interviewing versus cross-examining," for example. An interviewer might be a journalist, a television host, a researcher, or a telephone marketer. By contrast, a cross-examiner is likely to be working for an institution that needs to prove something, such as the police force or the armed forces or the barristers in a court of law.

The words we say to each other and the way we say these words create the different worlds we live in. And because we have so many styles of speaking to and with each other, we have hundreds and even thousands of different words to describe our manner of speaking. While I have used the present participle form of the verbs to describe these manners of speaking, I could as easily have used nouns: "exaggeration, fight, argument, rumour, lecture."

The reason I use verbs rather than nouns to describe the ways we speak to each other is that verbs denote something that is moving through the present moment; nouns are fixed descriptions of things that stand still. Verbs drive the action; verbs are moving. Nouns stand for the event; nouns create inertia. If we want to change and improve our words and thereby our worlds, it is therefore easier to alter the verb form of what is going on than to alter the noun.

This process is very similar to the verbal de-escalation techniques that are used in situations where violence or even crises might occur. As the Reverend Jessica Schaap, priest at St. Paul's Anglican Church, stated in a recent sermon, this is a way of showing compassion to one another.

Citing an example will make this clearer. I'm with a friend and we are discussing a tricky point of negotiation. I feel our language heating up. I don't want to start arguing, and thereby risk estranging ourselves from each other. If I can observe how we are discussing this thing, I can more effectively stay on the gentle bantering side of things and avoid moving to the rougher side of trying to prove my point. I can recognize the continuous fluidity of the situation through the verbs I am using to describe the process in my mind. I allow my quantum wisdom of observing to improve my behaviour.

When we are the observers of what we are doing and being, we are able to pull ourselves out from our emotions. They are what tend to keep us stuck in one place because they are so closely allied with our ego. Emotions are to the ego what foot soldiers are to the general: enablers.

The less desirable alternative to using verbs to perceive what is going on is to use nouns. This way I would see us having a discussion that is bordering on being an argument turning into a full-blown row with horrible results. The event becomes fixed through the nouns I am using.

I challenge you, the next time you find yourself in a verbal situation that is going in a direction you don't want it to go, to pull back from your emotions and describe the exchange to yourself in your mind with a verb. Be the witness. Then find a verb to describe a gentler action of what is happening. In moments, you'll be employing the skills and tactics attached to that gentler verb, and the possible "situation" will have diffused. You will have just gentled your world.

What are your default modes of dialoguing? Can you observe yourself even as you "dialogue"? Can you adjust your verbal descriptions of the dialogue in the moment? Can you use verbs as descriptors so you can change them?

ॐ

~ *Singing Is Different from Speaking* ~

"I turned to Sy. 'Sing "Happy Birthday" for me, will ya? Come on, Sy. Sing!'
"He stared at me in utter disbelief. Then he did it: he began to sing."
Allan J. Hamilton, M.D., FACS[177]

Did you know that we speak from one part of our brain and we sing from another? I learned that in *The Scalpel and the Soul*, by neurosurgeon Allan J. Hamilton, M.D. How amazing! Once the chief of neurosurgery and chairman of the Department of Surgery at the University of Arizona Health Sciences Center, Hamilton proved this with a patient of his.

Hamilton describes how his friend and fellow neurosurgeon, Sydney Sonnenberg, M.D., asked him to carry out a difficult surgical procedure to remove a brain tumour wrapped around the speech centre in Sonnenberg's brain. Through the intricacies of the surgery, Dr. Sonnenberg lost his power of speech. Dr. Hamilton was devastated at the outcome, despite having saved his friend's life.

Concurrently, Dr. Sonnenberg agreed to be guest of honour at the opening of a new wing at the Arizona Alzheimer's Research Center, having raised the funds and been one of its specialists. He prepared a speech for his wife to deliver on his behalf.

Dr. Hamilton continued to agonize over the outcome of the surgery that had silenced his friend, until he remembered a theory that "had been developed by a brilliant neurologist named Norm Mueller.... One of Mueller's keen observations was that there were cases recorded in the medical literature about people who could not speak but could sing. Mueller was struck by the fact that the human central nervous system did not process musical sounds the same way it did the auditory patterns of speech. He had found and described several patients with strokes involving the left hemisphere who were aphasic [could not speak].... They couldn't utter a word. But ... they could still sing!"[178]

[177]Allan J. Hamilton, M.D., FACS, *The Scalpel and the Soul: Encounters with Surgery, the Supernatural, and the Healing Power of Hope* (Jeremy P. Tarcher, Penguin Group, 2009), p. 151.
[178]Hamilton, *The Scalpel and the Soul*, p. 151.

Dr. Hamilton told his friend to sing "Happy Birthday." And that became a breakthrough for Sy Sonnenberg to express himself vocally, on pitch. Using the simple melody of "Pop Goes the Weasel," Dr. Sonnenberg gave a unique speech to great approval.

I remember a *Style by Jury* episode in which a woman had no voice, not because she had had surgery but because life had taught her to diminish her presence; she could not even express her anger at the injustices in her life in anything more than a whisper. Program experts encouraged her to recast her life story like an opera plot and to sing aloud her challenges. Encouraging her bit by bit, the vocal coach had the candidate proclaim her words to the world louder and louder until she was able to feel she was in charge of her life.

In this instance, singing helped a woman to reclaim her autonomy, her freedom from the influence of past unpleasant memories.

Singing can be a wonderful way for someone to "find their voice." Singing involves every aspect of ourselves—our physicality, emotions, thoughts, and connection with the deepest aspect of ourselves where our Divinity resides. And our voiceprint is as unique as our fingerprint, as well known to our loved ones and friends as our faces.

Do you sing? Where do you sing? Do you sing for the fun of it? In preparation for a performance? Alone? With others? What sort of songs do you sing? Do you sing your own songs?

~ *Unintentional Negative Affirmations* ~

"Our deepest fear is not that we are inadequate.
Our deepest fear is that we are powerful beyond measure.
It is our light, not our darkness that most frightens us."

Marianne Williamson[179]

179 Marianne Williamson, *Return to Love, Reflections on the Principles of "A Course in Miracles"* (HarperOne, 1996), p. 190.

When we say, "I am," we voice who we are, which can contribute to our healing. Whenever we say, "I am" and follow it up with more words, the Universe does its best to ensure that whatever we have said is what happens.

Saying "I am" is like throwing the proverbial boomerang that returns to us. It is partly to do with our subconscious mind being a faithful servant to its master, our conscious mind. But it's more than that, because the "I am" statement affects those around us and even those who are far away, thanks to the Law of Attraction.

So, if someone were to say, "I am never going to finish this job," then, sure enough, they would never finish that job. Either that or it would take them a huge amount of effort and time to finish, and might not be that successful. If someone were to say, "I am short of time," then again that would be their experience.

We are co-creators of our lives.

"I am" as a statement is the topic of much spiritual writing. Wayne Dyer writes about it at length from a biblical perspective. "Run through as large an inventory as you can of the things that you would like to define your life. Then make the shift in your imagination from an *I am not* or *I am hoping* to become *I am*. You want what follows I am to be congruent with your highest self, which is God."[180]

Only claim those states that you recognize in yourself and wish to prolong. If you don't like the behaviour you're describing, don't describe it aloud. Find its opposite and state that aloud instead. Go from "I am never going to finish this job," to "I can see that I am going to finish this job soon." Things will improve.

There's more. Imagine a coin with negative affirmations that we dread manifesting on one side and positive affirmations that we welcome on the other side. The centre of this coin is the hard metallic position of non-affirmations in the middle.

"Non-affirmation" is a word I may have coined for a wish held inside

[180]drwaynedyer.com/blog/the-power-of-i-am

by someone who has recognized a desire and keeps silent about it. I have written about my passionate desire as a teenager to sing a solo, a wish I kept hidden, even from myself. Someone might hide their talent for drawing portraits; another might know that they would love to befriend a lonely old lady, but they do nothing about it in case it appears to be interfering.

The longer we stay silent and undemonstrative about our gifts, talents, and desires, the longer our paths become. Marianne Williamson captures the tone of a non-affirmation when she imagines someone saying, "Who am I to be brilliant, gorgeous, talented, fabulous?" She would answer, "Who are you not to be?"[181]

How do you want your life to improve? What are the words that describe that success? What do you yearn to do? Who do you yearn to be? Where do you yearn to travel? To live? How do you yearn to behave? What is stopping you? When will you *live* your one life?

~ *Apologizing* ~

"'I cannot apologize,' I repeated, 'because I have done nothing to apologize for.'
"More jeers.
"'A man—if he is a man,' I accentuated, 'will only apologize
if he has done wrong and then he must apologize.
Do you want me to lie to you?...
Are you asking me to give up my manhood
and lie like a coward just because I am being threatened?'"

Lawrence Anthony[182]

What does it mean, "to apologize"? When I apologize to someone for something—whether we are together or I am sending the energy of the

[181]Ibid.
[182]Anthony, *The Elephant Whisperer*, p. 212.

apology to them by email or phone or etherically—I feel I am taking some responsibility and offering some regret for what took place. The clause "I am sorry" can be the full extent of an apology.

Women say, "I'm sorry" more often than men do. And Canadians say it more than other nationalities. It's a self-effacing statement, but it doesn't always mean the person is taking responsibility for what took place; often it just offers regret without the responsibility; it offers regret that the other person is having to endure something: "I empathize with your situation."

It's clear in the quotation above that Lawrence Anthony had no intention of apologizing to the Zulu hearing over land disagreements between neighbouring tribes, as he felt that an apology would imply his guilt. He stood his ground and, eventually, hostilities settled down.

Implicitly, an apology seeks forgiveness. *A Course in Miracles* says, "Fear condemns and love forgives" (Lesson 46). And the only person we really have to forgive is ourselves.

I am reminded of ho'oponopono, the forgiveness prayer used in ancient

times by Hawaiian Kahunas and recently developed by Ihaleakala Hew Len, Ph.D. for modern day use. The prayer in my usage goes like this: "Please forgive me. I forgive you. I'm sorry. I love you. Thank you." It's simple and powerful.

It takes responsibility and offers regret and does more.

As always, the intention that we attach to our petitions is the most important piece.

If you want to know more about the power and effectiveness of ho'oponopono, there's plenty on the internet about it. Hew Len, Ph.D., and his co-author, Joe Vitale, Ph.D., have written several books about it and there is more at zerolimits.info. What is intriguing is that Dr. Hew Len healed a ward of mentally ill criminals by reading their case studies and repeating the ho'oponopono, again and again. I've read that he worked only on himself; he healed himself and, in healing himself, he healed the criminals to the point where they could be released from prison.

What more powerful example can show us that we are all one? Is there an apology you would like to offer someone? Would you like to be forgiven an action, a behaviour, a thought? Is there someone you would like to forgive? Do you feel unforgiven? Forgive yourself.

Riting

~ Creating a Spiritual Practice ~

"The spiritual path is not an escape from life's duties but the fulfillment of them."
Barbara Y. Martin and Dimitri Moraitis[183]

On top of my piano, I have a display of seven-metal singing bowls, bowls that are also known as "standing bells." Some of them are old, traditional Tibetan bowls that have faded markings inside, faint memories of their original use as bowls for serving food. One of them is pristine in its newness, its purposeful manufacturedness. I almost didn't buy this one, because it was created to be a singing bowl rather than for some other purpose; somehow the original Tibetan bowls held more meaning for me. But then I heard the tone of the new bowl and it spoke directly to my ear and my heart. It sings easily with a purity that I found appealing. Its note is G above middle C, the note that many associate with the throat chakra.

Toning a note in harmony with a singing bowl is a desirable way for me to find my inner peace, to be present to myself, to seek home through *Om*. When I do it, it becomes a spiritual practice, like a ritual. It assists me in finding my own "unique frequency and vibration"—myself.[184] I find myself through other ways too—walking, writing, singing, and acting.

Creating a spiritual practice is very different from choosing a religion.

[183]Martin and Moraitis, *Change Your Aura, Change Your Life,* p. 65.
[184]Ibid.

Religion and spirituality are two different animals. While a church service is ritualized into a shared public liturgy, creating an individual or shared spiritual practice is totally personal and may be as varied as lighting candles, walking on the seashore, counting stars, sitting quietly in meditation, and gardening. Children's author and singer/songwriter Jasmine Bharucha says, "When you show your love and take care of the planet, you are loving and taking care of yourself. And everything on the planet loves and takes care of you."[185]

We can also make a spiritual practice of opening ourself up to inspired writing on a daily basis (see the section in chapter eight, "Writing").

These days, I'm following James Twyman's *A Course in Miracles* 2015 Revival Movement. And doing Barbara Y. Martin's Higher Self Meditation. And singing. And more.

Do you have a regular spiritual practice? Has it evolved over time as you have evolved? Is it as meaningful now as it once was? Is it serving its purpose of deepening your knowledge of yourself as spirit? Can you remain aware of your spiritual nature without a spiritual practice?

~ *Superstitions* ~

"If an actor speaks the name 'Macbeth' in a theatre prior to a performance,
he or she is required to leave the theatre building,
spin around three times, spit, curse, and then knock to be allowed back in."

Marjorie Garber[186]

When ideas and beliefs become habits with emotions attached, they can move into the realm of superstitions and even obsessive–compulsive disorders.

---

[185]Jasmine Bharucha, *Who Am I?* (North Vancouver: Influence Publishing, 2014).

[186]Marjorie Garber, *Shakespeare's Ghost Writers: Literature as Uncanny Causality* (Methuen, 2010).

I have played more than twenty roles in plays and musicals in the fourteen years between 2001 and 2015. Theatre carries its own superstitions, like never speaking the name of Shakespeare's play *Macbeth* inside a theatre but calling it "the Scottish play"; never whistling backstage; never wishing anyone good luck before a performance.

I do so much theatre because it is fun and it's a great test of my ability to build my self-confidence and keep my memory active. The other reason is that each role gives me an opportunity to step into someone else's shoes, if only temporarily. I get character roles—a wife who gets murdered, a mother who tries to amend, or the "scabby old bat" guest at Fawlty Towers who tries everyone's patience. In that way, I find out how cantankerous people create a cantankerous world around them, fearful people create a fearful world, and loving people create a loving world. Acting is an opportunity to live multiple lives in my one life.

A superstition is no more than a ritual created around something that errs on the side of danger, darkness, pain, anger, or fear. Once we understand how the superstition arose in the first place, we can release the fear and just honour the common sense. Maybe! Unfortunately, *Macbeth* is mired in superstitions seemingly unfounded in reality. But, just in case those listening allow superstitions to run live their lives, I avoid saying "*Macbeth*" in a theatre.

At one time, backstage crew used a variety of whistles to communicate to each other which backdrop or piece of set to fly in at a specific moment. Whistling at other times might encourage crew to fly something in and injure those onstage. Nowadays, crew use an intercom system with headsets between the stage manager, the booth operator (for lights and sounds), and the rest of the crew. So whistling is no longer dangerous. But I still don't whistle inside a theatre.

And I never wish anyone good luck before a performance. I say, "Break a leg!" The best explanation for the basis of that habit is that the full-length curtains one waits behind before an onstage entrance are called "legs." As soon as an actor walks between the legs, she has "broken the legs."

What superstitions do you honour? How did you first accept them? Are they still useful? If they aren't, can you drop them?

~ *Planning Silence* ~

"Silence, in the corridor!"

Howell's School prefects[187]

Often, we can share as much honesty and clear messaging in loving relationships through silence as through chatter. Just being in the same space, driving somewhere, sitting side-by-side at a coffee counter, at the dinner table, in the evening reading books, can create a very comforting silence that is intimate and familiar.

We know the shared mood between ourself and someone else that exists during silence. We know whether the mood is angry, fearful, relaxed, or content. Such emotions vibrate around us as loudly and clearly as any radio channel with a clear reception.

At Howell's School, one of the most difficult rules was the one of silence. We girls were to be silent in the corridors, silent in the assembly hall, silent when lining up for lunch, silent before saying grace, silent in class until called upon to respond. There were many other rules, too, such as not running in the halls. But the most difficult rule was to hold our tongues.

I was a fairly quiet child. I had been very shy when young and only gradually learned to speak out. So it was sometimes easier for me to not chatter to my girlfriends when I was lining up for lunch, walking in the corridors, and at my desk. I gradually learned to be silent. It became a mark of respect. It became a way in which I was able to develop the awareness that I was more than my body, because it helped me develop my observer. And now, I think it is one of the ways in which I become more self-aware.

In 2013, I had my first opportunity to enjoy a full day of silence.

[187]In the late 1950s and 1960s.

Actually, it wasn't a day of silence so much as a day of only toning and not talking. It was day six of the 2013 Sound Healing Intensive. Toning is harmonizing with each other on one note with one vowel for one breath. And then breathing and toning again. One can also tone alone or with a singing bowl or another instrument.

I wondered, as the planned day came close, how I would manage. Perhaps I thought back to when I had been a girl in high school, struggling to keep quiet at times when I was bursting to say something.

When the day came, I was astonished how much I enjoyed the release of the responsibility of having to speak. I didn't have to be clever, witty, funny, droll, succinct, topical, intelligent, current, or polite. I could just acknowledge the other person with a bow of my head and continue thinking my own thoughts. These days, I enjoy thinking more than I enjoy talking; perhaps I always have.

The day passed easily and smoothly. I spent it more alone than usual. When I wasn't toning, I was mostly walking outdoors, observing, thinking, listening, enjoying, and appreciating the sounds and shapes of nature all around me. I found it to be a very creative day.

Do you allow yourself to be silent sometimes, to access your deepest recesses and your connection with nature around you? Could you be silent for an hour, a day, a week?

~ *Intentional Affirmations* ~

"I'm gorgeous!"

High Commander Dick Solomon[188]

I love watching episodes of *3rd Rock from the Sun*; the sense of humour is so refreshing, pointing out the absurdity of the ways we behave on Earth, as portrayed by a bunch of "aliens" from another "rock." John Lithgow is

[188]Performed by John Lithgow in TV series *3rd Rock from the Sun*.

particularly refreshing when he claims, "I'm gorgeous!" What a wonderful affirmation!

We can attune to a state in which we enable our ego to step aside and allow our own Divine truth, the full truth of who we are, to come through. We are accessing quantum wisdom. When we can speak with such wisdom, we are channelling ourselves and our Divine knowledge.

Sometimes we might read an article or a book and think to ourselves, "That person is certainly full of themselves." There is a difference between "being full of ourselves" in an egoic way—boastful and inflated because of our accomplishments—and being full of our Higher Selves, allowing ourselves to be a mouthpiece for that Divine part of ourselves and our Source in a way that recognizes we are here as Divine beings having a physical experience, again, to learn and progress.

When we stand aside from our physical self and our ego, we can see our accomplishments more easily for what they truly are. This is wonderful.

About ten years ago, in an effort to recognize my path at the time, I took a piece of paper and wrote on it all the activities, all the actions that I did and enjoyed. Then I took the first letters of each of the words that remained on the page after I had crossed off some of the less favourite ones; I had twelve letters left. I moved them around as though I were trying for the fifty-point bonus in a game of Scrabble®. I came up with a word that made some sense to me: *Wrasmadascle*. I pronounced it raz-ma-'dazzle. At the time, I wanted to shine a little more brightly, so the sound of "dazzle" really appealed. I was honouring Marianne Williamson's appeal for each of us to recognize how great our potential is.

I registered Wrasmadascle in British Columbia's registry of companies as a single entrepreneurship. Some years later, because I found that my customers could not pronounce the word (I was selling natural products online at the time), I shortened the name to *Wrasma*. The acronym still described six of my favourite roles and activities: writer, researcher, author, singer, musician, and actor.

Gathering all my favourite descriptors of myself into one word launched my ability to connect with my foundational energies and find a harmonious way to run my online business. By recognizing the energies in myself that I most identified with, I was able to be myself more fully.

My soul-counselling clients were often amazed to hear that our purpose in life is to be who we are as fully as possible. It is a blessing that my clients' particular skills and attributes came through clearly and accurately through the Soul Realignment™ process, allowing them to see themselves more clearly through someone else's words.

When we recognize ourselves clearly in this way, it's easier to get on to our path, the one we follow when we are most closely aligned with our Divine selves. Joseph Campbell encourages us to "follow your bliss."

Recently, I did the exercise again. I was easily able to recognize the energy bringing me the greatest joy and affinity: "editor." Although I had performed the task of editing for decades, it was not in my original list of beloved roles. This year I pluralized *Wrasma* with an "e" to include this favourite role and made it *Wrasmae*.

So, I thought, "I am an editor," someone who would soon advertise her editorial skills and experience, get new business cards, and so on. The name for the website would be "The Healing Pen." For some reason or reasons, I did not do any of those steps. I continued to carry my "holistic healer" business cards and just edited the page on my Whole Health on Purpose website that said I am available to edit. But I still recognized very strongly within: "I am an editor."

Because of this awareness that editing is a strong skill set for me and that I am most attracted to the spiritual and inspirational genres, I am now working as an editor for a publisher of spiritual and inspirational books.

The more specific chain of events is fascinating. Indeed, I often find chains of events fascinating. It's as though someone is stepping on all the right stepping stones across the pond and getting to the new land on the other side without falling in. At times, it's nothing short of miraculous.

This chain of events started in the late 1990s when an intuitive and generous man called Brock Tully opened a wonderful metaphysical store on Denman Street, just around the corner from my home. I am always drawn to metaphysical stores—the sweetness of the incense and beeswax candles, the bright colours of imported clothing and silk scarves, the figurines of Hindu gods and goddesses, the tinkling timbre of the wind chimes, the inspiration pouring out of all the books. The store didn't stay long. There is a very fast turnover on Denman Street; lease rates are constantly rising, and the tourist season is short. But I never forgot Brock, the big-whiskered guy who has biked around North America with three different fund-raising campaigns (totalling 50,000 kilometres) to create a kinder world. He lives the philosophy.

Fast forward I-don't-know-how-many years to a Saturday morning in 2014 when I saw Brock on the sidewalk of my street selling his beautifully calligraphied, charmingly illustrated book of heart sayings. We chatted, I think for the first time. I told him how much I had loved his bookstore and how sorry I had been to see it close. He told me about the books he has written—and calligraphied—and I bought one: *Reflections for Sharing Dreams*. I gave him my business card, after taking a pen out of my purse and adding the word "editor" to it so he would remember our discussion.

He told me he was getting his book published that fall with Influence Publishing. Small world, I thought. Another person I knew, Karen Tyrell of Dementia Solutions, had told me that her book—*Cracking the Dementia Code*—was being published that fall with Influence Publishing. A busy publishing house, I thought! We said farewell and I went home, perusing the charming images and reflections in his book.

Some weeks later, unbeknownst to me at the time, Brock was sitting in Influence Publishing's office in North Vancouver, reviewing his manuscript in its latest version, when he learned they were looking for an editor. He remembered me, told Julie, and then, he emailed me to tell me, suggesting I phone Julie because she needed an editor. And, as they say in England, "Bob's your uncle," which means everything gets sorted out as it should, though I have no idea how such an expression could come to mean that!

The moral of the story is that it is not egotistical to claim who we are and to tell our friends, colleagues, family, and even total strangers what it is that we love to be and to do. What we love to do is frequently who we are. And when we know who we are, we become that bit more whole in body, mind, and spirit.

What are the affirmations (read "I am" statements) you use to describe yourself? Are they appropriate? Are they inadequate, demeaning, and critical? Or are they accurate, honest, and intentional?

~ *Ways of Loving* ~

"I was in love: in love with Greg and in love with Canada....
I struggled to remember if I ever felt this way about Graeme;
yet didn't my journal notes describe being 'in love' in the same way?
Do we fall in love with the idea of being in love?"
Julie Salisbury[189]

I decided a while ago to see whether it were true that the classical Greeks had many different words for what English speakers call "love." Online sources led me to merely seven: *eros, philia, agape, philautia, pragma, ludus,* and *storge.* I learned that our love for one another often combines several styles of love. Here they are in their purest forms.

Eros is the erotic and sexual love through which a man and woman seek to procreate.

Philia is love for one's brother.

Agape is the love that Jesus commanded we share with each other: compassionate caring, unconditional love. We may follow this

[189] *Around the World in Seven Years,* p. 217.

commandment in small ways, for example, by holding open a door while others pass through, or by shining a light forward into the dark. Or we follow this commandment in large ways, as did actor and author Janet Walmsley, the mother of Jenny Story, a young woman whose autistic symptoms appeared at the age of twelve months following her immunization. By constantly seeking the best options, doctors, caregivers, daycare, and practices for her daughter, Janet Walmsley shows her love. Her book—*The Autistic Author and Animator*—is a guidebook of how to express one's love for another human being.

Nadine Sands' love for her husband Michael encompassed all three—*eros, philia,* and *agape*—while she cared for him through his diagnosis and decline into debilitation from ALS (Amyotrophic Lateral Sclerosis), a disease which is better known as Lou Gehrig's disease. Mike learned to let go of the strength and independence he had once had; Nadine learned to adjust to their new relationship as she became his principal caregiver. Through the process, their trust and faith in God grew, as described in her gentle, touching, and humorous book, *Hold On, Let Go.*

Roman Krznaric, founding faculty member of The School of Life in London, writes about the first six in his article, "Have You Tried the Six Varieties of Love?" in the online magazine *Sojourner.*[190] He says that *philautia* refers to self-love, which comes in two forms: narcissism and self-compassion. This makes sense to me—as a lover of etymology I realize that *philia* refers to a form of love—because I recognize the beginning of the word *philautia* as the basis for "philharmonic," the descriptor for an orchestra that plays for the love of playing; and "philanthropist," denoting someone who loves other people enough to share his or her wealth with them. And the second half of *philautia* is reminiscent of the words "autograph, autobiography, autodidact," in which "auto" means "self-created."

Internationally acclaimed artist Pamela Masik described how she felt during the hardest time of her life, "'I had to learn self-love. I would stand there with my hand trembling trying to paint—worried that the

[190]With permission from sojo.net/blogs/2013/12/05/have-you-tried-six-varieties-love

next brush stroke would mess up the whole thing. I had to overcome that fear.'"[191] Masik overcame her fear and has gone on to create a prodigious body of work through paintings, sculptures, and performances.

I'm particularly intrigued by the type of love termed *pragma,* because it seems to be the root of "pragmatic." According to Krznaric, *pragma* means "mature love ... the deep understanding that develops between long-married couples." Just the other day, my husband and I were playing bridge with a couple who recently celebrated their sixty-eighth wedding anniversary. The husband of the couple said something that the wife ignored. He repeated it and she still ignored it. He then joked that she often ignored him. To which she responded, "That's why our marriage has lasted so long!" We all broke up into peals of laughter. If her lack of response wasn't pragmatic, I don't know what is.

The form of love that the Greek word *ludus* describes is a cheating, lying kind. A recent episode of BBC's *Mr. Selfridge* revealed that Miss Nancy Webb's love for Harry Selfridge was heavily overlaid with deception: she was hoping he would provide her with a life freed from her conniving, fraudulent past.

Storge describes the kind of love that can grow over time, say, for instance, between a betrothed couple who do not meet until their wedding day.

Whom do you "love"? Which style of love do you have for each person you love? Could you make a rite of loving someone, by bringing them food, making their bed, wiping their nose, listening to their stories for the hundredth time? How are you displaying your love? Do you want to love better?

[191]Masik's story is one of ten stories about unique individuals which Marilyn R. Wilson captures in *Life Outside the Box.*

Chapter 9—Integrating Body, Mind, and Soul

Dis-Ease

~ Sin Is Not So Sinful As It's Credited to Be ~

"One struggles, for forcible feeding is an immoral assault as well as a painful physical one, and to remain passive under it would give one the feeling of sin; the sin of concurrence."

Joan Bryans[192]

The word "sin" is scattered liberally throughout the Bible, the Quran, the Vedas, and other sacred texts. I used to see sin as being horrendous; now I understand it in a different way—as any thought, word, or deed that takes me away from my awareness that I am a spiritual being living a physical life on Earth. I see it as being an error, a mistake, some way I've strayed from Divine truth. I see it as confusion.

The sin of concurrence is going along with the status quo because it's easier than fighting. The sin of not trying is staying stuck in one place, going nowhere. The sin of fear is lacking the courage to follow your joy. The sin of worry is wasting mental energy on an outcome that you are not working to prevent or mitigate. The sin of regret is repeatedly wishing an event had occurred differently rather than bringing about a better event.

Even doubt is a sin if it makes me unaware of my own Divinity, my own connection with the Divine. I am as Divine as a mollusc, a daisy, a grain of corn, an arbutus tree. So are you.

What about the sin of expectation, an expectation being something we can take for granted? We expect to be healthy; to be happy; that life should be fair; that we should have enough; that if we can only reach a

[192]*Rebel Women*, Scene 12

nameable goal, all would be well; that a range of things can compensate for the lack of love. What about the sin of disappointment? We must have had an appointment with an expectation if we are disappointed.

What about the sin of assumption, assumptions being events and experiences we regard as probable? We assume that illness comes unbidden; that problems arise outside ourselves; that we can always choose; that the past is written in stone; that we are entitled to the anger we feel; that we are entitled to condemn; that we are special.

Of all these, the only two that are true are that we can choose and that we are special. Each of us is. The rest are lies we tell ourselves, to maintain our separation from our Divinity.

When I feel someone is creating a problem for me, my ego thinks the other person has the problem. The sort of thing I might say in the heat of the moment is, "The problem with you is . . . ." However, my soul realizes that if I feel someone is creating a problem for me, then indeed, it is "I" who has the problem: "I have a problem." The only way for me to solve that problem is to acknowledge the situation and forgive the person for whatever I feel they have done.

In *Merlin*, the medieval fantasy series for BBC One TV, Merlin is a young warlock training under the gentle eye of Gaius, Camelot's court physician, consulting with the Great Dragon, and saving Prince Arthur (later, King) time and again. Merlin "sins" in one of the final episodes when he loses faith in his powers of magic: "I am nothing without my magic." His deceased father answers, "Merlin, you are more than a son of your father. You are a son of the Earth, the sea, the sky. Magic is the fabric of this world. And you were born of that magic. You are magic itself. You cannot lose what you are." Merlin's father suggests Merlin believe what his heart knows to be true—"that you have always been and always will be. . . . Soon you shall awaken into the light."[193]

Merlin experiences a sudden loss of knowing who he is, having decided he is nothing without his magic. Replace Merlin's "magic" with our "mystery" and the "sin" becomes understandable.

---

[193]Julian Jones, Jake Michie, Johnny Capps, and Julian Murphy, creators of *Merlin*, TV series, 2008-12.

Few of us are aware from childhood of how integral we are to the mystery and how integral it is to us. It is something we have to learn along the way, to find our true, authentic self.

A friend told me recently that at three different times of his life, her father wrote about being a young man. The first and second occasions were separated by ten years, the second and third by fifteen years. What intrigued my friend was that the three versions of her father's life as a young man all carried the same elements of where he had been born, who his parents were, what he had done with his life, and how he'd dealt with his challenges. But the lenses through which he saw himself as a young man were totally different. He might have been three different young men.

The absolute reality of our Self does not change. If a person's identity changes, it is not their true identity. When we "awaken into the light" like Merlin, we find our essence, our authentic selves, our core; some of us would call this our spirit. I would.

How do we get there? By relaxing, resting, letting go, and "knowing" in a big way, a Divine way. Perhaps by meditating, being open to Divine guidance, or walking with nothing on our mind. When we notice synchronicities, large and small, we can use them as stepping stones to get to the next place along our path.

Can you identify your "sins"? Can you see that they are just tangents that take you from your path? Distractions? Excuses? Can you believe that magic and mystery are the fabric of this world and that you, like Merlin, were born of that magic and mystery?

~ *Dark Night of the Soul* ~

"Genuine healing rarely takes a safe path;
it takes a path that incorporates the whole of your life."
Caroline Myss[194]

Caroline Myss, an author of writings to which I respond particularly well, says that a lack of honesty and integrity, particularly between heart and mind, frequently underlies illness.[195]

Starting in March 1998, I began to experience a dis-ease in my eyes, which I have referred to several times before. Going through this illness became my "dark night of the soul"; healing myself from it became a "spiritual crisis" and my "mystical journey," as Caroline Myss says.

Bit by bit, I found I couldn't read, because some of my eye muscles had become so weak that they couldn't control the movement of my eyes. We have six eye muscles for each eye, to move each eyeball to the right, to the left, up, down, and to rotate the eye obliquely. The dis-ease began in the left eye and stayed there for several months. Then it eased and moved to the right eye for several months. And so on, back and forth, a very slow oscillation, with only one eye in extreme pain at any one time. The eye muscles became watery and weak, and, gradually, scarred. They could not control my eye movements. Within a year, my eyes were looking in two different directions—my vision was no longer fused into three-dimensional depth. The doctors called the disease "giant cell myositis."

My view of the world turned inward. It was my only choice. I had been wanting to do more soul work for some time. The irony of suffering from an eye dis-ease as a way to segue into soul work was not lost on me. The eyes are considered by many to be the windows into the soul. This dis-ease was certainly my entry into my own insight, my own learning,

---

[194]*Defy Gravity*, p. 72.
[195]Interview with Adoley Odunton on July 16, 2010 during the Wellness Revolution Summit series on the internet.

my soul work. When I finally recovered, although my eye muscles were scarred, the scars on my soul were cleansed and healed.

Initially, everything fell gradually away, one by one—communications work at Agriculture and Agri-Food Canada, taking French lessons, singing with the Vancouver Bach Choir, driving—until nothing was left, except things that I could do sitting at home alone, not moving my eyes. I knitted—I made a Romeo and Juliet coat of many colours after a design by master knitter and designer Kaffe Fassett; I painted small watercolours of my children; I listened to talking books; I scribbled poetry and prose; and I did soul work.

I enjoyed walking on the beach, especially when the tide was out, with our little cocker spaniel, Ginger. Off would come my shoes, off would come Ginger's leash, she would run and chase the seagulls, and I would feel the sand shifting under my feet and walk through the waves, singing as I went. The songs were my own compositions, generated by the white noise of the waves, large and small. I felt as though they were coming directly to me from Spirit; I was inspired! There was no requirement to write the pieces down, to do anything with them, just to enjoy their creation, their moments of being, for their truth and connection to nature and to the Divine.

Unfortunately, Ginger wasn't supposed to be off her leash—that's illegal on Vancouver's beaches—and a cop spotted me and gave me a ticket! I even contested it—I forget on what grounds—and I still had to pay the fine. Somehow, that discouraged me from going on with my wonderful wave songs. Just the memory of that time, though, brings a lightness to my soul.

Double vision persists in my peripheral vision; I see the world as double first thing in the morning and when my eyes are tired. I had surgery to correct my gaze and have a prism in my glasses. But otherwise, I have recovered fully from the eye-muscle dis-ease. And I retain my ability to "see" the world through my inner vision. What a gift.

The next scene is a journal entry from when I lived through that dark night.

Have you had a dark night of the soul? What did you lose? What did you gain?

~ *The Way I See Things* ~

"Above all else I want to see things differently."

A Course in Miracles[196]

When I am awake and I am ready, I look over at the top of the bookshelf to see how far apart are my images of the Spanish black wood carving of a peasant man.[197]

Where did I buy that carving? Costa del Sol? Tenerife? Mexico? All Spanish-influenced. Wherever it was purchased, it stands now above Christian's side of the bed, determined yet bored in its twosomeness, judging the state of the health of my eyes. One image is fainter, more blurred up to the right, the other with more colour and down to the left with books running through it.

Seeing with double vision gives strength to the notion that this world is an illusion. If I touch the right eye's image, it is there; the left eye's image is there also. Bowls of fruit appear in the middle of people, their heads disappearing behind paintings on the wall. Are we insubstantial?

I walk carefully to the bathroom, holding the furniture, touching the walls, scarily watching obstacles slide out of my path. Hall and bathroom floor tiles fan like a deck of cards, white spots for pips, black background instead of white.

I blink my left eye because it's easier to blink than my right. Moving carefully to the kitchen, I reach for a glass that isn't quite there, not lifting it too early for fear it will crash to the floor. Ah, there it is. If I can't see it where it is whole, how will I see it in shattered fragments? I fill it with bottled water and place it carefully in the microwave to warm before swallowing my calcium pills; I've mopped up too many glasses of spilled milk and water.

I note my own slowness, my deliberation where once such tasks would be unnoticeable, not tasks at all. I remember the days in early spring 1998

[196]Lesson 28, Foundation for Inner Peace.
[197]This scene is from my year 2000 journal.

when, after many weeks of pain and headaches, difficulty in moving my eyes, I began to have double vision. I would look down and see two sets of feet and legs and then my vision would focus and I would get dressed, eat, and go to work.

Now as I write, I have to decide which image to write on. I see my right hand twice: below to the left and above to the right, each image shadowing the other. An almost identical image, the one is blurred by my sweater, the other by carpet.

I remember going to the opera *La Bohème*; my eyes spread into double vision for the first time. I wrongly blamed the large person in front of me for blocking my view of the stage. All night long, I could only hear the opera; I could not watch it. That was the beginning of the walking nightmare.

I once walked across Burrard Street Bridge; I remember because it was so bizarre. It was while having double vision before wearing an eyepatch. My two images of the bridge came together at me, as I walked into them, the water and railing on my left, the bikes and cars and other people on my right, constantly walking through spaces where obstacles had been one or two seconds and footfalls earlier. Stuff of bad dreams and horror movies. So strange.

After I had struggled with walking into a double-imaged world for a week or more—like walking into a hall of distorted mirrors at the fair—my mother came to stay. It was her idea—not my clever doctors'—to look for a patch, to halve the images of my world. And then it was she who found it, not the clever and knowledgeable staff at the pharmacy.

What a boon! The world was one again, though flat, two-dimensional, lacking the depth of colour, at times blurry on close appraisal, but one world. Without three-dimensional depth perception, things were not where they seemed to be. I learned to touch the door first to know its location before inserting the key.

Christian didn't like to leave me alone, torn between staying with me and running the café down south. When he was home, I would kiss his two faces, my lips knowing his face better than my eyes.

I forget when I gave up driving; what a freedom abandoned for my safety and the safety of others. So often when I was walking, people would come to my patched left side and were in front of me, in my path, expecting me to have adjusted to their intentions, before I was aware of them. If that person were a car, how many near collisions would there be? Hang up the keys and be grateful that all my children now drive. How wonderful! That was once a scary thought: "These young boys, Grant and Ian, set loose in the streets!" Now, it is comforting and freeing.

For seven months or so, I wore my patch. At best, it was called "sexy" and "mysterious." At worst, it made me a freak for children to stare at and query their mothers about. And occasionally they would query me. "Is your eye broken?" I should have answered that my eye wasn't broken but my sight was.

One day I sat on a Davie Street bus, my eyepatch in place, when a young man in dirty jeans boarded and sat in front of me. He had an air of mystery that made me fearful. Why? He wore an eyepatch! It was like looking into a mirror and seeing someone else altogether.

While I was on the cross-Canada train with Jessica, a young boy asked, "What have you done to your eye?" Always there was concern over only one eye; yet both eyes were inflamed, taking turns, first the right, then the left, then the right, then the left. The question felt so intrusive. Jessica was protective, dispelling the hurt.

It was on that trip that I first abandoned the patch. For a day or two I forgot where I'd put it—actually in the glove compartment of the rented car. I even thought I could drive and offered my services, but I said the road seemed to bounce up and down a great deal. Both Jessica and I rejected my offer.

Then came the drive from hell through Newfoundland, wind and rain driving at us. Jessica held on fiercely to the steering wheel to keep us in our lane. "Stay awake, Mum. I don't know the road." We needed to get the ferry back to the mainland. And then came another big flare-up in my left eye and I wanted to increase my prednisone. When I was at the hospital in Halifax to have the stab wound stitched—I had accidentally stabbed right through an avocado pit into my hand—I asked the doctor whether I should increase the prednisone as my symptoms were flaring up and he suggested phoning my doctor, Jack Rootman, M.D. in Vancouver. On Dr. Rootman's advice, the prednisone went up and the patch went back on.

The way I see it, I was scared to look ahead into the future. It was easier to see duality: either things will continue as they are or they will not; either things will get worse or they won't; either things will get better or they won't. So I don't have to look and decide.

I began to look inside myself, taking a step at a time. Standing on that ledge, taking in the view, becoming accustomed before moving a little deeper, and looking again. A hand was holding mine, befriending me, my Higher Self, throwing light on the shadowy walls that enclosed me, just a little at a time, as I could manage.

I remember the first day I walked in Stanley Park without my patch, my eyes improving. I saw in three dimensions as though for the first time, saw the green world as a whole. What breath-taking beauty! I would stand still and allow my eyes to move up the mossy, green-stained trunk of a great oak to where it burst against the sky. I was in awe! What a glorious mix of green and blue and brown. And the swans, ducks, and geese showed off their skills and their feathers in the dappled water. The other people walking around Lost Lagoon were unaware of its beauty. My eyes were looking afresh, seeing nature as it is, without a veneer of tired worldliness. The eyepatch was on and off, and on and off. In the morning, my eyes are apart and then they come together somewhere during the morning, perhaps over my breakfast, perhaps later. Shall I walk with my patch? Yes, I'll need it. No, I won't. Leave if off just a little longer. There, I can cope.

I get tired and my eyes spread apart, the world becomes a blur of humanity moving, rushing past, unaware that I'm an obstacle that doesn't move as they do. I cannot anticipate their moves. I stand still, waiting for the rush to rush by. Now, I'm using a cane, to help with my balance and to avoid falling again. One fracture is enough.

I take out my memories and look at them one by one to see what they mean, what bearing they have on today. And I cleaned out some clutter in my mind and forgave myself and others of past wrongs and injustices, and chose to see things differently.[198]

I now can focus on much of the world without my glasses and sometimes even with my glasses (where my eyes focus is not necessarily where my glasses would have me focus). So now, I sometimes see things clearly as one. And then the images slip apart, the pain growing between my eyebrows.

And what of the pain? Lines of pain across my eyes, aches in my nose, inescapable pains across my forehead. "Intractable pain," said Dr. Rootman on one of the myriad of forms. Rubbing my forehead to relieve the pressure would not relieve the pain, just my anxiety. The pain is forgettable though. When it is not there, it's gone.

My physical body cannot remember the labour pains I endured to give birth to four wonderful people—Alun, Jessica, Grant, and Ian—yet it was quite real at the time. Now, I don't have so much pain, because I don't do the things that hurt, like focussing on words and details, except just a little at a time.

When I don't do so much, because of pain, I get bored and wonder what it's all for: it's for my Self, for this life I'm living and choosing to see and perceive as I see it. I am giving birth to my Self with these pains, this doubling and singling of views on my world. The birth is not all at once. It comes and goes, but for every backward step there's another step forward, gaining vision and sight. I need to realize that. And gradually my sight clears.

[198]One of the processes I used to clear the clutter in my heart and mind was creating mind maps with coloured pens on good paper, linking this with that through words, images, arrows, heart images, and doodles.

~ *Listening to My Body* ~

"Let go of the past and move forward."

My body's message to me[199]

I woke up at 4:32 a.m. this morning (numbers that already suggest I am going backwards), feeling aches and pains in my left knee, my sigmoid colon, and later, my left hip. I decided to follow two pieces of advice that psychiatrist and intuitive Judith Orloff, M.D., prescribes in her excellent book, *Dr. Judith Orloff's Guide to Intuitive Healing*. Her book is one of two texts for the seventh and final course in the American Institute of Health Care Professionals' Spiritual Counseling Program, a program I followed for two years to give greater authority to the spiritual counselling I gave clients.

Dr. Orloff suggests I use my own hands to direct healing energy intentionally from my heart chakra to those parts of my body that are painful. Pain is a frequently used method our bodies use to get our attention. I am no stranger to directing healing energy through my hands to myself and others, having taken Reiki Level I, in which I learned to channel Universal energy.

Let me return to Dr. Orloff's guidance. Somehow, it feels a little different from Reiki. I think it's the fact that her book encourages me to listen while placing my hands on my body. I lie in bed with my right hand on my left knee and my left hand on my heart. The heart is far more central in the chest cavity than I once realized. From the fact that our family doctor, Dr. Emrys, placed his stethoscope over my left rib cage, I got the impression that my heart was on the left. It was years later, during physiotherapy training, that I learned that the left ventricle, which is the lower left of the four chambers of the heart, lies under the left rib cage. It is the contraction of the left ventricle as it pushes oxygenated blood into the aorta and thereby the arteries of the whole body that creates our

[199]In the early hours of November 15, 2013.

left-positioned heartbeat. So my hand over my heart is in the centre of my chest.

The second piece of advice that Dr. Orloff gives is to listen to the message that the pain carries. "The body responds anyway; it's just that we're not aware of what's going on."[200]

For me, the intuitive message from my body that morning was to "Let go of the past and move forward." I followed the advice.

The next time you get a pain in some part of your body, ask your body what it is trying to communicate. Listen to the answer. And, having heard your body's response, follow its guidance. When you don't follow your body's guidance, it eventually stops trying to communicate clearly, and brings you instead all sorts of symptoms of discomfort and even dis-ease. Do you listen to your body?

Ease and Courage

~ *Rules for Living Life* ~

"I remember hearing the rules and, even as I was astonished
to know that they were so simple,
I started to feel myself waking from the dream state."
Timothy J. Doyle[201]

Recently, I came across three references to there being three rules for living life; I read them all within a small timeframe of about three weeks. (I always have several books on the go at once, for different times of the day.) Three by three by three! Of course, they're different rules. That caught my attention. Let's take a look.

[200]Video at drjudithorloff.com
[201]*How to Play the Game of Life: Beginner's Version*, pp. iv-v.

Doyle writes about three simple rules in *How to Play the Game of Life: Beginner's Version*. He refers to them in this way:

"I remember one Sunday evening, just after I'd gone to bed and was already in the dream state, that a Spiritual being said to me, 'I am going to tell you the three rules of life.' At the time, what he told me was so simple; I couldn't believe that these rules could ever be broken. He went on to say, 'Follow these three rules and everything in your life will be perfect.'...

"When I awoke in the morning though, all I could remember was learning about three simple rules and descending back into my body. What was so simple to remember in my spirit body in the dream state while in the presence of Spirit was impossible to remember in my denser physical body. I hope these three simple rules are registered within me somewhere."[202]

Later in his book, Doyle lists thirteen rules for playing the game of life. He writes, "I believe that the revelation dream of the three simple rules is also integrated into these thirteen rules." His thirteen rules include "I live in a free-will Universe; I do not entertain guilt or shame; and I love others to the degree that I love myself."[203]

Neurosurgeon and near-death experiencer Eben Alexander, M.D., received his three rules when he was on the other side, during his near-death experience. His guide—whom he called the "girl-on-the-butterfly-wing"—shared them with him: "Without using any words, she spoke to me. The message went through me like a wind, and I instantly understood that it was true. I knew so in the same way that I knew that the world around us was real—was not some fantasy, passing and insubstantial.

"The message had three parts, and if I had to translate these into Earthly language, I'd say they ran something like this:

"'You are loved and cherished, dearly, forever.'

"'You have nothing to fear.'

"'There is nothing you can do wrong.'

[202]Timothy J. Doyle, *How to Play the Game of Life: Beginner's Version*, pp. iv-v.
[203]Timothy J. Doyle, *How to Play the Game of Life: Beginner's Version*

"The message flooded me with a vast and crazy sensation of relief. It was like being handed the rules to a game I'd been playing all my life without ever fully understanding it."[204]

I wonder whether Tim Doyle's three simple rules are the same as Dr. Alexander's.

I also find it interesting that two of Dr. Alexander's rules are expressed in the negative, stating what does not have to happen. Why would these profound rules for life be stated negatively? Could Dr. Alexander's two negatively expressed rules be "Love is all there is" and "Everything you do is perfect"?

Leo Tolstoy states the third group of three rules in his story, "The Three Questions." I paraphrase the king's three questions: When is the right time to act? Who should I pay attention to? What affair needs my immediate attention? The answers in order are simple: Now. Those you are with. The one where you can do the most good.

Over time, many others have shared their rules for life. In 1925, metaphysical author Florence Scovel Shinn wrote *The Game of Life* and, later, several other books of advice. Cherie Carter-Scott, Ph.D., a human-development coach, wrote *If Life Is a Game, These Are the Rules* in 1998. Her ten rules are listed on her website.[205] The series of books by Jack Canfield titled *Chicken Soup for the Soul®* includes four subtitled *Life Lessons* for different phases of life. If we learn by example, and most of us do, then a huge percentage of non-fiction books provide rules for life.

With that in mind, I thought it would be useful if we examined our own rules. What are the rules you have absorbed into your subconscious? They're probably hard to see—just as it's hard to see the forest for the trees. I become so absorbed with the trees in my vicinity—their bark, their branches, their beauty, the small birds and animals that inhabit them, their leaves, their flowers, their seeds, their habit of dropping leaves, flowers, seeds, or branches on our lawns and sidewalks—that I

---

[204]Eben Alexander, M.D., *Proof of Heaven,* p. 41. With permission.
[205]"*The Ten Rules For Being Human*" on drcherie.com

stop seeing the urban forest they create with the rest of the trees in my neighbourhood.

In chapter ten, there is a scene about habits (Posing Questions Brings Results, ~ Kaizen Your Habits ~); habits are those behaviours that support our rules and our beliefs, so our behaviours might indicate what our rules are.

Let me give some examples of the difference between our rules and our habits. One rule I accept is Divine Source loves me, because Divine Source—what you might call God or Infinite Mind or *Om* or any number of other nomenclatures—is Love. So Divine Source can only love. Divine Source cannot not love, cannot withhold love, cannot punish; Divine Source can only love. Divine Love loves me. Divine Love loves everyone I know: my spouse, my children, my grandchildren, my sister, my departed loved ones, my friends, and even my enemies. This is one of my rules for living life. It's very similar to Dr. Alexander's rule, "You are loved and cherished, dearly, forever."

What would be some habits I have that support this? I have a habit of doing some sort of ritual as close to daily as possible, because I want to align with Divine Love and infuse my life with that unconditional love.

I also realize that if I am loved unconditionally, then I might as well forgive myself when I make some kind of mistake, because Divine Source has already forgiven me. Actually, Divine Source did not at any time even consider that what I did was a mistake. Remember the reiteration of one of Dr. Alexander's rules? "Everything you do is perfect." So it wasn't a mistake and I don't have to withhold any energy from myself in the form of guilt or shame.

This becomes another habit that I work hard to enact constantly—to forgive myself when I make mistakes *before* berating myself. Viewed in this light, the human habit of withholding forgiveness from oneself or from another person is absurd. It is one of the most cruel and common forms of self-flagellation on the planet.

Another rule that I hold dear grows out of the previous one. My greatest potential for spiritual growth is through my conscious connection with Divine Source. Let me explain. Divine Source loves me and if I can accept that unconditional love, I can also accept Divine Source's infinite wisdom, infinite intelligence, abundance, and prosperity for the benefit of myself and others. I do this at my High Heart Chakra through my godspark connection with my Higher Self. As I accept these Divine gifts, their energies spread throughout my physical and subtle bodies.

Each of us is a spark that came from and is potentially still connected to Divine Source. I say, "potentially still connected," because many people on the planet have disconnected themselves from their own Divinity for different reasons: perhaps in order to put those in religious authority on a higher platform than themselves; or to deny Divine Source any place in their lives; or because they somehow consider themselves unworthy. It is very reassuring to know, though, that we all have the potential for equal worth and full connection with Divine Source.

I shall limit myself to three rules:

- Divine Source loves me.
- My greatest potential for spiritual growth is through my conscious connection with Divine Source.
- Everything happens for a reason.

Do you know your rules? Can you state them? Once you do that, you can zero in on them more accurately.

If you can't figure out what your rules are already, can you create three rules for yourself? Once you create—and write down—what you think your rules are, then some of your actual and most important rules will start to show up. Life rules make life more acceptable, more understandable, more bearable; they make me realize that it is possible to grow and improve, that I am here for a higher purpose.

Try out some of the rules I've suggested. Or create your own by working with some of the following sentences.

I am ______
Life is ______
What has happened so far in life is ______
The purpose of life is _____
I am here on Earth to _____
What do your rules do for you? How do they help?

ॐ

~ More Typing ~

"One of the well-documented findings in the study of attributions is that we are more likely to ascribe traits to others, whereas we explain our own actions according to the situations we are in."

Brian R. Little, Ph.D.[206]

As you will realize from the quote for this scene, "typing" in this instance does not refer to touch-typing or hunting-and-pecking on a keyboard. It refers to the many ways we can figure out more about ourselves. The author of the scene quote is Brian R. Little, Ph.D., Fellow of the Well-Being Institute at Cambridge University in the UK. In an interview with CBC Radio One's Anna Maria Tremonti, Dr. Little described how to discern one's behaviour between high and low self-monitoring as an excellent way to know more about ourselves. I realize that I am a high self-monitor and my husband is the opposite—more impulsive and likely to respond in the moment. This explains why he constantly responds in circumstances where I would remain silent.

One of the ways of typing that Dr. Little discussed with Tremonti is the Big Five Personality Traits of openness, conscientiousness, extraversion, agreeableness, and neuroticism. With an acronym of "ocean," these five

---

[206]*Me, Myself and Us*, p. 3.

are named for traits at one end of the scale. Thus, openness is the opposite of being closed to new experiences; conscientiousness is on the other end of being disorganized; extraversion opposes introversion; agreeableness opposes being competitive and manipulative; and neuroticism, the only "negative" within the acronym, is on the other end of being emotionally stable and less likely to react to stressors.

Dr. Little believes, however, that, while there are relatively stable dispositions ("fixed traits"), we have the capacity to act out of character through "free traits" and these offer a more optimistic view of how personality influences our well-being.

Another useful personality typing system is the Myers-Briggs Type Indicator, developed from Carl Jung's sixteen personality types that are based on the combinations of four traits in a person's behaviour: Extrovert or Introvert; Thinking or Feeling; Sensing or Intuiting; Judging or Perceiving. Though not directly useful to help with growth along a spiritual path, knowing our personality style certainly helps us understand our interactions with others and, as many people say, we learn the most in community with others.

Have you taken the Myers-Briggs test? Where are you with the Big Five Personality Traits? Are you a high or a low self-monitor? Are you aware of other styles of being?

~ *Recipes for Spiritual Growth* ~

"Quinoa Porridge
2 cups water
sea salt to taste
½ cup mixture of quinoa, millet, and buckwheat
2 heaped tablespoons of cranberries (two small handfuls)
2 tablespoons of mixed raw flaxseeds, sunflower seeds, and almonds
½ cup fresh or frozen blueberries (two generous handfuls)"
Nina Shoroplova[207]

Several years before retiring from the public service, I decided to take a retirement course. This is the sort of thing that the Canadian federal government does extremely well—looking after the training of its people. The trainer was excellent, sharing many promising ideas about how to make the years leading up to retirement and retirement itself some of the best years of life.

I love living a somewhat planned life. That must be to do with the fact that numerologically my destiny number is 13/4. Tania Gabrielle says 13 has to do with sudden shifts, transformations, changes, and letting go of past beliefs, whereas 4 means grounding ideas into reality, architecture, building, planning, patience, and a diligent work ethic; these describe me well.

I learned at the retirement course that the federal government offered an initiative to encourage imminent retirees to cut back on their days of work (and of course, their accompanying pay). The incentive was that the smaller paycheques for two years before retiring would not affect the amount of the person's pension. This plan appealed to me as a way to segue into less money as well as less responsibility, so afterwards I researched it further and ultimately signed up.

---

[207]"Quinoa," ninashoroplova.ca

As a result, I slid into "retirement," which, for me, has never looked anything like withdrawing from activity but more like putting on fresh new tires! In fact, three days before my official retirement began—I was still using up my last holiday hours—I went back to school, starting a year of holistic nutritional training.

I have arrived at the topic of this scene—recipes. Registered as a nutritionist, I can now take almost any recipe and "nutritionalize" it. Isn't that a great word? It means improving the ingredients and the process of a recipe so that it meets my body's needs more effectively. For instance, I would nutritionalize a recipe for bread that uses white wheat flour by replacing some or all the white flour with any mixture of whole grain wheat flour, whole grain rye flour, coconut flour, pea meal, or other whole flours.

Did you know that you can claim a recipe as yours by changing a certain number of its ingredients? I have read that the number of ingredients that have to be different are six, but then some recipes don't even have as many as six ingredients.

If you're changing the process—such as going from frying in oil to water-sautéing—that definitely becomes a new recipe.

The course I enjoyed most in that year back at school was the Body-Mind-Spirit course. In fact, the whole year moved me along my spiritual path, as it launched me into Reiki, followed by ThetaHealing™, spiritual counselling, and other great modalities. I sought out esoteric authors such as Barbara Y. Martin, Drunvalo Melchizedek, Doreen Virtue, Ambika Wauters, and Paramahansa Yogananda.

I also started looking back on my life, connecting the milestones on my spiritual path. I became far more aware of my progress. We are always in the process of becoming: I have always been becoming a spiritual seeker. Whenever I think I have recalled or captured the very first stepping stone on my spiritual path, something or someone comes along to make me remember an earlier stepping stone.

Do you remember the beginning of your spiritual journey? What have been some of the more recent stepping stones? Where are you moving now? What is your recipe for life? For health?

~ *Creating Health* ~

"We can only speculate how far evolution will take us,
but there are dramatic instances where the mind refused
to believe in disease and the body suddenly followed."

Deepak Chopra, M.D.[208]

While editing *Baby Comes Home* by Paul Roumeliotis, M.D., I acknowledged his warning about the dangers of "Invisible or Not-So-Obvious GERD."[209] He also calls it a "non-regurgitant form of reflux" and says, "An irritation of the esophagus [is] caused by the acid that refluxes back up" from the stomach.

I experience reflux occasionally. Actually, my brother-in-law died of esophageal cancer. What a warning that was.

I am always "watching" my health and dealing with any ache or pain right away in medical and alternative ways. At the risk of provoking a barrage of disagreement over the specifics of my particular self-healing discipline, I write a list of the actions I can take to avoid getting reflux. These will help keep me healthy.

- **Get up at 6:30 a.m.** I feel fine when I wake then; it's only when I sleep until 7:00 a.m. or later that I feel some stomach acid has entered my esophagus. Since working for myself, I love not setting the alarm clock. Often I wake up naturally just before 6:00 a.m., but if I'm feeling tired I allow myself to sleep another hour or so. And then sometimes when I awake around 7:00 a.m., I know I have had a bout of reflux.

[208]*Perfect Health*, p. 18.
[209]"GERD" stands for gastroesophageal reflux disease.

- **Have sufficient salt in my diet.** Salt is required to keep the sphincter at the top end of the stomach strong—I first learned that from Jonn Matsen, N.D., and his book, *Eating Alive.*
- **Don't eat too much**. Born after the Second World War and raised during the years of rationing in Wales, I always try to finish what is on my plate; and when there are a number of plates on a table, I try to have a little of everything. As my eyes are often bigger than my stomach, I try to notice before I get full and stop eating.
- **Don't eat anything after 7:30 p.m.** Not a nibble. Digestion slows down at night and anything that is undigested at 7:30 p.m. might not be digested throughout the night.
- **Get to bed by 10:00 p.m.** I love to read, so that will allow me to read for half an hour and still get eight hours' sleep before 6:30 a.m.[210]

After writing that list—just the bolded words—I saw three of my daily emails, from TUT (Thoughts from the Universe by Mike Dooley), A.R.E. (Edgar Cayce's Association for Research and Enlightenment), and Reverend Christina Lunden. Today, they are perfect, synchronistic, and integrated. They cast a new light on the situation.

- TUT asks, "Tell me, when you think of taking consistent action in the general direction of your dreams, Nina, do you imagine discipline, stamina, work, sacrifice, monotony, courage, and strategies, or are you thinking adventure, discovery, new friends, excitement at the crack of dawn, magic, surprises, fun, laughter, and, on occasion, the Macarena?" TUT then signs off for the Universe by adding, "Cool! Me too! HEY!"[211]
- Reverend Lunden says, "Dear Nina, Today's affirmation is 'I AM blessed because I AM.'"

[210]Being habits only loosely embedded in time, these too have changed since I wrote them out.
[211]©Mike Dooley, tut.com

- A.R.E. quotes Edgar Cayce's Reading 254-68, "Think on This—Blessed, then, are they that make their wills one in accord with Him, as they seek to know, 'Lord, what would thou have me do!'"[212]

I see synchronicity in these three readings: I AM Blessed (as is each of us, though we seldom acknowledge that fact), and I am here on Earth to reach my potential. I have been receiving nudges of what to do about reflux for some time. I have had symptoms since I was a girl—a frog in my throat and an edge to my voice that my singing teacher Elizabeth Taylor noticed. So now, instead of seeing the list of ways to live my life as restrictive, I am going to follow the advice from the Universe via Mike Dooley, and make them into play, fun, and adventure. Especially, "excitement at the crack of dawn." That is when the sun always casts a new light on the day.

According to Deepak Chopra, M.D., perfect health is ours by Divine right. And yet, we certainly don't exhibit that. I strongly believe that our ability to heal rests in our belief system, in other words, in our mind. I have three examples to call on. You will know of more.

One day when he was not yet in his teens, my eldest son showed me quite a well-developed wart on his hand. I told him that if I were to buy it from him right then with a twenty-cent coin (we were living in Australia at the time and a twenty-cent coin was legitimate currency) and he were to bury the coin I gave him, the wart would fall off overnight. He agreed, not liking the very secure, unsightly bump. I gave him the twenty-cent coin, he buried it, and the next day, the wart fell off. It hadn't even been loose the day before.

People who exhibit multiple personality disorders (also known as "dissociative identity disorders") present the most fascinating and persuasive proof that our health is governed by our mind. Take for example a person with a multiple personality disorder in which one of

---

[212]Edgar Cayce Readings © 1971, 1993-2007 by the Edgar Cayce Foundation. Used by Permission, All Rights Reserved.

the personalities is allergic to orange juice. Such a case was recorded by the *New York Times* in 1988.[213] If the personality that was not allergic to orange juice disappeared and the one who was allergic appeared, there would be an instant reaction of hives. If the allergic personality disappeared once again, the hives would settle instantly.

Anita Moorjani, author of *Dying to Be Me,* was admitted to a Hong Kong hospital in a coma in the final stages of terminal cancer, her organs riddled with tumours, when she had a near-death experience. Moorjani instantly began to recover from her terminal health condition and, within a short time, she was enjoying full health once more, her organs clear and functioning well.

When I had a complete hip replacement under emergency surgery in April 2014, my surgeon told me that people with hip replacements can make a full recovery. And so, I have. I am doing everything I did before breaking my hip.

Is any part of your health restricting your life? Do you believe it should keep you restricted? Do you know of anyone who has recovered or regained complete functionality despite having the same condition you have? Is it just luck that some people recover? Or is it a factor of their beliefs?

Wholeness

~ Birth of a Soul ~

"At our end of the emporium under an archway the entire wall is filled
with a molten mass of high-intensity energy and … vitality….
From the mass a swelling begins, never exactly from the same site twice.
The swelling increases and pushes outward, becoming a formless bulge.
The separation is a wondrous moment. A new soul is born.
It's totally alive with an energy and distinctness of its own."

Michael Newton, Ph. D.[214]

[213]Daniel Goleman, "Probing the Enigma of Multiple Personality," June 28, 1988; accessed December 23, 2014, www.nytimes.com/1988/06/28/science/probing-the-enigma-of-multiple-personality.html

One of our lessons on Earth is to recognize the connection of every living thing to Divine Source. Another is to integrate ourselves in body, mind, and spirit—physically, mentally, emotionally, and spiritually—to become whole, to become healed. This is the actual meaning of being "holy." Mindfully selecting the words we use and the ways we hear, think, speak, read, and write them is one choice through which we can speed up those integrating and healing processes, bringing ourselves closer to Divine Source, if we choose to do so.

Even while I have the goal of integrating myself physically, mentally, emotionally, and spiritually, I recognize that there are many souls on this Earth plane who have lost all knowledge of their Divine connection; but if you are reading this book, it is highly likely that you are well connected with your Higher Self. The souls who have lost knowledge of their Divinity have either severed their Divine Source connection (albeit temporarily—we are all given endless chances to reconnect) by plugging their godspark into some negative energy source, or they have chosen to ignore their Divinity, much as an ostrich puts its head in the sand.

We are souls living in physical bodies on the Earth plane, one of the most challenging places in our universe. We are here to test ourselves and learn further life lessons. I am connected to Divine Source, my Divine parent, through my godspark connection with my Higher Self, which is that part of me that always remains in Spirit, between and during all my incarnations. My godspark connection is my Divinity, that Divine part of myself. By logical deduction, as there is a Divine part of me—even if it is as small as an infinitesimally small spark from the immeasurably immense and infinite ball of fire that is our Source—then I am Divine.

The place where my godspark resides is in the centre of my sternum—my breast bone—right over the thymus gland, in the area that Reverend Christina Lunden calls the High Heart Chakra. I believe that when I put my hand over my sternum, I am connecting with my Divine spark, my Divine umbilical cord, up which I travel nightly when I am asleep to

[214]Michael Newton, Ph.D., *Destiny of Souls: New Case Studies of Life Between Lives*, © 2000 Llewellyn Worldwide, Ltd. 2143 Wooddale Drive, Woodbury, MN 55125, p. 127. All rights reserved, used by permission.

recharge my "Divine battery" so that I can continue living on this planet.

If I say, "My name is Nina Shoroplova," and signify myself with my left or right hand on my body, most often I put that hand on my High Heart Chakra, in the area of my breast bone.

Try it for yourself: signify yourself with your left hand while naming yourself aloud in a full sentence like mine.

Where you just placed your hand is more than likely the location of your High Heart Chakra. You too are Divine. Everything that I have said above to describe myself as being Divine is true for you.

I choose to believe this.

I recently read some insights about choosing.

"I AM what I AM. I AM what I choose to be. I choose to be love. I choose to be happy. I choose to be One."[215]

Natalie Goldberg questioned her past choices when she looked back at the incubation period for her book *Writing Down the Bones*: "Actually, when I look at my old notebooks, I think I have been a bit self-indulgent and have given myself too much time to meander in my discursive thoughts. I could have cut through sooner."[216]

Laraaji Nadananda, a musician who pioneers "in the arena of ambient music, sound, and consciousness"[217] explains that "Ten steps towards God are a hundred steps away from God, but one step AS GOD and I arrive."[218] As soon as I claim, "I am God," I am there, united with Divine Source.

With these suggestions in mind, I choose to align consciously with Source and to follow the path that my godspark invites me to follow.

What "I am" choices are you making? Are they healing choices, ones that will integrate your body, mind, and soul? Are there other choices you would like to make?

---

[215]Reverend Christina Lunden, "Angel Affirmation," June 21, 2013.
[216]Natalie Goldberg, *Writing Down the Bones*, pp. 17-18.
[217]Sound Healing Intensive handbook, 2013.
[218]In a personal email; reprinted with permission.

~ *Soul and Spirit* ~

"The soul of man is like a seed that God plants in the garden of creation. All the potential for realizing its divine nature is already in the core of the soul. To realize that potential, the soul must embark on a pilgrimage through creation where it grows, eventually making its way back, fully realized, to God."

Barbara Y. Martin and Dimitri Moraitis[219]

The women's suffrage movement in England and elsewhere was inspired with determination and drive to continue striving for the enfranchisement of women against all odds—confrontations with police and public, imprisonment, forced feeding, and years of denial of their equal citizenship with men. It was women's souls that enabled them to continue the fight. "They have suffered their imprisonment, have come out of prison injured in health, weakened in body, but not in spirit."[220]

I struggled at length to discern the difference between spirit and soul. I now call that part of my spirit inhabiting my body "my soul." The purpose of this life is to live out my soul lessons as best I can. And it is my spiritual connection that somehow keeps me on track and connected with these soul lessons. My spirit is that eternal part of myself that is both here on Earth (as my soul) and waiting on the other side as my Higher Self, ready to provide me with guidance when I seek it. I see my spirit as a nebulous vertical column into the ineffable.

There is a difference between the spirit that I am and the capital-s Spirit, which to me is the amalgamation of All That Is on the other side, hierarchical and benevolent, available in every moment to assist us and get us back on track. Capital-s Spirit comprises ordinary souls who incarnate, Ascended Masters who, from time to time, choose to come to Earth and other planets to assist beings to re-member their Divinity, and souls who don't incarnate, such as Angels, Archangels, Seraphims,

---

[219]*Change Your Aura, Change Your Life*, pp. 82-3.
[220]Joan Bryans, *Rebel Women*, a play about the Suffragette movement in Great Britain, partially inspired by Emmeline Pankhurst's *My Own Story*.

and Choirs of Angels. In my own experience and that of teachers I have met in person and in books, our souls and our spirits are accompanied at all times by angelic beings, whenever we ask them to be with us. Angels light our way.

Paramahansa Yogananda describes how his guru Swami Sri Yukteswar was able to enter a state of *Samadhi,* "a superconscious state of ecstasy in which the yogi perceives the identity of soul and Spirit."[221]

Synchronous events these days show me how much I am on the right path in my writing and learning. I wrote some of this scene on a Saturday. The next day just happened to be the feast day of St. Michael and All the Angels. And so in church I sang about the hierarchies of angels as described in the hymn by John A.L. Riley (1858-1945).

"Ye watchers and ye holy ones,
Bright seraphs, cherubim, and thrones,
Raise the glad strain, Alleluia!
Cry out, dominions, princedoms, powers,
Virtues, archangels, angels' choirs,
Alleluia! Alleluia!"

Knowledge of the order of the angelic hierarchy entered humanity during the time of Abraham, the first of the Jewish patriarchs. Angelology still intrigues us.

Do you call on your angels and know that they will be with you? Do you seek their help to ease your path, share your pain, bring you joy, and light your way? Do you have a different understanding of soul and spirit? Capital-s Spirit and spirit?

[221] *Autobiography of a Yogi,* Chapter 12.

~ Holistic Nutrition ~

"Let food be thy medicine and medicine be thy food."

Hippocrates

As a "mature" university student, some of my favourite courses were in linguistics, the study of words and language: how nouns and adjectives function, how sentences are compiled, how the English language has changed. The foundation of linguistics looks at the etymology of words; where they came from; what their history is. To look at the history of a word is to discover its roots, revealing what the word originally meant, even though it may have morphed through centuries.

Take for example the verb "to heal;" my etymological dictionary says the word "heal" comes from the Middle English word *helen* and the Anglo Saxon word *hēlan,* both meaning "to make whole." When I look up the word "whole," I find it comes from the Middle English words "hole" and "hool." From these words, we have several derivatives: "holistic" (meaning "to see the entire organism as one unit"), "hale" (a rather old-fashioned term often used together with "and hearty" to describe vigorous health), "healthy" (easily understood), and "holy" (misunderstood through its usage to describe someone who is religious).

So, even though the words "heal" and "whole" have the same etymological roots as the words "holy" and "holiday," the word "holy" has now come to mean "sacred." "Holiday" originally meant "a festival for a holy day"; now it means taking time away from work to do something completely different, such as travelling. How fascinating that when we are on holiday, we are usually at our most relaxed, not doing as much as regularly, just being. For after all, we are human "beings." And so, when we relax on holiday, we come closer to being our true Divine selves, to being holy.

Understanding that, I find it easier to realize that "to heal" is to get closer to being whole: it is to integrate myself physically, mentally, emotionally, and spiritually; it is to balance, harmonize, and align myself; it is to accept myself as I am; it is also to recognize my connection with Divinity. It is to whole myself; again, it is to become more "holy."

Until I trained as a Holistic Nutritionist with the Canadian School of Natural Nutrition, I didn't understand the term "holistic." Now I do. Holistic nutrition sees the way we nourish our bodies as including not just the food we eat but the mood in which we eat, where we eat, what time we eat, whom we eat with, what we are discussing around the table as we eat, what music is playing as we eat, whether the television is on or not, when we ate our last meal, when we plan to eat our next—and much more. In other words, holistic nutrition views the ingredients we put in our mouths as only a very small aspect of the way we nourish ourselves.

In a way, this entire book looks at ways of nourishing our Selves holistically, with provocative ideas, ways to discern our emotions, methods to increase self-awareness, and ways to connect with our souls.

Do you treat yourself holistically? How do you nourish your body, your mind, your heart, your spirit? Do you see yourself as a whole human, a holy human?

~ *What Is Healing?* ~

"'Heal' means 'make whole.'

The person torn apart by his fears, hates, or greeds is not a whole person.

He is a circle with one or more segments missing."

Frederick Bailes, M.D.[222]

As I described in the previous scene, the word "heal" linguistically is connected with being whole. We are whole when we are in spirit. When each of us incarnates into a physical body in the Earth plane, we leave part of our spirit behind. Were we to import our entire spirit into our physical bodies, we would blow our circuits. Our personal infinitesimally small portion

[222]*Basic Principles of the Science of Mind*, p. 12.

of Divine mind—of Infinite Intelligence—is far more than our finite human brains can handle.

For writers, editors, poets, actors, singers, playwrights, lyricists, bloggers, journalists, speakers, lecturers, teachers, counsellors, translators—people who live life through their fifth chakra of communication—words are our tools. It could be said that we have fifth-chakra gifts.

Fourth-chakra gifts are those of loving and healing. I am particularly referring to healers who are communicating spiritual ministration in some way—New Age authors, channellers, self-help bloggers, psalm writers, priests, rabbis, inspirational poets, and spiritual coaches. It helps us when we understand the Divine Wisdom words we share deeply, phenomenally, expansively, and even funnily, as well as understanding the many, many ways that we can use them.

The word "healing" might suggest that there is to be a cure, but healing means something different from curing. I believe that healing is one of the main tasks that each of us came to Earth to accomplish: to heal ourselves and, by doing so, to heal others. According to Nasiri Suzan, a sound therapist, "Therapists are healed through their clients' healing." And every healing lifts all of us.

Healing begins when we acknowledge that we are not whole, that something is separating us from our true Self.

Edgar Cayce, the sleeping prophet, says, "All healing, mental or material, is attuning each atom of the body, each reflex of the brain forces, to the awareness of the Divine that lies within each atom, each cell of the body."[223]

I also find it useful to look etymologically at the words that have the phoneme *spir* within them: "inspire, inspiration, expire, expiration, respire, respiration." I expect you can see where this is going. Actually, I first considered this when I took singing lessons and learned to get out of my own way and allow Spirit to come through with my inbreaths as I inspired.

When we breathe in, we carry out the act of inspiration; we bring spirit (also known as "breath") into our bodies. The physiological function of respiration—carried out by the nostrils, trachea, bronchi, lungs, ribs, intercostal muscles, diaphragm—comprises two actions: breathing in is inspiration and breathing out is expiration.

[223]Reading 3384-2.

We come into this life on an in-breath as we inspire our bodies with spirit. We leave on an out-breath—an expiration—as our spirit leaves our body. The process of dying is no more than ceasing breathing. We breathe out our last breath and breathe in no more.

Have you ever been with someone who took their last breath? They took it and they breathed out. You waited for the next inbreath and it never came. And that was it. You may have heard of someone's date of death as the date he or she "expired." The time a person dies is far more difficult to pin down. Death is a nebulous moment. You can look at the clock, but when did the "death" happen?

It is so perfect that the word "inspiration" means both "to breathe in" and "to draw spirit into ourselves." By common usage, "inspiration" also means "to give ourselves other-worldly ideas."

Our major purpose on Earth is to heal and integrate ourselves to become whole by recognizing our spiritual connection to Divine Source. A mindful selection of the thoughts we think, the images we see, the senses we feel, the emotions we acknowledge, the words we use, the ways we hear, speak, and write these words, and the actions we take are choices through which we can speed up that integrating and healing process.

According to Gregg Braden (*The God Code*), we have great potential in each life to choose to become more healed, more whole, more holy, growing purposefully closer to God, closer to our Divine nature.

What are the choices you are making while on Earth? Are they healing choices? Are you integrating yourself, body, mind, and spirit? Are you healing others?

Part IV ~ Moving Forward

Chapter 10—Being Fully One's Self

Now Orientation Brings Peace

~ Live the Spiral of Life ~

"Before enlightenment; chop wood, carry water.
After enlightenment; chop wood, carry water."
Zen proverb

Much of life seems cyclical—the seasons of the year move through spring, summer, winter, and fall. Water falls as rain, collects into rivers, travels to the ocean, rises as moisture, gathers as clouds, falls as rain. A seed falls from a plant, germinates in the ground, grows into a plant, flowers, and goes to seed. The Earth turns 360° on its axis, a rotation that seems to us on Earth as taking us toward and then away from full sunlight, from day to night and back to day. At birth, a female child's body contains all the eggs that will ever mature there; if she has a child of her own, the cycle continues.

When we go with the flow of our cyclical lives, we can find the peace of living day to day, oriented to the "now" of life.

We also live our lives not just in cycles, but in ascending spirals. At first, we come around and around again to emotions, sensations, thoughts, and words (words being one of the ways we express ourselves), and we rise in wisdom as repeated exposures make us more aware. These basic tools of awareness are discussed in Part I. If we do grow in awareness, we can start to improve our actions.

Spiralling up from action that is conscious and altruistic is the next level: increasing awareness of the mystery that is all around us, much of it ignored and disregarded. As our awe at the mystery and our awareness of it grows, our thoughts, words, goals, and actions become more Divinely informed. This second stage is discussed in Part II.

Part III offers a myriad of ways to live the highest life on Earth by observing our processes, incorporating the mystery (which also means *embodying* the mystery through self-awareness), and integrating body, mind, and soul. Incorporating this, we live more responsibly, more consistently, more consciously. We no longer have to strive to find our precious life—it will find us.

As the Zen proverb opening this scene claims, our actions may be the same after we reach a higher spiral as before, but the motivation for any action may change.

~ *Mind the Gap* ~

"God exists within the thought of Divinity itself, within our mind,
nowhere outside of us,
not even inside the definition that we've held of who we are,
because it's only by releasing that definition that we experience this."
James Twyman[224]

Written on station platforms in the London Underground is the caution "Mind the Gap." It sounds like meditation advice. Meditators say there is a gap—a space—between one thought and the next. So, would it be a case of minding or unminding the gap, or mining the gap, if we want to meditate successfully? There is so much we can do when we want to re-mind ourselves of our spiritual reality, our Divine consciousness, our connection to our real home.

On January 25, 2015, Tania Gabrielle sent out an inspirational quote

[224]2015 Revival reflection on *A Course in Miracles,* Lesson 30.

advising her followers to "remember that prayer and devotion are songs to the divine. Hear the music of the spheres in the ethereal space between your sentences, breaths and thoughts."

And so to "Mind the Gap" means to bring Divinity into the spaces between breaths, between thoughts, between thoughts and actions, within actions. It means to become observers of our lives, to live in the moment, to let go of control, to invite the Divine in, and to accept the events of our lives. We can find our Divine selves in the gap—I AM as God made me. While praying is considered to be talking to God and meditating is considered to be listening to God, "minding the gap" means being intentionally in a receptive state more constantly, perhaps always.

When I was pregnant with each of my children, I knew in every single moment of every waking day that I was carrying another life in my uterus. It was a constant awareness from first thing in the morning to last thing at night. Nowadays, I know that I am first and foremost a spiritual being; I know in every single moment of every waking day that I am Divine; and so are you.

~ *Connect with the Life Force Consciously* ~

"God is the energy that connects all living things."

Unknown source

Our Divine Source vibrates with the energy of love. Divine love vibrates so fast that it becomes Divine light. This is our nature—love and light—because each of us is part of the whole.

In order to grasp ideas about our origins, I accept the analogy that the Great Creator of All That Is *aka* Divine Source is an infinite ball of light, rather like our Sun, only infinite in time and space. We live here on the

Earth in a finite world of time and space, within the infinity of all-time and all-space—Divine Source.

Just as our sun emits solar flares and coronal mass ejections, our Divine Source flares and erupts parts of itself; some of these ejections separate long enough to become individuated souls, as described in the quote introducing the scene "~ Birth of a Soul ~" in chapter nine. The journey of each soul is unique.

We who choose to incarnate into a physical, emotional, and mental planet such as Earth live through multiple incarnations—we reincarnate time and again. Each time we die, we review our life in Divine love's light and embrace, never being judged, only ever judging ourselves. In whatever way we find ourselves wanting—by judging our previous life—we declare this lack of growth to those souls who are on our spiritual council and, with their guidance, select the lessons we want to work on in our next life. An example of a type of wanting could be a lack of patience, a lack of the ability to show love, a lack of empathy, a lack of initiative. It could be even worse—it could be a wrongdoing such as injuring another, being dismissive, or neglecting one in our care.

In that other world—what some call "the other side" and others call "Heaven"—we spend time with our soul group, compare notes, help each other grow and understand. We review the Akashic Record of our past lives; and as our time to reincarnate gets closer, we choose our next life, our next parents, and our next challenges. Then we focus on the fetal body we will soon inhabit, starting to spend some time there, absorbing our mother's emotions, being triggered by her thoughts. And then, one fine day, we are born into a new physical body.

For most of us, somewhere between our day of birth and our sixth birthday, the veil of forgetfulness descends completely between ourselves and Divine Source. Only some children are able to hold on consciously to the memories of their life between lives, their past lives, and their origins. For most of us, myself included, we forget. By forgetting where we come from, we live an easier life; we face our tests without expectations; we come once more to self-awareness of our spirit's journey; and we receive the gifts that come from learning.

Over time, I have compiled my understanding of a spirit's journey from writings by Frederick Bailes, Edgar Cayce, Deepak Chopra, Tim Doyle, Wayne Dyer, Andrrea Hess, Christina Lunden, Barbara Y. Martin, Michael Newton, and Paramahansa Yogananda. If you read all their words, you might not come up with the same understanding that I have. Even so, this is my truth and it is the truth upon which I build my life. It is my bias.

Eighty-five years ago, in 1930, spiritual philosophers and quantum physicists began bringing their fields of understanding closer together. At that time, English physicist, astronomer, and mathematician Sir James Hopwood Jeans (1877-1946) delivered the highly esteemed Rede Lecture at the University of Cambridge, England. An impressive array of such lectures has been presented by Fellows of one of the Colleges at Cambridge every year since the late 1660s.

Sir James Jeans's lecture was also published as a book entitled *The Mysterious Universe*. I am intrigued by his conclusions. Initially, Sir James states that "the universe appears to have been designed by a pure mathematician";[225] he claims that mathematical thought is pure thought. Having proven this theory satisfactorily for himself, he quotes his fellow Englishman George Berkeley, Bishop of Cloyne (1685-1753), an idealist philosopher who suggests that just because we humans do not know about certain things with our minds, those things "'must either have no existence at all, or else subsist in the mind of some Eternal Spirit.'"[226] He uses the obvious existence of the planet Pluto before that planet was discovered to prove his argument.

After agreeing with this premise, it's a short move to the statement that makes Jeans famous: "the universe begins to look more like a great thought than like a great machine. Mind no longer appears as an accidental intruder in the realm of matter; we are beginning to suspect that

[225]James Jeans, *The Mysterious Universe*, p. 115.
[226]Ibid., p. 126.

we ought rather to hail [mind] as the creator and governor of the realm of matter—not of course our individual minds, but the mind in which the atoms out of which our individual minds have grown and exist as thoughts."[227] Let me repeat Sir James Jeans' most intriguing premise: "the universe begins to look more like a great thought than like a great machine."

Jeans moved from quoting Bishop Berkeley on his term "Eternal Spirit" to referring to an omniscient, omnipresent, and eternal mind. It's a short leap from this to seeing that we are co-creators with Divine Source. We engage as co-creators through our thoughts, words, and actions, creating and re-creating ourselves and our environment.

What I find fascinating is that more than three millennia ago, the Sanskrit Vedas of ancient India were describing the world as an illusion, as *maya*. And what is an illusion if not a thought? It was when I was reading Paramahansa Yogananda's *Autobiography of a Yogi* that I first heard this paradigm-changing idea that actually confirms such sonic creationist myths as "In the beginning was the Word."

All the emotions, thoughts, ideas, and actions that make us believe in the turmoil of the world and doubt that we are Divine are negative, destructive emotions, thoughts, ideas, and actions. By contrast, those emotions, thoughts, ideas, and actions that serve to align us more closely with our Divine nature—our personal knowledge of our own Divinity—our Life Force—are positive and creative. Day after day, I consciously choose to connect with the positive side of life.

[227]Ibid., p. 138.

Posing Questions Brings Results

~ *Asking and Answering Questions* ~

"I KEEP six honest serving-men
(They taught me all I knew);
Their names are What and Why and When
And How and Where and Who.
I send them over land and sea,
I send them east and west;
But after they have worked for me,
I give them all a rest."

Rudyard Kipling[228]

Questions have a huge potential for healing, which is why I have used them so prominently in this book. In an episode of BBC's *Lark Rise to Candleford*, Minnie, to me the most endearing of the characters, asks a very personal question of someone who has recently lost his wife; everyone else has been tiptoeing around the topic, recognizing the pain attached. The question is something like, "What was it like when your wife died?" You can hear the indrawn breaths from the other four people present. But the widower actually settles back, answers fully and then says (this is the gist of his words), "Thank you. That's the first time anyone has asked me that question. What a relief and even a joy it is to be able to express some of the pain in my heart."

Too often, we tiptoe around the elephant in the room, careful to ignore and sidestep any questions that might expose another person's emotional pain. Such efforts just solidify the idea that such pain is best left buried, which is exactly the opposite of how we release emotional pain.

I say, "Good on ya, Minnie!" like any true Aussie.

---

[228] *Just So Stories*, p. 31.

If we don't ask questions when presented with a puzzle, we make assumptions. To *assume* is to make an *ass* of *u* and *me*. Miguel Ruiz says, "The way to keep yourself from making assumptions is to ask questions."[229]

Some of the most frequent questions asked by spiritual seekers are "Why am I here? Why are we here? What is my purpose? What is my story?"

The Reverend Lois Boxill peppered a June 2014 sermon at St. Paul's Anglican Church with questions: "Whose are you? Who do you serve? What do you serve? Who controls you? What controls you? What does your identity say about who you are? What intrigues you? What do your actions say about you? Do they betray you?" She ended with the clincher, "Who are you with your dogs and cats?"

Well, I don't have a pet any more, but I know what she means.

She designed these questions to help us get to the core of our identity and to question who or what dictates how we live our lives. She said we are labelled by what we do, how we are perceived, and how we act. I wonder; does someone else's perception make us who we are? She encouraged us—the congregation—to use our answers to her questions to help us adopt a Christ-like identity. Being more spiritual than religious, I have to translate "adopt a Christ-like identity" in my mind to "recognize I can attain Christ Consciousness" in all I do.

In reply to my request to use her words in this book, she emailed, "My only hope is for folks to draw closer towards greater integrity and awareness in their lives—which to me means conscious awareness of their truth as it is—unprettied and raw, without need for excuse, clarification, or adornment."

Alyson Jones—therapist, educator, and writer—recommends sixteen steps to live an exceptional life, the first and second of which are "Turn it up to eleven" and "Give up perfectionism and become an exceptionalist." In her book *M.O.R.E.*, where her titular acronym stands for movement,

[229]*The Four Agreements*, p. 72.

opportunity, reality, and exceptional living, she uses these steps to ask questions that enable her readers to get to the core of their lives.

My husband and I love watching movies. In *Don Juan DeMarco*, Johnny Depp in the eponymous romantic role tells the psychiatrist who becomes his greatest ally, "There are only four questions of value in life, Don Octavio: What is sacred? Of what is the spirit made? What is worth living for? What is worth dying for?" Then this modern-day Don Juan answers his own questions, saying that the reply to each is the same: "Only love." How right he is.

Questions are powerful. When we ask ourselves a question aloud, we bring out our inner authority. We answer instantly. If we settle into ourselves and think deeply about a question, we will always hear an answer and the deeper we settle into ourselves, the deeper the place it will come from, eventually coming as Divine wisdom.

~ *Positive Requests* ~

"Imagine the Universal Law as a shipping clerk in a large mail-order company.
He gets your order but has no idea who you are.
If the order says 'size 8,' he sends out size 8.
It's of no concern to him whether or not size 8 fits you.
He merely complies with your request."
Stuart Wilde[230]

We are sending our requests, daydreams, affirmations, wants, and wishes to the Universe all the time. Sometimes, we couch them in positive phrasing, sometimes in negative. The Universe does not understand negatives. Everything is positive. So when we say, "I do hope I don't fail my exam," the Universe hears, "I hope I fail my exam," and helps us fail.

[230]*The Three Keys to Self-Empowerment*, p. 17.

Someone who is always looking on the gloomy side of life—the have-not situations, the bad-luck scenarios, and the downright catastrophes—will be thinking something like, "What a terrible world we live in." The Universe will continue to provide that person with a terrible world to live in.

All through high school, I was the quiet girl sitting near the front of the class, seldom able to raise my hand with an answer or a comment during classes, certain my opinion didn't matter. I was the one who was so quiet during choir practice that it never occurred to me to ask the director if she would consider me for a solo, even though I just yearned to be asked. The choir director was also my piano teacher, Miss Cole. Can you imagine! I sat with my teacher for a half-hour lesson on the piano each week, yet it never occurred to me to ask that same teacher for a chance to sing a solo in her choir.

That's how strong one's inner critic can be. What was my inner critic telling me when I truly wanted to sing a solo? "I will never get chosen." I was certainly right there, with that mindset!

What else was my inner critic saying? "I don't speak Welsh." My high school was in Wales and Miss Cole was also the Welsh teacher; she asked mostly Welsh-speaking girls to sing her Welsh solos. That's an "aha!" for me, after all these years of thinking I wasn't good enough. What a bias for a teacher to choose only Welsh-speaking girls to sing the solos!

What else was my inner critic saying? "My voice is too light, too thin; it doesn't have the quality [I didn't know the word 'timbre' in those days] that Meghan's has or Sian's has. Could I sing out loud in front of everybody here? Would I remember the words? I would be too shy."

I waited decades before I sang a solo in my high school, and that was at my fortieth-year high school reunion.

When we want to turn to the next page in our lives, we must voice our desires rather than our misgivings and negative observations.

By choosing to live consciously and positively, by making positive requests for the situations we truly want and desire, we will find that life flows more easily in a direction that moves us forward.

~ *Kaizen Your Habits* ~

"The word Kaizen means 'continuous improvement.'
It comes from the Japanese words 改 ('kai') which means 'change'
or 'to correct' and 善 ('zen') which means 'good.'
Kaizen is a system that involves every employee....
Everyone is encouraged to come up with
small improvement suggestions on a regular basis."

Steve Stephenson[231]

Kaizen is a concept developed by the Japanese auto industry but with wide application for improving any process. I use the word as a noun and as a verb, so I can kaizen my habits by tweaking them until they are really working for me.

We all have odd habits. For instance, my husband only ever has butter on his bread in a restaurant; at home, he eats his bread "dry." What's that all about?

I grew up in South Wales in the fifties and sixties, when a big fry-up for breakfast on the weekend was a wonderful treat. Fried bacon and eggs took centre stage, with fried bread on the side. In addition, there was a wide array of further choices: fried tomatoes, black blood sausage, laver bread (chopped seaweed—a Welsh specialty), and one of my favourites, fried mushrooms.

In those days, it was hard to find mushrooms in the marketplace. My father would come home delightedly carrying a small paper bag with

[231]"What is Kaizen?" accessed July 15, 2014, www.graphicproducts.com/tutorials/kaizen/

half a dozen or more mushrooms, elderly mushrooms, already turning black under the gills. Because of their age, they were far tastier than the beautiful white-crowned field mushrooms we get these days. While the flavour of these mushrooms had improved, their caps were dry with age. And so we peeled the cap of every mushroom, habitually. This was a habit I continued, even with much younger mushrooms. I did it without questioning, until I looked more carefully at that habit. And adjusted it.

I kaizened my mushroom-peeling habit.

An intentional repetitive action carried out for twenty-one days in a row becomes a habit. This is how we can tweak and change habits that are not serving us. When I assigned homework to my soul-counselling clients, I asked them to repeat their transmutation prayer aloud for twenty-one days in a row and to start the twenty-one days over again if they missed a day.

We also have good and bad habits. Bad habits take us away from our alignment with goodness. Good habits serve our beliefs through our rules.

What are some of my beliefs and the rules supporting them? How can I kaizen them?

I believe that I am going to live a productive life until I am in my late nineties. I believe I am inhabiting the best body possible for living my life. I have a number of rules that I have ritualized into habits to support me in preserving this body in good shape over the next thirty years or so. Bit by bit, I kaizen these habits. Following are some good habits I've had in the past:

- practise yoga for half an hour each morning for strength, flexibility, and stamina;
- drink two large glasses of lemon water to get my digestive tract up and running;
- bring to the boil the porridge flakes and seeds that I've already soaked overnight;

- turn off the element and put the lid on the saucepan to allow the porridge to continue cooking in its residual heat;
- soak a scoop of porridge flakes and seeds in water with a couple of drops of apple cider vinegar in readiness for tomorrow; the vinegar is for starting the seeds' germination process;
- wait an hour after drinking the lemon water before eating;
- carry out a spiritual ritual before breakfast;
- at the end of the day, put a glass of filtered, alkalized water by my bed to hydrate myself through the night; and
- get a good night's sleep, aiming for eight hours.

Then on mornings when I wake up bursting with ideas for whatever I'm writing, I have to juggle everything around until it all gets done … or not!

The habits I've just described are excellent ones I developed during the year I began studying holistic nutrition. I've kaizened some of them since; in fact, I am rather vague about my spiritual ritual because it continues to evolve as I evolve.

Drinking lemon water first thing in the morning is an excellent habit that has also evolved. Although lemon juice is a very strong acid, it works in the body like a strong alkalizer, because its ash is alkaline. The ash of a food is what is left after it has been fully digested. These days the average diet veers toward being acidic—because of the high consumption of meat, processed foods, soft drinks, and candies, all of which require high quantities of the body's own minerals for digestion. Thus, these foods demineralize the body, turning it more acidic. Minerals alkalize the body. Lemon juice alkalizes the body. Additionally, lemon juice in that quantity boosts the peristaltic action of the digestive tract and thins the blood, as well as providing fresh vitamins.

The last time I visited my dentist, she and I realized that while the lemon juice was benefitting my digestion, keeping my blood thinner, and providing my body with excellent vitamins and minerals, it was not helping my teeth. In fact, over the course of the previous four or so years, the lemon juice has worn away quite a bit of tooth enamel. I explained that I wasn't about to give up the habit of drinking lemon juice in the mornings, and so she came up with a compromise. I now revert my oral pH back to alkaline with a special paste right after drinking the lemon juice.

Some habits are learned. I became aware of this when I first lived in Australia. Having grown up in Wales and lived much of my adult life in Canada, my geographical orientation had me thinking that January was in the winter, August was in the summer, the sun was in the south, and cooler climes were to my north. Of course, being in the southern hemisphere, Australia enjoys summer in January, winter in August, the sun in the northern sky, and cooler climes to the south. Completely opposite. It took strict learning to create new habits around my geographical orientation.

Research the System and Trust

~ *Seeing through I AM Christ Consciousness* ~

"There is another way of looking at the world—
through the eyes of Christ Consciousness or 'I AM consciousness';
[which is] to see things through the eyes of God,
when all things appear as light not as shadow."
James Twyman[232]

On August 16, 2009, I wrote a new affirmation in my journal—"I speak my truth from my heart." Such an affirmation helps me to be more honest, to reflect better on my emotions, to become more aware of my Divine nature. However, it sometimes has repercussions.

[232]2015 Revival reflection on *A Course in Miracles,* Lesson 33.

The next day was the Feast Day of the Assumption of Mary the Mother of Jesus into heaven. In the choir room that Sunday, the topic of Mary's immaculate conception arose. We were discussing the fact that the Roman Catholic Church claims that both Mary and her mother Ann were immaculately conceived; this belief came about so that the two women would be pure vessels to give birth to Jesus, the *only* son of God.

I spoke up and said I believe we are each the sons and daughters of God, and that each of us is Divine. And David Ryniker said, "Heretic, heretic. Burn her at the stake."

David said it in jest, which I partly knew. But it struck me to the core. I have felt fear and horror around stories of women being burned at the stake previously—for instance, when seeing Arthur Miller's *The Crucible* performed. I have a horror of flames. Was I burned at the stake in a previous life during those horrific times? If I wasn't, I certainly believe I saw my sisters being burned.

During the Assumption service, my mind and heart were reviewing what David had said, and I became very tearful as I thought about my beliefs, perceiving them as quite different from everyone else's in that church. I believe that Jesus did not die for our sins so much to redeem us as to demonstrate love and forgiveness. I believe in reincarnation; even that Jesus is a reincarnated Soul with a Higher Self; and that when we say, "He shall come again," I believe that that refers to each of us, that that time is now and that each of us has the opportunity to "put on Christ," raise our soul vibration rate, and follow in Jesus' footsteps. That for me means stepping into Christ Consciousness.

Jesus said, "Whoever believes in me will do the works I have been doing, and they will do even greater things than these, because I am going to the Father."[233]

I turned to David Ryniker and said, "Your comments cut me to the quick. Did you really mean that? Do you not believe that you are Divine?"

He replied, "Of course, I believe I have the Divine in me."

---

[233]John 14:12, NIV®.

I wept tears of relief, sadness, and confusion. It was a deep mood that was hard to shake off.

I have often felt that I am a fraud attending church and saying, "Jesus, the only son of God," when I don't believe that he is the *only* human who can be God's son. I see Jesus as being a pure vessel of Divine Source, as Christ Consciousness personified. I believe there have been other *only* sons of God—Mohammad, Buddha, Paramahansa Yogananda, to name just three—each of them living as pure Christ Consciousness, to be lights in our world, as models of Divinity. The desire of each of us as souls to gain Christ Consciousness is humanity's desire to reach Christ Consciousness, with the potential to become part of the Only Son of God, as pure as Jesus the Christ. We will do that by recognizing our own Divinity fully and denying our ego self, a tall order, but there are others who have done it. If that were not the case, what would be the purpose of reincarnating?

There in that place of worship, I was stuck in the doctrine, the dogma, the liturgy, stuck in my emotional body. And until I had talked it out, crying all the while, with other choir members and my husband, I couldn't shake off my sadness at the confining nature of organized religion, which puts such walls around the spiritual potential of ordinary mortals like me.

Eventually, I checked in with my angels, my Higher Self, who told me, "It is part of your growth to know that your heart is deeply connected to the Divine and that the worldly words of a church cannot alter your beliefs, only strengthen you where you align with the beliefs, and help you clarify your beliefs where they do not align with the liturgy." How interesting that we don't get altered at the altar.

We come to our lessons and our teachers when we are ready. Feed your curiosity about your spiritual potential and let the strength of that curiosity move you forward.

~ *Writing a Letter to Your Future Self* ~

"You are invited to attend a day-long workshop entitled 'Between the Retirement Party and the Funeral.'"
Sharon Coates, Maggy Kaplan, and Yvonne Stuart[234]

Those commenting on how hard it is to live in the "now" often say that we live regretting our past, dreading our future, and seldom enjoying this very moment. And this moment. And this moment.

Yet, by thinking differently of our past, we can learn from it and see more clearly the dots that, once connected, mark our path. By thinking differently *from* our future *back* to our present, we can trace a path that we can follow from this moment forward. In fact, that is one of the best ways for us to create the steps that are essential for completing a goal. And for completing a life beneficially.

Some years after the temenos I was in had folded, the original Vancouver temenos organizer got together with a couple of other women and organized a workshop entitled "Between the Retirement Party and the Funeral." I attended. One of the exercises was to write a letter from our ninety-year-old selves to our current selves. Initially, it was strange to imagine myself aged ninety but somehow not strange to look back at my current self from the future. After connecting with my inner wisdom, I perceived myself in my nineties being a sage elder whose wisdom was evident in what she wrote and said to others. I was deeply grateful to my younger self (me, now) for the steps I took (am taking) to get myself to that wise state. The exercise built a bridge that has made it much easier to walk in that direction.

From this workshop seven years ago emerged a group that goes unnamed—some just call it "the group"—though I call it the Eldergarten (compare with "Kindergarten"). If youngsters—*kinder*—can have fun and learn at a Kindergarten, then surely we elders can have fun and learn

---

[234]An invitation by email, May 31, 2008.

at an Eldergarten. And we do have fun—we laugh a lot and we reflect on our lives. And we discuss issues that are important to conscious aging: "Yearning, longing, and the soul," "Uncertainty," "Differences between ourselves and our parents," "What is play?" "Beliefs and blind spots," "Being Alone," and "Loss."

The Eldergarten celebrated its fifth year together at Maggy's: Donna, Sharon, Sue, Ada, John, Diane, Karen, and me. Several of our group were out of town.

Life is rich with examples of topics suitable for reflection, for further learning, for growing self-awareness. What is important is to have ways of taking the time to reflect, to learn about what you actually believe about your Divine self, your life, your relationships with others.

Whatever your current age, writing a letter from your ninety-year-old self to your current self after connecting with your inner wisdom can open up a more expansive view of your life. It can help you build a bridge forward into your future and place some irresistible stepping stones along that bridge.

~ *Trust the Mystery* ~

"Is being of service in community the basic human condition, whereas money, materialism, and consumerism have made it all about the individual person?"
Julie Salisbury[235]

When we immerse ourselves in this life on Earth, we face constant challenges, surprising unknowns, out-of-the-blue pitfalls, as well as tremendous joys and shining opportunities. We may at some point wonder why we are here, what it's all about, and what our purpose is.

Before a pilot flies a plane that is sitting on the tarmac in Vancouver International Airport, the pilot researches, studies, learns, and embodies his part in utilizing the aerodynamics of mechanical flight. Then he trusts that the tried-and-true theory of flight, when carefully applied, will yield the miracle of a metallic object weighing 174,000 pounds or more rising into the air and flying from one destination in the world to another. Yet again!

Before a surfer takes to the waves at Whitesands Beach in West Wales and swims out to the north end of the headland, she learns about surfboards and weather conditions, the right gear and physical preparedness. And then she trusts that a particular wave will give her a spectacular ride back into the bay. What a rush!

Learning to ski provides the same challenges and similar thrills.

Life doesn't come with a handbook. I always wanted a handbook as a first-time mother. I knew I had learned to walk as a baby, but I wondered how I could teach my baby boy to walk. Then I let go and trusted that the example of other people walking would inspire my son to stand up and take his first tentative steps. He did.

Each of these exercises in trust represents a miracle, something that was once seen as magic; each one poses a mystery. What elements are

[235]Julie Salisbury, *Around the World in Seven Years* (North Vancouver: Influence Publishing, 2015), p. xiii.

involved? Research. Training. The embodiment of a system. Forward movement. Trust. Trust in the Mystery. An airplane is heavier than air, and yet it flies because of forward movement. A surfboard with a human aboard is heavier than the water it rests on, and yet it rushes forward, because of the force of the waves pushing into the angled board.

The best way to experience life and grow our soul is by being in community, being of service, contributing, doing whatever we love to do without counting the cost. For most of us, it is impossible to experience life without being in community with others. In chapter seven, the scene entitled "~ Your Team ~" will have engaged you in thinking about your communities. It is within these relationships that we do most of our growing.

In relationship, we have the opportunity to be in harmony with others, to talk with, to walk with, to travel, dine, joke, and discuss with others. We can trust, support, care, and serve others, whatever their size, beauty, age, colour, creed, or gender; no matter their wealth, power, influence, or lack thereof; whether we like, idolize, fear, or are revolted by them. Each of us carries the spark of Divine life within; we are here to help each other reach the next platform … and the one after that. We do that by doing what we can … in community … in relationship.

Bob McDonald of CBC Radio One's *Quirks and Quarks* interviewed Sandra Trehub, Doctor of Psychology and Professor of Psychology at the University of Toronto, Mississauga about the fact that every human culture past and present plays music. Professor Trehub's response was very revealing. "When people listen to music together, it seems to enhance social bonds. It does that even better when they participate actively in music. So, whether [that's] clapping, dancing, singing together, or playing instruments together, a very important aspect of the joint music making is our ability to synchronize our movement to music and to synchronize with each other, and one of the consequences of synchronous activity is enhanced cooperation. So music makes good sense for people living in groups."[236]

[236]The program aired on June 21, 2014.

I have trusted the mystery in writing this book. I have written it in the hope that it will inspire you to live a fuller life. If it does not, that is my fault for not sharing the wisdom I've received clearly enough, compellingly enough. If it does inspire you, I am truly grateful, and place all praise at the feet of my many teachers, whether they are people I have met personally, people I have met through their writing, whether they are my spiritual teachers, those who are with me every moment of every day.

I wish you every blessing you wish for yourself.

Live well and fully, and trust the mystery.

Epilogue

One mystery of life that I have barely mentioned is death. It's a huge mystery and a compelling topic, one that fascinates me because of the ways that death can inform life. It's a topic that many people spend much energy avoiding, which detracts from its power to enrich our lives.

Rather than dreading death, I would like to investigate it further. It will be the topic of my next book, as soon as I can write it!

Until then, Blessed Be.

Nina Shoroplova, February 4, 2015

Bibliography

Articles

Edgar Cayce Readings. Edgar Cayce © 1971, 1993-2007 by the Edgar Cayce Foundation.

Hopler, Whitney. "Sacred Roses: The Spiritual Symbolism of the Rose," angels.about.com

Lunden, Reverend Christina. Daily Angel Affirmations. christinalunden.com

McCraty, Rollin, Ph.D. "The Energetic Heart Bioelectromagnetic Interactions within and between People." Boulder Creek, California: Institute of HeartMath, 2002.

Terry Small Learning Institute. terrysmall.com

Books

Ananda, Raamayan. *Michael Jackson: The Man behind the Mirror.* North Vancouver, Influence Publishing, 2014.

Anthony, Lawrence. *The Elephant Whisperer.* Thomas Dunn Books, St. Martin's Griffin, 2009.

Bailes, Frederick, M.D. *Basic Principles of the Science of Mind,* Twelve Lesson Home Study Course, 1951.

Baxter-Holder, George, D.N.P. *Drugs, Food, Sex and God: An Addicted Drug Dealer Goes from Convict to Doctor through the Power of Intention.* North Vancouver, Influence Publishing, 2015.

Bharucha, Jasmine. *Who Am I?* North Vancouver, Influence Publishing, 2014.

Biblica, Inc.™ Holy Bible, New International Version®, 2011.

Bisson-Somerville, Michèle. *Voodoo Shit for Men: Flex Your Intuitive Muscle.* North Vancouver, Influence Publishing, 2014.

Braden, Gregg. *The God Code: The Secret of Our Past, the Promise of Our Future*. Hay House, 2005.

Brennan, Barbara. *Hands of Light: A Guide to Healing through the Human Energy Field*. Random House, 2011.

Cameron, Julia. *The Artist's Way: A Spiritual Path to Higher Creativity*. Tarcher, 2002.

Chopra, Deepak, M.D. *Perfect Health: The Complete Mind/Body Guide*. Harmony Books, 1991.

Chopra, Deepak, M.D. *Return of the Rishi: A Doctor's Story of Spiritual Transformation and Ayurvedic Healing*. Houghton Mifflin Company, 1988.

Cleese, John. *So, Anyway….* Doubleday Canada, 2014.

Couture, Eugenea. *Adoption Not an Option: A Métis Woman Torn from her Family and her 40 Year Battle to Find Them Again*. North Vancouver, Influence Publishing, 2014.

Donne, John. *Devotions upon Emergent Occasions, and Severall Steps in My Sicknes "Meditation XVII."* 1624.

Doyle, Timothy J. *How to Play the Game of Life: Beginner's Version*. 2013. *How to Play the Game of Life: Intermediate Version*. 2014. ThePathToOneness.com

Dumais, Sue. *Heart Led Living: When Hard Work Becomes Heart Work*. North Vancouver, Influence Publishing, 2014.

Dyer, Wayne. *There's a Spiritual Solution to Every Problem*. Harper, 2001.

Eisenstein, Charles. *Sacred Economics: Money, Gift, and Society in the Age of Transition*. Evolver Editions, 2011.

Fleury, Theo and Kim Barthel. *Conversations with a Rattlesnake*. North Vancouver, Influence Publishing, 2014.

Fox, Mem. *Reading Magic*. Harcourt Inc., 2001.

Gandhi, Mahatma, selected by Richard Attenborough. *The Words of Gandhi*. Newmarket Press, 1982.

Garber, Marjorie. *Shakespeare's Ghost Writers: Literature as Uncanny Causality*. Methuen, 2010.

Gardner, Howard. *Frames of Mind: The Theory of Multiple Intelligences*. Basic Books, 2011.

Goldberg, Natalie. *Writing Down the Bones: Freeing the Writer Within*. Shambhala Publications, Inc., 1986.

Goldstein, Leah and contributor, Lori Moger, M.Sc. *No Limits: The Powerful True Story of Leah Goldstein: World Kickboxing Champion, Israeli Undercover Police and Cycling Champion*. North Vancouver, Influence Publishing, 2015.

Goodheart, George J., Jr., D.C. *You'll Be Better: The Story of Applied Kinesiology*. AK Printing, 2000.

Hamilton, Allan J., M.D., FACS. *The Scalpel and the Soul: Encounters with Surgery, the Supernatural, and the Healing Power of Hope*. Jeremy P. Tarcher, Penguin Group, 2009.

Hawkins, David, M.D., Ph.D. *Power vs. Force: The Hidden Determinations of Human Behavior*. Hay House, 1995.

Hess, Andrea, *Unlock Your Intuition*. Soul Star Publishing, 2007.

Jeans, Sir James. *The Mysterious Universe*. Cambridge University Press, 1930.

Judith, Anodea. *Wheels of Life: A User's Guide to the Chakra System*. Llewellyn Publications, 1999.

Jung, C.G. *Memories, Dreams, Reflections*. Recorded and edited by Aniela Jaffé; translated from the German by Richard and Clara Winston. New York, Vintage Books, a Division of Random House, Inc., 1989.

Kipling, Rudyard. *Just So Stories*. CreateSpace Independent Publishing Platform, 2013.

Lee, Belynda. *Five-Inch Heels: When Women Step into Power and Success*. North Vancouver, Influence Publishing, 2014.

Leeming, David Adams and Margaret Adams Leeming. *Encyclopedia of Creation Myths*. Oxford University Press, 1994.

Lipton, Bruce, Ph.D. *The Biology of Belief: Unleashing the Power of Consciousness, Matter, & Miracles*. Hay House, 2011.

Little, Brian R., Ph.D. *Me, Myself, and Us: The Science of Personality and the Art of Well-Being*. HarperCollins Publishers Ltd., 2014.

Liu I-Ming. *The Taoist I Ching*. Translated by Thomas Cleary. Boston: Shambhala Books, 2005.

Luskin, Frederic, Ph.D. *Forgive for Good: A Proven Prescription for Health and Happiness*. HarperSanFrancisco, 2002.

Marieb, Elaine N., R.N., Ph.D. *Essentials of Human Anatomy & Physiology*. Old Tappan, NJ: Pearson Higher Education.

Martin, Barbara Y. and Dimitri Moraitis. *Change Your Aura, Change Your Life*. Spiritual Arts Institute, 2003.

Matsen, Jonn, N.D. *Eating Alive: Prevention thru Good Digestion*. Crompton Books, Ltd., 1987.

Matt, Daniel C. *The Essential Kabbalah*. HarperOne, 1996.

McGowan, Linda. *Travelling the World with MS in a Wheelchair*. North Vancouver, Influence Publishing, 2014.

McKeown, Max. *Adaptability: The Art of Winning in an Age of Uncertainty*. Kogan Page, 2012.

Melchizedek, Drunvalo. *The Ancient Secret of the Flower of Life*, Volumes I and II. Light Technology Publishing, 1998.

Michel-Brown, Bell. *Message from the Gods: Soul Secrets from 500 BC*. Cadbury Hill Publishing, 2007.

Myss, Caroline. *Defy Gravity: Healing beyond the Bounds of Reason*. Hay House, 2010.

Newton, Michael. *Destiny of Souls: New Case Studies of Life between Lives*. Llewellyn Publications, 2011.

Oleson, Terry. *Auriculotherapy Manual: Chinese and Western Systems of Ear Acupuncture*. Elsevier Health Sciences, 2013.

Orloff, Judith, M.D. *Dr. Judith Orloff's Guide to Intuitive Healing: Five Steps to Physical, Emotional, and Sexual Wellness*. Three Rivers Press, 2000.

Padgett, Jason and Maureen Ann Seaberg. *Struck by Genius: How a Brain Injury Made Me a Mathematical Marvel*. www.jasonpadgett.com and Amazon Books, 2014.

Roumeliotis, Paul, M.D., CM, MPH, FRCP. *Baby Comes Home: A Parent's Guide to a Healthy and Well First 18 Months*. North Vancouver, Influence Publishing, 2014.

Ruiz, Miguel. *The Four Agreements: A Practical Guide to Personal Freedom*. Amber-Allen Publishing, 1997.

Salisbury, Julie. *Around the World in Seven Years: A Life-Changing Journey*. North Vancouver, Influence Publishing, 2015.

Sands, Nadine with Michael Sands. *Hold On, Let Go: Facing ALS with Courage and Hope*. North Vancouver, Influence Publishing, 2015.

Satori, Judy. *Sunshine before the Dawn*. Satori Incorporated, 2011.

Schucman, Helen, with William Thetford. *A Course in Miracles*. Foundation for Inner Peace, 1996.

Selby, Julie. *Infertility Insanity: When Sheer Hope (and Google) Are the Only Options Left*. North Vancouver, Influence Publishing, 2015.

Sisu, Kristina. *How to Get Out of Your Own Way: Inspiration and Transformational Techniques to Open Space for Miracles*. North Vancouver, Influence Publishing, 2014.

Staveley, Carole. *Conquer Your Pain in 9 Steps: Building the Mindset and Team You Need to Suffer Less and Achieve More*. North Vancouver, Influence Publishing, 2015.

Stevenson, Ian, M.D. *Twenty Cases Suggestive of Reincarnation*. University Press of Virginia, 1974.

Stone, Joshua David, Ph.D. *Soul Psychology: How to Clear Negative Emotions and Spiritualize Your Life*. Light Technology Publishing, 1994.

Tagore, Rabindranath. *Gitanjali*. tagoreweb.in

Tully, Brock. *Reflections for Sharing Dreams*. Brock Tully Press, 2011.

Tzu, Lao, and translation by Victor H. Mair. *Tao Te Ching*. Bantam Books, 1990.

Voskamp, Ann. *One Thousand Gifts: A Dare to Live Fully Right Where You Are.* Zondervan Books, 2011.

Walmsley, Janet. *The Autistic Author and Animator: A Mother's View of a Daughter's Triumph.* North Vancouver, Influence Publishing, 2015.

Walsh, Michael G. *Thinking Big Is Not Enough: Moving Past the Myths and Misconceptions that Stop Business Growth.* North Vancouver: Influence Publishing, 2015.

Webb, Wyatt, with Cindy Pearlman. *It's Not About the Horse: It's About Overcoming Fear and Self-Doubt.* Hay House, 2002.

Wheeler, Woody. *Look Up! Birds and Other Natural Wonders Just Outside Your Window.* North Vancouver, Influence Publishing, 2014.

Wilde, Oscar. *The Importance of Being Earnest.* Dover Thrift Editions, 1991.

Wilde, Stuart. *The Three Keys to Self-Empowerment: Miracles; "Life Was Never Meant to Be a Struggle"; Silent Power. Hay House, 2004.*

Williamson, Marianne. *Return to Love: Reflections on the Principles of "A Course in Miracles."* HarperOne, 1996.

Woolliams, Nina. *Cattle Ranch: The Story of the Douglas Lake Cattle Company.* Douglas & McIntyre, 1979.

Yogananda, Paramahansa. *Autobiography of a Yogi.* gutenberg.org

Yukteswar, Swami Sri. *The Holy Science.* Self-Realization Fellowship. 1984.

Movies and Videos

Dooley, Mike. *Thoughts Become Things.* YouTube, youtube.com/watch?v=8x4sVR67wCk

drjudithorloff.com/video-archive/how-to-listen-to-your-body

Lunden, Reverend Christina. *"'Light' Angel Soul Teaching."* BlogTalkRadio.com, December 12, 2011.

Author Biography

Since the seventies, Nina Shoroplova has been on a spiritual path, interacting with others as a Holistic Nutritionist, a Soul Realignment Practitioner, a Spiritual Counsellor, and a Healing Minister. Six decades of contrasting environments have enriched Shoroplova's life—on three continents, in the heart of cities and in cattle and sheep country; through life-challenging dis-eases and perfect health. Growing through self-expression, she has been a wife, a mother, a best-selling non-fiction author, a singer, an actor, and is Influence Publishing's senior editor. Her journey has taken her through a wide variety of teachings, from the bible to *I Ching*, texts old and new, various trainings, courses, workshops, and readings, and through the lessons she has gained from the spiritual books she has edited.

To learn more about Nina Shoroplova, please visit

NinaShoroplova.ca

TrusttheMystery.ca

Twitter@healthy_Nina

LinkedIn Nina Shoroplova

Facebook Author Page FB.com/AuthorNinaShoroplova

To provide feedback about this book, please contact Nina Shoroplova at Nina@NinaShoroplova.ca

If you want to get on the path to becoming a published author with Influence Publishing please go to www.InfluencePublishing.com

More information on our other titles and how to submit your own proposal can be found at www.InfluencePublishing.com

CPSIA information can be obtained at www.ICGtesting.com
Printed in the USA
LVOW10s0805270815

451692LV00006B/122/P

9 781771 411301